closing the EU east-west productivity gap

foreign direct investment, competitiveness and public policy

closing the EU east-west productivity gap

foreign direct investment, competitiveness and public policy

David A. Dyker
University of Sussex, UK

ICP
Imperial College Press

Published by

Imperial College Press
57 Shelton Street
Covent Garden
London WC2H 9HE

Distributed by

World Scientific Publishing Co. Pte. Ltd.

5 Toh Tuck Link, Singapore 596224

USA office: 27 Warren Street, Suite 401-402, Hackensack, NJ 07601

UK office: 57 Shelton Street, Covent Garden, London WC2H 9HE

Library of Congress Cataloging-in-Publication Data
Dyker, David A.
Closing the EU East-West productivity gap : foreign direct investment, competitiveness, and public policy / David A. Dyker.
p. cm.
Includes bibliographical references.
ISBN 1-86094-629-1
1. European Union--Europe, Eastern. 2. Europe--Economic integration. 3. Investments, Foreign--Europe, Eastern. I. Title.

HC240.25.E852D94 2006
337.1'420947--dc22

2006041747

British Library Cataloguing-in-Publication Data
A catalogue record for this book is available from the British Library.

Typeset by Stallion Press
Email: enquiries@stallionpress.com

Printed in Singapore.

CONTENTS

LIST OF TABLES AND FIGURES

PREFACE

This book is the product of the Framework V research project *EU Integration and the Prospects for Catch-Up Development in CEECs — the Determinants of the Productivity Gap*, project No. HPSE-CT-2001-00065. The editor and authors wish to thank the European Commission for the financial and moral support extended to the research group over the three-year life of the project. In this connection, they would like especially to thank Mr. Peter Fisch of the European Commission. We are also heavily indebted to one of our number, Dr. Johannes Stefan of the Halle Institute of Economic Research, who undertook the colossal task of organising and coordinating the project as a whole, in addition to making invaluable research contributions to a number of the workpackages within the project. Finally, we must thank the numerous discussants at our workshops who were so generous with their help, advice and patience. The final product is certainly the better for their interventions.

David A. Dyker

CHAPTER 1

INTRODUCTION: PRODUCTIVITY AND SOCIAL CAPABILITY — A HISTORICAL AND ANALYTICAL FRAMEWORK

David A. Dyker and Leonardo Iacovone

The failure of Soviet-type socialism, in particular its failure to catch up with the developed industrial countries in terms of basic GDP and standard of living indicators, was in essence a failure of productivity. To a degree, low levels of productivity under socialism reflected misallocations of resources. But even in the Soviet Union itself, allocative efficiency in the broad factorial sense was not so bad (Whitesell, 1990). Basic process productivity was not so bad either. What cut average productivity to a fraction of the levels reported in comparable plants in the developed countries was the inefficient (in terms of what would be rational in a market economy) organization of ancillary functions. Thus in the Soviet engineering industry in the early 1980s, repair, tool-making and transport/warehouse work accounted for 38% of the total workforce, compared to just 11% in the USA (Kulagin, 1982). Of course, these functional patterns were perfectly rational in the context of the classic weaknesses of central planning. Central planning is incapable of providing efficient supply networks, so that lead factories have to make the bulk of their tools and components themselves. Once central planning is gone, however, the rationale for this distorted kind of Fordism goes with it. In practice, old habits die hard, and Soviet-style industrial 'do-it-yourself' has survived into the transition period (Dyker and Radoševć, 1994; McDermott, 1997). This reflects more than just conservatism and the forces of inertia. It also reflects the fact that the building of supply networks is neither costless nor instantaneous. Effective supply networks, *inter alia*, are based on elements of *social capability*, and their development is constrained by considerations of *technological congruence*, just like other elements of X-efficiency, i.e. organizational and motivational efficiency (Leibenstein, 1966; 1978).[1]

In purely statistical terms, there is nothing unique about the productivity problem of the transition countries. Thus, for example, productivity in the British steel industry in 1967 was only some 35% of productivity in the US and EEC steel industries (Cockerill, 1974, p. 32). After some muscular restructuring and radical downsizing, the British industry largely closed the gap. What is special about the productivity problem in the transition countries are the factors that make it difficult to close the gap, therefore still difficult to catch up with the developed industrial countries. These factors form the focal point of this book. Before trying to dig deeper into the essence of the problem, we pause to give precise definitions to our terms.

Social Capability and Technological Congruence

In the simple but incisive theory of catch-up put forward by Verspagen (1999) following Abramovitz (1979; 1994), the scope for catching up is defined in terms of the scope for diffusion of technology (in the broadest sense, including 'soft', organizational technology — see Chapter 2) from the advanced countries to the catch-up countries. Just as the level of GDP per head (i.e., the level of social productivity) in the former countries is determined by their human capital and knowledge stocks, and the efficiency with which they use those stocks, so the ultimate limits to economic growth in the latter countries are determined by their ability to assimilate those knowledge stocks and bring their own human capital stocks up to the same level. If economic development is universally dependent on the same productivity-enhancing factors, and assuming no critical constraints on the supply of basic factors of production (land, raw labour and physical capital), what is to stop all countries ending up at the same level of development?

We have already identified the two main groups of factors which may inhibit catch-up through technological diffusion — *technological congruence* and *social capability*.[2] Verspagen defines the first in terms of

[1] 'The deviation between the optimal levels of effort from the firm's point of view and the actual level that individuals are motivated to put forth determines the degree of X-inefficiency in the system'. (Leibenstein, 1978, p. 204)

[2] Among other factors that can affect the rate of technological diffusion are, for example, cultural and geographical factors, and the dimension of political stability. There is, in fact, little

> The match between the technologies in use in the advanced country and those most fit for introduction in the backward country. If there is a mismatch between the two, the opportunities for catch-up-driven growth are reduced. The sectoral distribution of economic activity is one important factor in congruence. For example, one may well imagine that most technologies developed in the industrialized market economies are not very relevant for the most backward economies, which are often still largely agricultural societies. But there are also other factors in congruence, as in the case where the technologically leading country applies very scale-intensive technologies, for which investment opportunities and/or domestic markets in the backward country are too small. In such a situation, technological incongruence would prevent successful catch-up. (Verspagen, 1999, p. 31)

The second he defines in terms of

> Institutional factors such as educational systems (which supply the human capital necessary for assimilating spillovers), the banking system (which supplies financial capital for catch-up related investment), the political system etc. (Verspagen, 1999, pp. 31–32).

The concept of social capability is clearly related to that of *social capital*. Thus Putnam (1993), following Coleman (1988), argues that

> Stocks of social capital, such as trust, norms, and networks, tend to be self-reinforcing and cumulative. Virtuous circles result in social equilibria with high levels of cooperation, trust, reciprocity, civic engagement, and collective well-being..., Defection, distrust, shirking, exploitation, isolation, disorder, and stagnation intensify one another in a suffocating miasma of vicious circles. This argument suggests that there may be at least *two* broad equilibria toward which all societies that face problems of collective action

evidence that geographical factors present any absolute barriers to technological diffusion, while the political stability variable can be subsumed under the category of social capability (see *passim*). Culture is more difficult to tie down. Landes (1998, p. 516) argues that 'if we learn anything from the history of economic development, it is that culture makes all the difference'. We would argue that cultural factors, important though they are, impact on economic development primarily *through the medium* of social capability.

> (that is *all* societies) tend to evolve and which, once attained, tend to be self-reinforcing. (Putnam, 1993, p. 177)

In the present context, however, the notion of social capital presents two critical difficulties. Firstly, it focuses on *inputs* rather than *outputs*, and offers no explanation of how social capital interacts with other inputs — other forms of capital, and other factors of production. Partly for that reason, it says little about productivity, or indeed about any other key economic development indicator.

> Whilst much effort has gone into examining the indices of social capital in both qualitative and quantitative terms, much less attention has been devoted to the mechanisms by which such measures of social capital lead to discernible differences at the economic level. Does more social capital, for example, lead to a higher growth rate or merely to a different growth path or the same growth rate on a higher base? (Fine, 2001, p. 92)

Because the notion of social capability focuses on outcomes, and because it subsumes the dimension of learning, it avoids these difficulties: it provides a supple framework within which issues of development and catch-up can be assessed. Vicious circles of poverty and virtuous circles of prosperity can be accommodated by the framework, but in social capability analysis, no country or society is condemned to eternal backwardness. The productivity gap may be deep-seated and obdurate, but with time and appropriate policies it should be possible to remove it completely. None of this stands in contradiction to the social capital approach — it simply makes it more precise and focused.

The distinction between social capability and technological congruence is in theory clear enough. In the real world, shortfalls in social capability may constrain the establishment of technological congruence, and indeed incomplete technological congruence hampers the development of social capability, where governance is heavily technology-dependent (e.g., in relation to computer and software systems). The ability of a given group of workers to cope effectively with a flexible production system is clearly a dimension of technological congruence, yet it must surely also relate to elements of social capability within the society in which the group of workers is nested. To the extent that the dichotomy is not recognized by the principal actors whose behavior we are analyzing (a fate shared by many economic concepts), the distinction will not help us to understand decision-making, though it may still help us to understand outcomes. Thus while the social capability/technological congruence dichotomy provides a sound initial basis for our empirical work, we will not cleave rigidly to it in working out the details of the analysis.

Why Trade Enhances Productivity

Productivity varies in function of social capability and technological congruence. It also varies in function of patterns of exchange. More specifically and most importantly in the present context, it varies with the extent and pattern of foreign trade, and of the degree of mobility of capital stocks between countries/societies. In this section, we look at the general question of the linkage between trade and productivity. The more specific question of how foreign investment affects productivity we address, in a preliminary way, in the following section.

Traditional trade models offer no conclusive answer

Standard trade models, assuming perfect competition, imply that once a country reforms its trade regime it benefits from a 'one-shot' improvement in the allocation of resources. This does not imply by itself that firms become more efficient or productive, i.e. produce more output with the same inputs, but implies merely an allocative improvement throughout the economy, with increased specialization on the things that economy does best, and a consequent increase in overall output (Tybout, 1992). It follows that the allocative effects of a trade reform are not the most important in the present context. In order to understand more fully the linkage between trade and productivity, we have to relax some of the traditional assumptions present in trade models based on the perfect competition paradigm (Corden, 1997).

So, are we back with X-efficiency?[3]

The 'empirical observation' behind the X-efficiency argument is simple, and has been a constant theme in all discussions surrounding trade reform. Firms do not always aim to maximize profits, and are less efficient than they could be. These patterns of behavior are not random, but are systematically

[3]This section draws heavily on Corden (1997), Leibenstein (1966; 1978), Martin and Page (1983), and Martin (1978).

related to the existence of trade restrictions. The intuitive inference is that trade works as competition policy, and that trade can 'bring in the cold shower of competition'.

The X-efficiency argument is formally developed by Martin and Page (1983) and Corden (1974). Given a certain technological 'state of the art' and a given tariff level, the efficiency of each company is a function of the manager's effort. The utility level of that manager is in turn a function of leisure time and profits. When a tariff increases, the profits of that industry rise, *ceteris paribus*, and consequently the marginal value of managerial effort will rise. The X-efficiency argument, however, leaves aside the substitution effect that would push the manager to increase his/her effort, and rather concentrates on the related income effect. It posits that some of the income gains will be traded for more leisure time, which will lower effort, and therefore X-efficiency. This argument rests on four important assumptions:

(1) The increased level of protection produces an income effect larger than the substitution effect;
(2) The income elasticity of demand for managerial leisure is positive;
(3) There is a positive and direct causal relationship between effort and efficiency;
(4) The effect of the tariff increase is limited to one, import-competing sector, with no secondary effects on other, export-oriented, sectors.

All these assumptions are questionable, and it is not clear that they hold in reality. Corden focuses his critique on the last assumption, showing that we need to use a general equilibrium approach to take into account the effect of the tariff on other sectors. In fact, following the logic of the X-efficiency argument, we should conclude that the tariff increase has indeed a positive impact on the X-efficiency of export-oriented sectors, not to mention the impact on the relative prices of service sectors producing leisure goods. At the same time, Corden considers that the X-efficiency argument can be saved, as the increased level of protection can increase the degree of monopoly and therefore produce a redistributive impact that increases profits at the expense of wages, translating into a decrease of X-efficiency. Analogously, a situation where firms compete through technology choice can mean, in the context of a protectionist trade regime, the emergence of an oligopolistic equilibrium with domestic firms colluding to avoid costly modernization. On this scenario, opening up the trade regime may create an incentive to break the collusive equilibrium (Rodrik, 1988) and thus increase X-efficiency. The fact remains that, while we may consider a whole range of channels through which trade reform and X-efficiency may be linked, assumptions must always be made, and the proposed linkages cannot be considered *a priori* certain.

Dissecting the logic behind the X-efficiency argument does not ultimately devalue the argument itself, because X-efficiency considerations, in distinction to those of allocative efficiency, may affect the whole output of the firm concerned, not just marginal output. For instance, let us assume the introduction of a tariff that increases import-competing output by 5%: while the resultant loss in efficiency through misallocation of resources is confined to the marginal increase of output (only 5%), the potential loss in X-efficiency would impact on all the output, including the intramarginal units. The crucial implication is that the linkage that the X-efficiency factor creates between trade and productivity is important, but is not uniform throughout the economy; it may, however, be particularly important in some sectors. It is clear, therefore, that the theoretical model does not exhaust the debate surrounding X-efficiency. Only on the basis of empirical analysis can we hope to understand how this factor may work out in concrete cases.

Increasing returns and economies of scale

When we allow for the existence of increasing returns, and economies of scale, it becomes evident that an increase in market share may lead to a reduction in real production costs. The traditional argument here has been that opening up the domestic market to the world market exposes the domestic firm to a larger market, which permits economies of scale and therefore productivity increases (Nishimizu and Page, 1991). This argument also suffers from some problems — it is at best incomplete, as the positive relationship between trade reform and productivity may be reversed if increasing returns to scale are present in import-competing, protected, industries (Rodrik, 1992). In this case, domestic firms, exposed to world competition, will be pushed back up their (decreasing) cost curves. Thus the linkage between trade and productivity under economies of scale is ambiguous. The precise outcome will depend on the cost or ease of entry and exit, and the type of competition in place in the particular case.

A slightly different version of this theory assumes free entry and exit of firms, and argues that in the presence of increasing returns to scale, a protected market will be 'overcrowded', because protection attracts 'too many' new entrants. In this case, liberalization may lead to a more efficient structure of the industry with fewer firms operating at higher levels of productivity. This argument fits in quite well with the observation that protected markets tend, especially in developing countries, to show high variations in productivity levels. But it is crucially dependent on the not very realistic assumption of free entry and exit. Even more important, it fails to explain why the stronger firms in these overcrowded protected markets do not enter export markets even without liberalization. Thus the theory is only valid if we assume myopic entrepreneurs (Rodrik, 1992).

Technological catch-up

In a very similar vein, various formal models that link technological catch-up with trade regimes have been presented. Rodrik (1992), assuming that the firm's rate of catch-up to international productivity levels is a function of its market share, shows theoretically how opening up to trade may speed up the process of catch-up in export-oriented industries, whilst slowing down the transition towards the world frontier for import-competing industries. In a different model, Rodrik (1988) demonstrates that, if we assume that domestic companies do compete through 'choice of technology', those in protected markets may collude and fail to update their technology. Trade liberalization may push firms away from the 'colluding equilibrium' but, as with other theoretical models, the net results are ambiguous and crucially dependent on the assumptions made. What Rodrik's work does make clear is that the notion of technological congruence cannot be abstracted from market structures and trade regimes.

Uncertainty and externalities

In a world where there is uncertainty regarding not only production processes, but also the success of a given 'business model' in a new country, the first to enter the market will be exposed to higher risks, but also obtain higher rewards (Hausmann and Rodrik, 2003). If we assume that experience acquired through production leads to 'publicly observed improvements in technology' (Jovanovich and Lach, 1989) followers will be able to embody more easily than leaders the latest techniques, and general levels of social capability will rise; but at this point, output prices will be lower than for first entrants. Trade liberalization can shift the demand for products involving new technologies, and also affect expectations about future demand, thus modifying incentives for producers. Further, in a world where final productivity depends on the menu of intermediate inputs available through the medium of supply networks, trade openness increases it by encouraging the introduction of new products, because bigger markets imply more demand for any particular new product variety, even where they are up against stiff competition from the variety of substitute products already existing (Grossman and Helpman, 1990).

Finally, there is an important linkage between trade liberalization and productivity through the 'uncertainty channel', because trade policy influences demand and, consequently, through expectations, the investment decisions of producers. When uncertainty about demand is higher, due to uncertain trade policy, entrepreneurs may prefer to under-invest or invest in less capital-intensive technology because of the sunk costs that capital investments imply (Baldwin, 1989).

In this section, we have surveyed various models that explore the potential linkages between trade and productivity. What emerges is that each model relies crucially on specific assumptions, and different assumptions can lead to very different conclusions. Thus theoretical models are unable to give an unequivocal and universal answer. In the next section, we see how much difference it makes when we introduce international investment flows as a variable into the equation.

Foreign Direct Investment, MNCs and Productivity — Some Initial Generalizations

Foreign direct investment (FDI) is the *deus/diabolus ex machina* of international economic development. As the main vehicle for the globalization of the activities of multinational corporations (MNCs), it is alternately lauded as a key instrument of technology transfer, and more generally of economic modernization, and condemned as a weapon of exploitation and socio-political subjugation. These are not, of course, mutually exclusive interpretations, and indeed some authors have integrated both elements into their analysis (Ellingstad, 1997). Any assessment of these issues by us must clearly come at the end of the research, not at the beginning. But we do start off with certain assumptions about MNCs as initiators of FDI which are either true by definition, or strongly supported by the standard literature. Let us look briefly at the development of that literature.

The standard theory of international trade: The traditional approach to the analysis of FDI, rooted in the standard theory of international trade, can be traced back to MacDougall (1960), with his partial equilibrium comparative static analysis approach. The principal insight here is that FDI will raise marginal productivity of labor and reduce marginal productivity of capital in the host country.

The 'Dependency School': Key early contributions to the analysis of the impact of FDI on developing countries in the 1960s–1970s can be found among the Dependency School thinkers. They considered FDI harmful for the long-term growth of the 'peripheral' (i.e. developing) countries, because, they argued, MNCs, through FDI, were controlling and extracting resources in developing countries that could have been used for 'development objectives'. They thus stood accused of perpetuating a global division of labor and distribution of profits in the global economic system that was unfavorable to developing countries.

Industrialization theory and spillover effects: In the late 1970s, the study of MNCs started to move away from the standard neoclassical theory of trade and portfolio flows, to focus increasingly on the role of FDI inflows in the industrialization process. Neoclassical theory, based on the Heckscher–Ohlin (H–O) model, assumed immobility of production factors and identical production functions across different nations; within such a framework, there is no role for technology transfer, as technology flows are assumed to be a global public good, hence instantaneous and without costs. In the neoclassical financial theory of portfolio flows, MNCs simply act as 'arbitrageurs' of capital, reacting to changes in rates of return in different countries and therefore focusing only on the transfer of financial resources and nothing else (Xiaoquin Fan, 2002). Hymer (1960) was the first to move away from these perspectives and analyze FDI as a 'package' involving technology, management techniques and 'also capital'. Similarly, Caves (1974) pointed to the importance of transfers of 'intangible assets' (i.e. technological skills and knowledge) to subsidiaries, though he still did not explicitly model the benefits and costs of transferring them. The pioneering models in this literature were firstly developed by Koizumi and Kopecky (1977) and Findlay (1978).

The Koizumi and Kopecky model assumed that the rate of technology transfer between the MNC and the subsidiary is a positive function of the proportion of the host country's capital stock that is owned by foreign residents; the actual transmission of the 'technological knowledge' is 'automatic', because the technology is treated as a 'public good'. Findlay's model is based on two main concepts; first, the 'contagion theory' developed by Arrow (1971), which modeled technological diffusion analogously to the spread of contagious diseases (i.e. direct contact between the carrier and receiver is required for the diffusion of the knowledge)[4]; second, the classical model of catch-up of Solow (1957), and Gerschenkron's (1962) idea that the wider the 'development gap' between backward country and world frontier, the faster the catch-up rate. Findlay's model generates two main propositions

- That the larger the technological gap between the MNC and subsidiary, the bigger the spillovers will be;
- That the rate of technical change is proportional to the degree of penetration of FDI, defined as the proportion of the host country's capital stock owned by foreigners. (As, indeed, Koizumi and Kopecky had proposed.)

What these models did not address explicitly was the issue of the 'forces' determining the transfer of technology from the 'advanced' MNCs to the local subsidiaries in the backward regions. This question was taken up by Das (1987), whose model predicates that FDI has two effects. The first is voluntary transfer of knowledge and intangible assets to subsidiaries; the second is involuntary transfer to other domestic firms through 'knowledge leakages'. Das analyses the decision to transfer knowledge through FDI using a model from oligopoly theory. Following the same line of thought, but using a more complete and complex model, Wang and Blomström (1992) show how the process of transfer of technology from MNCs to subsidiaries and other domestic firms emerges from the process of strategic interaction between MNCs and host country firms. They replicate Findlay's assumption about the positive impact of the technological gap on spillovers, but explicitly recognize the cost of transferring technology within MNCs, as well the learning costs of host country firms, following Teece (1977). Wang and Blomström derive a set of conditions that

[4]The contagion theory was subsequently developed and systematized into the theory of tacit knowledge, which posits that key elements of technological knowledge are only transferable between individuals working closely together within the framework of a single organization. See main text below.

impact on the rate of technology transfer between MNCs and domestic subsidiaries:

(1) the level and cost-efficiency of the domestic firm's investment in learning (positive);
(2) the subsidiary's discount rate (negative);
(3) higher operating risks in the host country (i.e. political instability) (negative);
(4) the cost of transmitting knowledge from the MNC to the subsidiary (negative).

A final interesting characteristic of this model is that the authors analyze the reasons behind sub-optimal levels of investment in learning activities among domestic firms, explaining this in terms of the presence of externalities in learning investments.

The foregoing literature, varied though it is, does have in common two important features that have recently come in for strong criticism. First, it assumes, with different degrees and in different manners, that technological knowledge does have a 'public good' nature. Second, it builds upon Findlay's hypothesis that technological gaps positively influence the rate of transfer of technological knowledge from MNCs to subsidiaries and host countries.

FDI as an embedded element in growth models: The literature analyzing FDI within a growth theory framework is not as abundant as we might expect (Xiaoquin Fan, 2002). Two relevant exceptions are Wang (1990) and Walz (1997). Wang's model analyses the interaction between international capital flows and growth, with human capital playing a crucial role in determining the rate of return on physical capital, and accordingly affecting the magnitude of capital flows. In the Wang model, FDI has a beneficial impact on backward economies because it facilitates domestic technological change, consequently increasing the growth rate. Walz (1997) incorporates FDI into a dynamic general equilibrium model with endogenous technical change, where MNCs acquire knowledge through R&D in advanced countries and invest in less advanced, lower-cost countries, to produce goods using the knowledge accumulated elsewhere. In this model, the idea of trade-related international spillovers developed by Grossman and Helpman (1991) is extended to FDI, with these spillovers making innovation through imitation in the lower-cost, less developed country profitable. Walz's central message for policy makers is that policies promoting FDI will have a positive impact on growth.

The fundamental weakness of the growth models which seek to embed FDI is that they concentrate primarily on the transfer of technology between MNCs and subsidiaries, and simply assume that the spillovers to other domestic firms are proportional to the degree of FDI presence. In these models, as in the underlying contagion model of Arrow, the nature of technological knowledge is treated in an essentially simplified manner, with technological progress being considered a sort of black box. In the next section, we try to open that black box.

Social Capability, Technological Congruence and Foreign Direct Investment

God or devil, MNCs are always *exogenous* to the host country and its institutions. When they invest in a given country they always introduce new ideas, breaking the mould of existing patterns of business relationship and giving new impetus to dynamic entrepreneurial development. This is as true for EU countries, for the US or Japan as for any emerging or developing economy. Thus, for example,

> Inward FDI...acted as a conduit for the spread of Japanese organizational and managerial practices to other countries during the 1970s and 1980s. The comeback of the United States automobile industry and, more generally, the recovery and growth of United States manufacturing productivity, is due partly to the successful adaptation of Japanese organizational and managerial practices. Similarly, in developing host countries, foreign affiliates have often acted as conduits for the transfer, or catalysts for the adoption, of numerous improvements in organization and management by indigenous enterprises (UNCTAD, 1995, p. xxxii).[5]

Note that we are not saying that the new ideas are always good ones, or that the new entrepreneurial developments are always profitable ones. International investment has its failures as well as its successes, and it is only reasonable to assume that that will also be the case in the transition

---

[5]It is equally striking that, against the background of the extended recession that affected the Japanese economy in the 1990s, the Japanese government has recently targeted increased inward FDI as a key instrument for the redynamization of the domestic economy.

countries. But FDI is always a *new broom*, and this is particularly important in countries like the transition countries, where legacies from the past may hang more heavily than in other emerging economies. More specifically, MNCs dominate the international trade in technology and innovation.

> An important feature of international production is the overwhelming importance of TNCs in trade and innovative activities . . . TNCs account for a large proportion of global R&D, perhaps as much as 75%–80%. Judging from German, Japanese and United States data — between two-thirds and nine-tenths of intercountry technology flows are also intra-firm, that is, within TNC systems. (UNCTAD, 2000, p. 17).

It would be wrong, however, to assume that, because MNCs always start with a clean page, that therefore their commercial and technological vistas are unlimited. On the contrary, all the literature on FDI in general stresses that MNCs are generally cautious in their assessment of socio-technological options for FDI. They usually look to invest in host industries/plants of more or less similar factor mix to the 'mother' industries/plants (Ozawa, 1979; Wells, 1983). In our terminology, they are *averse to technological incongruity*. That is why, automotive MNCs, for example, tend to invest in medium-developed countries with (by international standards) relatively high wages, rather than in undeveloped countries with very low wages, even though car production is relatively labor-intensive. In more positive terms, MNCs generally place considerable stress on the importance of being able to impose their own *technological culture* on subsidiaries, and indeed on some categories of supplier, as a way of guaranteeing control over productivity (in this case, of course, *plant* productivity rather than social productivity), and thereby control over the crucial wage/productivity relationship (much more important than the level of wages as such).

As far as subsidiaries are concerned, the point hardly needs elaboration. With respect to suppliers, its implications are more complex. Where the relationship is essentially a commodity one, delivery conditions are the only things that matters to the MNC. In the extreme form of *outward processing*, raw materials are supplied to the partner for processing and redelivery at a precontracted price. Neither wage nor productivity levels at the partner plant are of any interest to the MNC. Where there are hierarchies of supplier, as in the automotive and electronics industries, the same can be said of *second-* and *third-tier suppliers*, which generally supply components to higher-level suppliers, without any direct link to the MNC at all. In relation *to first-tier suppliers*, the situation *may* be rather different. Because first-tier suppliers are involved in the design as well as the production function, the lead firm may want to integrate the first-tier supplier into its own technological culture, in order better to integrate the latter's design function into its (the lead firm's) design function. But this goes beyond the sphere of *a priori* analysis. It is, indeed, one of the research questions we have to ask.

Finally in this section, MNCs do not build, or maintain, schools. Indeed one of the factors that inhibited brownfield FDI in the former Soviet Union is precisely the fact that the majority of big formerly Soviet plants did take responsibility for most of the social functions affecting their workforce, and the expectation that a foreign buyer would in turn take over this commitment. But MNCs do build and maintain R&D units, and do spend a great deal of money on training. In terms of our jargon, they have policies on social capability, but policies that operate within constraints. One of the goals of our research is to find out exactly where those constraints are located.

References

Abramovitz, M.A., "Rapid growth potential and its realization: The experience of the capitalist countries in the postwar period." In E. Malinvaud (ed.), *Economic Growth and Resources*, Vol. I, London and New York, The Macmillan Press (1979).

Abramovitz, M.A., "The origins of the postwar catch-up and convergence boom." In J. Fagerberg *et al.* (eds.), *The Dynamics of Technology, Trade and Growth, Aldershot*, Edward Elgar Publishing (1994).

Arrow, K.J., *Essays in the Theory of Risk-Bearing*, Amsterdam, North-Holland (1971).

Baldwin, R., "Sunk-costs hysteresis." NBER Working Paper No. 2911, March (1989).

Caves, R. E., "Multinational firms, competition, and productivity in host-country markets." *Economica* **41**, 176–193 (1974).

Cockerill, A., The Steel Industry. International Comparisons of Industrial Structure and Performance, University of Cambridge, Department of Applied Economics, Occasional Paper 42 (1974).

Coleman, J., "Social capital in the creation of human capital." *Amer. J. Sociol.* **94**, S95–S120 (1988).

Corden, M., *Trade Policy and Economic Welfare*, Oxford, Clarendon Press (1997).

Das, S., "Externalities and technology transfer through multinational corporations: A theoretical analysis." *J. Int. Econ.* **17**, 188–206 (1987).

Dyker, D.A. and S. Radošević, "Industrial Restructuring in the Baltic Countries." PSBF Briefing, Royal Institute of International Affairs, Russian and CIS Programme, No. 3, December (1994).

Ellingstad, M., "The Maquiladora syndrome: Central European prospects." *Europe-Asia Stud.* **49**, 1, 7–21 (1997).
Findlay, R., "Relative backwardness, direct foreign investment, and the transfer of technology: A simple dynamic model." *Quart. J. Econ.* **92**, 1–16 (1978).
Fine, B., *Social Capital Versus Social Theory*, London, Routledge (2001).
Gerschenkron, A., *Economic Backwardness in Historical Perspective*, Massachusetts, Belknap Press of Harvard (1962).
Grossman, G. and E. Helpman, "Comparative advantage and long run growth." *Amer. Econ. Rev.* September, 796–815 (1990).
Grossman, G. and E. Helpman, "Trade, knowledge spillovers and growth." *Europ. Econ. Rev.* (papers and proceedings), **35**, 3, 517–526 (1991).
Hausmann, R. and D. Rodrik, *Economic Development as Self-Discovery*, Cambridge MA, Harvard University Press, (2003).
Hymer, S., "The international operations of national firms: A study of direct foreign investment." D.Phil. thesis, MIT, MIT Libraries (1960).
Jovanovich, B. and S. Lach, "Entry, exit and diffusion with learning by doing." *AER*, **79**, 690–699 (1989).
Koizumi, T. and K.J. Kopecky, "Economic growth, capital movements and the international transfer of technical knowledge." *J. Int. Econ.* **7**, 45–65 (1977).
Kulagin, G., "Trudno byt' universalom." *Pravda*, p2 (1982).
Landes, D., *The Wealth and Poverty of Nations. Why Some are so Rich and Some are so Poor?* New York & London, W.W. Norton (1998).
Leibenstein, H., "Allocative efficiency vs. X-efficiency." *Amer. Econ. Rev.* Vol. lvi, No. 3, June (1966).
Leibenstein, H., *General X-Efficiency Theory and Economic Development*, New York, Oxford University Press (1978).
McDermott, G.A., "Renegotiating the ties that bind: The limits of privatization in the Czech Republic." In G. Grabher and D. Stark (eds.), *Restructuring Networks in Post-Socialism*, Oxford University Press (1997).
MacDougall, G.D.A. "The benefits and costs of private investment from abroad." *Econ. Rec.* **36** (1960).
Martin, J.P. "X-inefficiency, managerial effort and protection." *Economica* **45**, 179, 273–286 (1978).
Martin, J.P. and J.M. Page, "The impact of subsidies on X-efficiency in LDC industry: Theory and an empirical test." *Rev. Econ. Statist.* **65**, 4, 608–617 (1983).
Nishimizu, M. and J.M. Page, "Trade policy, market-orientation and productivity change in industry." In J. De Melo and A. Sapir (eds.), *Trade Theory and Economic Reform*, Cambridge, Basil Blackwell (1991).
Ozawa, T., *Multinationalism, Japanese Style*, Princeton University Press (1979).
Putnam, R., *Making Democracy Work. Civic Traditions in Modern Italy*, Princeton University Press (1993).
Rodrik, D., "Imperfect competition, scale economies and trade policy in developing countries." In R. Baldwin (ed.), *Trade Policy Issues and Empirical Analysis.* University of Chicago Press (1988).

Rodrik, D., "Closing the productivity gap: Does trade liberalization really help." In G.K. Helleiner (ed.), *Trade Policy, Industrialization and Development: New Perspectives*, Oxford, Clarendon Press (1992).
Solow, R.M., "Technical progress and productivity change." *Rev. Econ. Statist.* **39**, 312–320 (1957).
Teece, D., "Technology transfer by multinational firms: The resource cost of transferring know-how." *Econ. J.* **87**, 346, 242–261 (1977).
Tybout, J.R., "Linking trade and productivity: New research directions." *World Bank Econ. Rev.* **6**, 2, 189–211 (1992).
Verspagen, B., "A global perspective on technology and economic performance, and the implications for the post-socialist countries." In D.A. Dyker and S. Radošević (eds.), *Innovation and Structural Change in Post-Socialist Countries: A Quantitative Approach*, Dordrecht, Kluwer, 29–44 (1999).
Walz, U., "Innovation, foreign direct investment and growth." *Economica* **64**, 253, 63–79 (1997).
Wang, J.-Y., "Growth, technology transfer, and the long-run theory of international capital movements." *J. Int. Econ.* **29**, 3–4, 255–271 (1990).
Wang, J.-Y. and M. Blomström, "Foreign investment and technology transfer: A simple model." *Europ. Econ. Rev.* **36**, 1, 137–155 (1992).
Wells, L.T., *Third World Multinationals*, Cambridge, MA, MIT Press (1983).
Whitesell, R., "Why does the Soviet economy appear to be allocatively efficient?" *Soviet Stud.* **42**, 2, 259–268 (1990).
Xiaoquin Fan, E., "Technological Spillovers from Foreign Direct Investments — A Survey, Economic and Research Department." Asian Development Bank, Manila, Philippines (2002).

CHAPTER 2

IDENTIFYING THE CHANNELS AND MECHANICS OF FDI-INDUCED TECHNOLOGY TRANSFER

David A. Dyker, Leonardo Iacovone and Cordula Stolberg

Own-Plant Effects and Spillovers

Given that MNCs possess specific assets that give them a competitive edge over domestic companies, it follows that foreign ownership will normally increase the productivity of domestic firms. An explicit vehicle for analyzing the process of technology transfer is built by Wang and Blomström (1992). They develop a model in which international technology transfer through foreign direct investment emerges as an endogenized equilibrium phenomenon, resulting from the strategic interaction between the subsidiaries of multinational corporations and host country firms. The model explicitly recognizes two types of costs — the costs to the multinational of transferring technology to its subsidiaries, and the learning costs of domestic firms (cf. earlier discussion of the work of Teece). The analysis points to the importance of the learning efforts of host-country firms in increasing the rate at which MNCs transfer technology, as well to the incentives and risks of leakage faced by the MNCs when deciding their pattern of 'engagement' in the process of international technological transfer. Spillovers to domestically-owned firms can be further broken down as follows.

Horizontal spillovers

Imitation: This is a classic mechanism through which domestic firms can acquire MNC knowledge; one example, common for both process and product technologies and widely practiced in the old socialist economies, is that of 'reverse engineering'. But imitation can work also for managerial and organizational knowledge (Wang and Blomström, 1992). In this case, it is commonly said that MNCs increase domestic productivity through 'demonstration effects'.

Movement of labor: Through this mechanism, domestic firms can acquire human capital accumulated within the subsidiaries of MNCs, by means of learning and investment in human capital accumulation. Some researchers have argued this is the most important of the various spillover channels, and evidence for this has been found in empirical research (Fosfuri, Motta and Ronde, 2001; Djankov and Hoekman, 1999).

Export spillovers: Domestic firms can 'learn to export' from MNCs through collaboration or imitation. This channel assumes, consistent with empirical evidence, that exporting implies 'sunk costs' like having established distribution networks, capacity to learn about consumers' preferences, etc., that domestic firms tend to lack compared with MNCs (Aitken *et al.*, 1997). Further, the entry of MNCs into the domestic market can encourage the entry of specialized providers of business services that can also be used by domestic firms (i.e. international trade brokers, accounting services, etc.). Even where there is no marginal-cost-reducing (and productivity-enhancing) effect, there is evidence that multinational firms which penetrate third markets from a foreign base reduce entry costs for other potential exporters from that base (see Aitken *et al.*, 1997). Such spillovers may stem from informational externalities, and are more likely to lower fixed costs than marginal costs of production.

Competition: With the entry of MNCs, domestic firms are put under competitive pressure to increase X-efficiency, which can lead to an increase in productivity. In some cases, this has been identified as a major source of productivity gain. Competition may, furthermore, increase the speed of adoption/imitation of new technology (Görg and Greenaway, 2003). The X-efficiency argument is important for our analysis of the linkage between FDI and productivity, because it reminds us that we cannot assume that inputs will unequivocally be used to achieve the maximum feasible output. The efficiency of firms is indeed relative, and the X-efficiency argument underscores the importance of the dimension of managerial effort. In the long run, the competition/X-efficiency effect can only be positive. It must be noted, however, that if competitive pressures reduce the level of output of domestically-owned firms in the presence of increasing return to scale, the short-term impact on productivity in those firms will be negative.

Once we have identified the 'spillover channels' that allow domestic firms to benefit from the presence of MNCs, it remains for us to pose the question: why does this process unfold differently in different contexts? This question has been tackled by the theoretical literature, and the central focus has been on the 'relative technological distance' between the new technologies brought in by MNCs and domestic technological capacities. While earlier work tended to suggest that the strength of spillovers may be positively correlated with 'relative backwardness' (Gershenkron, 1962; Findlay, 1978), more recent work has rather argued that relative backwardness determines 'absorptive capabilities', and that the bigger the 'technology gap', the lower tends to be the technology transferred and the potential for spillovers (Glass and Saggi, 1998). There is a clear link here with the social capability/technological congruence approach discussed earlier.

Vertical spillovers

Vertical spillovers run up and down the 'value-chain', or, if you like, the columns of an input–output table. They can thus be divided into backward and forward linkages. Blalock (2001) suggests two theoretical explanations lying at the base of vertical spillovers (he analyzes mainly backward linkages, but the argument is a general one.) Firstly, a rational MNC has an incentive to improve the productivity of its suppliers, which it can promote through strategic cooperation with, and training of, those suppliers; it may at the same time diversify its supply links, so making domestic suppliers more productive and attracting other MNCs. Secondly, MNCs will outsource domestically inputs that domestic suppliers are already able to produce within the constraints of domestic absorptive capabilities; these are precisely the product areas where we may expect narrower technological gaps and therefore stronger spillovers.

In a recent paper, Pack and Saggi (2001) emphasize that downstream buyers in developed country markets will benefit from technology diffusion among potential suppliers in developing countries, since such diffusion increases competition among those suppliers. In their model, increased competition flowing from technology diffusion in the developing country market can increase demand in the upstream market,[6] and may

[6]The increase in demand flowing from MNC sourcing requirements.

consequently induce entry into marketing, thereby increasing competition in the downstream market. While they model trade rather than FDI, it is not hard to see how their model can be applied to understand the consequences of technology diffusion within the framework of FDI rather than that of exporting.

Rodriguez-Clare (1996) develops a formal model of linkages and shows that multinationals improve welfare only if they generate linkages over and beyond those generated by the local firms they displace. The key question in the present context, however, is whether the generation of linkages can be expected to result in technology diffusion. In that context, vertical spillovers can operate through a number of channels (Smarzynska, 2002), viz.,

1. Direct knowledge transfer from foreign customers to local suppliers.
2. Higher requirements regarding product quality and on-time delivery introduced by multinationals, which provide incentives to domestic suppliers to upgrade their production management or technology.
3. Indirect knowledge transfer through movement of labor.
4. Increased demand for intermediate products due to multinational entry, which allows local suppliers to reap the benefits of scale economies.
5. Competition effect — multinationals acquiring domestic firms may choose to source intermediates abroad, thus breaking existing supplier–customer relationships and increasing competition in the intermediate products market.

The literature suggests that the following factors may also influence the intensity of vertical spillover effects.

1. *Market orientation*: It is generally supposed that domestically-oriented MNCs tend to purchase more locally than export-oriented ones (Altenburg *et al.*, 1998). This is normally explained in terms of export-oriented multinationals tending to impose more stringent quality requirements; and tending to form part of international production systems, and being therefore more dependent on global sourcing policies defined centrally by home headquarters.
2. *Ownership structure*: It is normally assumed that wholly-owned subsidiaries, and also greenfield investments, will tend to source supplies externally, while joint ventures will be more inclined to rely on the existing network of local suppliers.

Negative spillovers from FDI

These can take the following form:

1. 'Brain drain'
2. Raising wages
3. 'Market stealing'.

Aitken and Harrison (1999) formalize negative spillovers as the outcome of the joint impact of positive spillovers and market stealing. In their formalization, domestic firms are imperfectly competitive, and face fixed costs of production. The entry of FDI has a positive effect on average costs, with the curve being shifted backward (in Fig. 2.1, the movement is from AC_0 to AC_1.) However, the MNC, with lower marginal costs than its domestically-owned competitors, will have a stronger incentive to expand production, which will reduce the output of the domestically-owned firms, and move them along the new cost curve from A_1 up to B, where their productivity level will be lower.

Market stealing may clearly have an important impact on productivity. But it does this directly, rather than through the medium of technology transfer and learning processes, so that it is not of primary concern to us. Increases in wages consequent on FDI are only a problem if productivity has *not* increased. And brain drain carries with it at least as many possibilities of positive learning spillovers for the host economy as of the opposite result. While, therefore, it is important to take cognizance of these possible forms

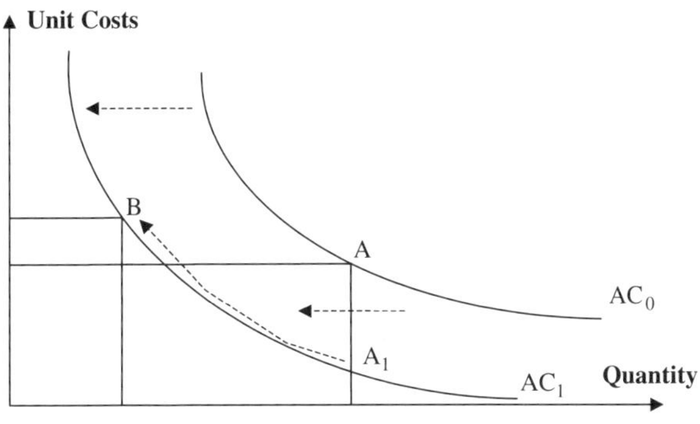

Fig. 2.1. The impact of 'market stealing' on costs.
Source: Aitken and Harrison (1999).

of negative spillover, none of them impact significantly on the research questions we are addressing.

Foreign Direct Investment and the Mechanics of Technology Transfer

Technology transfer is the key to catch-up, and MNCs are identified as key vehicles of technology transfer. How exactly does this transfer take place? There are two main schools of thought, which we may describe as the *OLI/spillover school* and the *network school.*

The OLI/spillover approach

There are any number of immediate reasons why an MNC may invest in another country: lower wage costs, tax advantages, exploitation of economies of scale, tariff jumping, and exploring new markets are just a few of those reasons. In order to be able to make such an investment, the firm itself needs to fulfill a range of prerequisites. How can we make sense of these complex patterns in a general way? The OLI paradigm (Dunning, 1981) addresses the problem by asking two simple questions: what generalized advantages is the firm seeking to exploit? And why does it seek to exploit them through FDI, rather than through arm's-length trade? The OLI answer is that the firm will seek an *O*wnership-specific or firm-specific advantage and a *L*ocational advantage, and will have to be convinced that *I*nternalization is the only way to access these advantages. The ownership advantage might be a cost advantage (that outweighs the disadvantage of doing business abroad) or some intangible asset the firm possesses, such as in the area of product or process technology, management or marketing. For horizontally structured MNCs, the locational advantage may lie in transport cost minimization and in access to large markets in host countries. Economies of scale at the plant level are connected to this. Vertically structured MNCs may access a locational advantage by locating different activities along the value chain in different countries, according to the host countries' comparative advantage. In either case, the human capital stock, in terms of education levels, skills and work discipline, may be crucially important.

The management of agency problems is captured under the internalization heading. If the firm possesses some kind of intangible asset, FDI might be the best way to make the most of that asset. Both the ownership-specific advantage and the internalization factor are linked to a firm's technology. It is most commonly some form of technological leadership that constitutes the key ownership-specific advantage and secures a market-leading position. The firm will obviously be concerned to keep this technology, to some degree at least, within the boundaries of the firm. To the extent that it wishes to transfer that technology, it will want to do so in the most efficient way possible. Where technological leadership is based on a substantial body of *tacit knowledge*, technology transfer within the firm, e.g., through FDI, may be the only effective way of transferring the technology.

The next stage in the OLI analysis is to distinguish between an internal technology transfer and an external transfer of technology, i.e., a technology spillover as discussed above. When an MNC invests in another country, it will have to convey some internal technology to the new foreign affiliate. The scope of the technology transfer will be that much broader if the FDI is taking place in a country less developed than the one in which the MNC's headquarters are located. Such technology transfer is necessary to secure the MNC's product standards, management skills, economies of scale, production efficiency etc., which in turn are needed to gain a leading market position in the host country. The internal technology transfer can take the form of formal staff and management training workshops/courses, on-the-job-training, training courses in the parent company etc. Strategic restructuring of the production process (aimed at generating a more efficient production organization that allows for, e.g., economies of scale) is likely to be involved, too, and is also part of the internal transfer of technology. Moreover, and less obvious, technology can be transferred via the flow of exports and imports between the MNC headquarters and its foreign affiliates (Blomström and Kokko, 1996). When investing in a less developed country, MNCs often — at least during the initial period after the investment — export more sophisticated components/products for further processing to its foreign affiliates, in order to guarantee product standards. As a result, the affiliates see how the technology is used, and can thus actually learn at first hand how to introduce the technology into the production process themselves.

Whereas the intra-firm technology transfer benefits the overall performance and competitiveness of the foreign affiliate and hence of the MNC, the impact of external technology spillovers on the MNC is less obvious in the OLI theoretical framework. Furthermore, although technology spillovers should, *a priori*, be desirable from the host country's point of view, it has been argued that FDI and the consequent external technology transfer may disturb the host economy's equilibrium (Konings, 2000).

One formal model that has tried to break down the overall effect of FDI on the host economy is that developed by Markusen and Venables (1997). They distinguish between a *competition effect* and a *linkage effect*, both of which are triggered by FDI. When an MNC establishes an affiliate in a foreign country, that affiliate does not operate as an isolated firm in the industrial sector of the host country's economy, but is linked to other domestic firms in a number of ways. First, the affiliate has local suppliers. Though the number of domestic suppliers might be low, at least some components will be supplied locally, and, with the passage of time, the local content might rise. Additionally, the affiliate stands in direct competition to firms within the same industrial sector in the host economy. With the arrival of FDI, the demand and supply structures in the host economy will change. FDI, and with it the establishment of a new firm in the host economy, creates additional competition, particularly as the new firm is able to offer superior products to the local ones due to the superior technology provided by the MNC. This competition effect is likely to harm domestic firms in the same industrial sector as the new firm, because local firms will not be able to match the product standards offered by the new firm. However, although firms in the same industrial sector as the new firm might be harmed by the FDI, firms in other sectors will benefit from the FDI, e.g., via price reductions or via forward-linkages to customer firms of the new firm.

This linkage effect is of particular interest to us in our investigation of the link between FDI and technology transfer. In the Markusen–Venables approach, the linkage effect is generally beneficial to local firms and acts as a transmitter of technology. *Backward linkages* affect the domestic supply industry, i.e., the suppliers of the new firm. Since the foreign affiliate has to ensure that supplied components match the standards and technology of the product, it might initially provide suppliers with assistance regarding the production of components. It is likely that during that process technological knowledge will 'spill over' from the MNC/its foreign affiliate to local suppliers. Blomström and Kokko (1996)[7] summarize possible ways in which backward linkages might occur:

- MNCs might help prospective suppliers to set up production facilities;
- MNCs might provide technical assistance/information to raise the quality of suppliers' products/to facilitate innovations;

[7]Adapted from Lall (1980).

- MNCs might provide/assist in purchasing of raw materials and intermediates;
- MNCs might provide training and help in management and organization; and
- MNCs might assist suppliers to diversify by finding additional customers.

Thus, backward linkages are clearly a tool for technology transfer, beneficial for the host economy inasmuch as the competitiveness of the local supplier base is strengthened — not only domestically, but also on an international scale.

Forward linkages operate via the customer firms of the MNC, i.e. distribution networks and sales establishments. Here, MNCs can provide guidance in establishing an efficient distribution network, they can help to organize the necessary logistical, technological and marketing tasks, and can probably even help to establish consumer contacts. Again, the result is that local customer firms of the MNC have the opportunity to learn from the MNC. Since the MNC's technology is superior to theirs, the customer firms will try to adopt the MNC's technology. In that way, the technology of the MNC is transferred to the host country's domestic industrial base.

Finally, spillover effects can also occur via imitation of the MNC's products by domestic firms in the host economy, via labor turnover between the affiliate of the MNC and local firms, and via a *positive* competition effect, where domestic firms are forced to use their technologies more efficiently in the presence of the MNC as a competitor.

Although in this approach MNCs are seen as to a certain degree actively helping local firms in the host country to reach a higher level of technological sophistication, they are not seen as *planning* diffusion of technology to the wider industrial base of the host economy. There is no assumption that they co-operate closely with their supplier base/customer firm base on a long-term basis to establish a network structure and to share technological progress. Hence the technology transfer is seen as more or less 'involuntary'.

Though transfer of technology and spillovers are generally difficult to measure, several empirical studies have tried to do so. All studies conclude that there do exist spillover effects and linkages when an MNC invests in a foreign country (see e.g., Blomström and Kokko, 1997 and Weresa, 2001). With regard to linkage effects, backward linkages seem to dominate, but this may partly reflect the fact that backward linkages can be more easily captured empirically than forward linkages. There seems, in any case, to be a tendency for forward linkages to gain in importance (Blomström and Kokko, 1996; Altomonte and Resmini, 2001).

The strategic technology transfer/network-building approach

Whereas most formal economic models that predict a spillover effect use the Dixit–Stiglitz assumption, with imperfect competition and increasing return to scale, the alternative approach to FDI and technology transfer rests on classical economic thought, dating back to Adam Smith (1776) and his theoretical framework on the organization of production. Specialization and fragmentation are seen as the central issues here, and a sharing of technologies amongst networks of firms, suppliers, customers, and research facilities are the main characteristics of the approach. MNCs not only transfer technology to local firms in the initial phases of investment in order to raise their technological standard to a predetermined absolute level, but continue to co-operate closely with these firms to develop new technologies on a cooperative basis, and thus strengthen the competitiveness of the whole industrial sector in the host economy.

Dluhosch's (2000) approach to economic integration and industrial location falls within this category of economic theory. While explicitly treating the impact of economic integration on the organization of production and the location of industries, Dluhosch implicitly treats the link between FDI and technology transfer, too. Contrary to the new economic geography models (e.g. Krugman and Venables, 1993 or Brainard, 1993), Dluhosch's approach rests on the classical lines of economic modeling, especially on Smith's thoughts about the organization of production, and with the central focus on the supply side. Economic integration — as in the case of EU accession of the CEECs — triggers a change in the organization of production, specifically in the pattern of specialization and fragmentation of production. Dluhosch develops a model in which economic integration has a horizontal as well as a vertical impact on the market. The horizontal impact operates in such a way that competition increases due to an increase in the elasticity of demand. This, in turn, reduces producers' mark-ups and forces producers to create additional economies of scale. In that context, the first source of economies of scale is the increase in individual output under a given technology. The horizontal effect then results in a vertical effect which is characterized by a process of specialization and fragmentation. As the number of components going into final products becomes larger and the components themselves become more dissimilar, more specific, with stronger and stronger complementarities, it becomes necessary to divide production into more narrowly defined production blocs.

Against that background, FDI emerges as an optimal tool to exploit the absolute and comparative advantage of regions when choosing a location for production units. Thus suppliers — especially those in peripheral regions — now have the advantage of specializing in niches, in which they enjoy a comparative advantage, and in this way benefiting from FDI. The technology transfer takes place through close co-operation between suppliers and the MNCs. Since components are carefully matched in advance, and since suppliers are directly involved in the planning and designing process, a direct and ongoing technology transfer from the MNCs to the local suppliers takes place. Though the link between FDI and the transfer of technology are not an explicit part of Dluhosch's approach, it becomes evident that a strategic technology transfer to the host country's industrial sector is a necessary condition for reaching the predicted outcome regarding the organization of production.

Best's (2001) approach to technology transfer fits in neatly here. While using a different methodology, Best's theory too, rests on the classical economic perspective, and he accordingly also emphasizes the aspects of specialization and fragmentation. In this configuration, the main prerequisite for and characteristic of the technology transfer is the so-called productivity triad (see Fig. 2.2).

The right business model, production system, and skill formation are here essential to guarantee technology transfer. By business model, Best means the processes of capability development within the firm. An

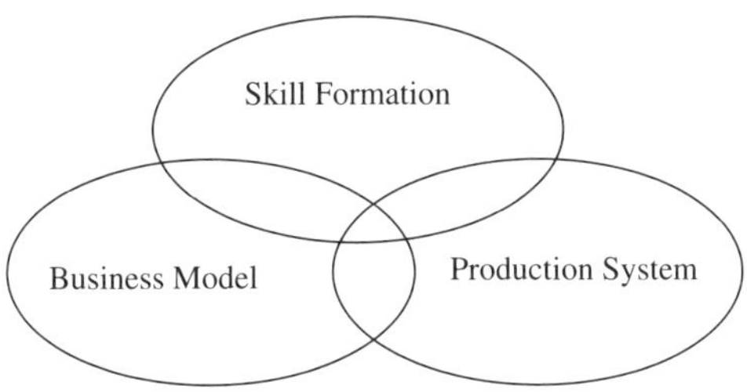

Fig. 2.2. The productivity triad.
Source: Best, M.H. (2001, p. 9).

entrepreneurial firm carrying out FDI should seek to use 'open system networks' (p. 11). These networks are characterized by the firm concentrating on its core abilities and using networks for complementary tasks. By doing so, the firm actively pursues 'techno-diversification' (*ibidem*), in which it not only makes use of the existing capabilities of other firms, but also creates opportunities by sharing technology-development tasks among the members of the network. As the different nodes of the network are connected, a technical change at one node means that all the other nodes will have to adapt to the change. Thus, technical opportunities and challenges are constantly created. Although it is likely that an investing firm will initially have to contribute more to the network, and to 'push' the concept of an open network, once the concept is established, the investing firm will gain as much as the local firms from the network. In this way, the process of technology transfer can be transformed from a one-way process to a two-way, and ultimately to an integrated, technology-transfer matrix.

Systems integration is the complement to open system networks at the level of the production system. The main features of systems integration are ongoing technological improvements and developments resulting in improved and new products; multi-disciplinary teams carrying out R&D tasks and able to identify different technological needs according to their professional background; management of the integration of independently developed technologies into the production process; and feedback effects from the various sub-systems of the production process (including the network). Thus new developments are shared among the network and are integrated in all sub-systems. Technology transfer is therefore internalized throughout the production system. This is obviously an ideal picture of systems integration. As in other aspects of dynamic business development, there may be failures as well as successes. The key, for our purposes, is the way that systems and sub-systems interact with networks.

To achieve a well-functioning open system network, a high-standard skill base among the employees of the firms in the network is essential. Accordingly, skill formation is the third aspect of the productivity triad. Links between firms and universities/research facilities represent one method of skill formation. This type of co-operation is not only beneficial for the firm in terms of new technologies, but also provides the opportunity to recruit the graduates and researchers who have proven to be most competent in their work. Whereas the firm transfers skills ('soft' technology factors) to the research institutions, the firm in turn receives a transfer of 'hard' technologies.[8]

Many other ways of transferring technology are embedded in the various patterns of interaction between the members of the network. Through these interactions, skills are transferred in an informal way by means of teamwork, changing firms, and the assimilation of new production methods. In this way, tacit knowledge is 'liberated'.

There are relatively few empirical studies analyzing this theoretical approach. That is largely due to the fact that very detailed and micro-level data would be required for such an analysis. Such data are in most cases not available. However, there do exist numerous case studies — many of them focusing on the CEECs — that investigate the approach. In these case studies, evidence can be found to support the proposition that such open networks, involving a re-organization of production towards fragmentation and specialization and an element of strategic technology transfer, are emerging (see e.g. Dörr and Kessel, 1997 and Meyer, 2000, for case studies on the automotive sector in the CEECs). There exists also empirical evidence specifically on open networks and strategic technology transfer (e.g. Diehl (2001) and Dyker and von Tunzelmann (2003). It seems, accordingly, that the theoretical framework discussed above can provide new and different perspectives on the link between FDI and the transfer of technology.

Technology transfer depends not only on the MNC, but also on the host country. The given industry in the host economy has to possess a certain degree of so-called 'absorptive capacity', in order to be able to make use of the new technologies. A sound base of relatively high-skilled workers, a good education system, a flexible workforce, and research facilities that focus on industry-relevant issues, are all part of the absorptive capacity and are necessary for successful technology transfer. Moreover, economic policy in the host economy influences technology diffusion, too. A stable macroeconomic environment along with supply-side policies that allow MNCs to establish production facilities and to run them efficiently are essential, not only to attract FDI, but also to generate technology transfer. That brings us

[8]NB there is a good deal of variation in the way that the terms 'soft technology' and 'hard technology' are used. Dyker (1999) defines them in terms of process/product (hard) and organizational (soft). Ivanova (1998) defines them in terms of the physical nature of the artefact concerned, so that the technology embodied in a machine is hard, whereas that embodied in drawings or other patent documentation is soft. Here we define hard technology as that embodied in physical capital, and soft technology as that embodied in human capital.

back to the issues of social capability with which we began the discussion, and points forward to the areas and issues subjected to detailed research in Chapters 3 and 4.

References

Aitken, B., G. Hanson and A. Harrison, "Spillovers, foreign investments and export behaviour." *J. Int. Econ.* **43**, 1–2, 103–132 (1997).

Aitken, B. and A. Harrison, "Do domestic firms benefit from direct foreign investment? Evidence from Venezuela." *Amer. Econ. Rev.* **89**, 3, 605–618 (1999).

Altenburg, T., W. Hillebrand and J. Meyer-Stamer, "Building systemic competitiveness. Concept and case studies from Mexico, Brazil, Paraguay, Korea and Thailand." *German Develop. Stud.* Berlin, No. 3 (1998).

Altomonte, C. and L. Resmini, "Multinational corporations as catalyst for industrial development: The case of Poland." Working Paper No. 368, ISLA-Bocconi University, Milan (2001).

Best, M.H., *The New Competitive Advantage — The Renewal of American Industry*, Oxford University Press (2001).

Blalock, G., *Technology from Foreign Direct Investment: Strategic Transfer through Supply Chains*. University of California, Berkeley, Haas School of Business (2001).

Blomström, M. and A. Kokko, "The impact of foreign investment on host countries: A review of the empirical evidence." Stockholm School of Economics Working Paper (1996).

Blomström, M. and A. Kokko, "Regional integration and foreign direct investment." NBER Working Paper No. 6019 (1997).

Brainard, S.L., "A simple theory of multinational corporations and trade with a trade-off between proximity and concentration." NBER Working Paper No. 4269 (1993).

Diehl, M., "International trade in intermediate inputs: The case of the automobile industry." Kiel Institute of World Economics Working Paper No. 1027 (2001).

Djankov, S. and B. Hoekman, Foreign Direct Investment and Productivity Growth in Czech Enterprises. World Bank (1999).

Dluhosch, B., *Industrial Location and Economic Integration — Centrifugal and Centripetal Forces in the New Europe*, Cheltenham, Edward Elgar (2000).

Dörr, G. and T. Kessel, Eine kreative, aber nicht ganz einfache Kooperation — Erfahrungen aus dem deutsch-tschechischen Joint Venture Unternehmen Skoda-Volkswagen, Wissenschaftszentrum Berlin für Sozialforschung Working Paper FS II 97–601 (1997).

Dunning, J.H., *International Production and the Multinational Enterprise*. London, George Allen and Unwin (1981).

Dyker, D.A. and N. von Tunzelmann, "Network alignment in firms in transition countries: A survey of Hungarian and Slovenian companies." In A. Tavidze (ed.), *Progress in Economics Research*, Vol. 6, Nova Science Publishers, New York, 69–88 (2003).

Findlay, R., "Relative backwardness, direct foreign investment, and the transfer of technology: A simple dynamic model." *Quart. J. Econ.* **92**, 1–16 (1978).

Fosfuri, A., M. Motta and T. Ronde, "Foreign direct investment and spillovers through workers' mobility." *J. Int. Econ.* **53**, 1, 205–222 (2001).

Gerschenkron, A., *Economic Backwardness in Historical Perspective*, Massachusetts, Belknap Press of Harvard (1962).

Glass, J.A. and K. Saggi, "International technology transfer and the technology gap." *J. Develop. Econ.* **55**, 2, 369–389 (1998).

Görg, H. and D. Greenaway, "Much ado about nothing? Do domestic firms really benefits from foreign direct investments?" Bonn, Germany: Institute for the Study of Labor (IZA) (2003).

Ivanova, N., "Strategic technology alliances (STA) in the Russian innovation system." Tacis-Ace Project No. P95-4003-R, IMEMO, Moscow, mimeo (1998).

Konings, J., "The effects of direct foreign investment on domestic firms: Evidence from firm level panel data in emerging economies." William Davidson Institute Working Paper No. 344 (2000).

Krugman, P. and A.J. Venables, "Integration, specialization, and adjustment." NBER Working Paper No. 4559 (1993).

Lall, S., "Vertical interfirm linkages in LDCs: An empirical study." *Oxford Bull. Econo. Statist.* **42**, 203–222 (1980).

Markusen, J.R. and A.J. Venables, "Foreign direct investment as a catalyst for industrial development." NBER Working Paper No. 6241 (1997).

Meyer, K.E., "International production networks and enterprise transformation in Central Europe." *Comp. Econ. Stud.* **42**, 1, 135–150 (2000).

Pack, H. and K. Saggi, "Vertical technology transfer via international outsourcing." *J. Develop. Econ.* **65**, 2, 389–415 (2001).

Rodriguez-Clare, A., "Multinationals, linkages and economic development." *Amer. Econ. Rev.* **86**, 4, 852–873 (1996).

Smarzynska, B.K., "Does foreign direct investment increase the productivity of domestic firms? In search of spillovers through backward linkages." World Bank, Washington, D.C. (2002).

Smith, A., "An Inquiry into the Nature and Causes of the Wealth of Nations." In E. Cannan (ed.), 1904, London, Methuen, 5th edition (1776).

Wang, J.-Y. and M. Blomström, "Foreign investment and technology transfer: A simple model." *Europ. Econ. Rev.* **36**, 1, 137–155 (1992).

Weresa, M., "The impact of foreign direct investment on Poland's trade with the European Union." *Post-Commun. Econ.* **13**, 1, 71–83 (2001).

CHAPTER 3

ANALYZING FDI IN CENTRAL-EAST EUROPE ON THE BASIS OF SAMPLE SURVEYS

Boris Majcen, Slavo Radošević and Matija Rojec

Introduction

In the course of intensifying integration of Central-East Europe into the economic region of the EU, firms in CEE are gradually being absorbed into international production and technological networks. By early 2000, the degree of integration of CEE within international production networks was comparatively high, especially in relation to GDP. Large-scale inflows of FDI have had a big direct effect on growth in CEE countries. The picture is much less clear when it comes to technological catch-up and long-term productivity growth via FDI. This chapter addresses that problem in a methodologically novel way. We try to understand the contribution of FDI to growth and productivity of the CEE by analyzing the technological positions of subsidiaries within their parent companies' networks. FDI is a micro–macro, i.e., *meso* phenomenon, and its growth and productivity effects on the host economy impact through the activity of local subsidiaries. In that respect, our paper provides an empirical basis for the new conceptualization of FDI and MNCs as differentiated networks of subsidiaries (Bartlett and Ghoshal, 1989). However, our primary interest lies in the effects of subsidiaries' positions and patterns of upgrading on growth and productivity in the host economy as a whole. In that respect, our empirical work follows the approach outlined by the literature focused on developmental subsidiaries and linkages between international business and endogenous growth theories (Ozawa and Castello, 2001). We report on the results of research based on data from 433 subsidiaries in five CEE economies (Estonia, Hungary, Poland, Slovakia and Slovenia). The subsidiaries are analyzed in terms of several attributes (product scope; given and enhanced mandates; autonomy of subsidiaries, etc.). In mapping subsidiaries' technological, production and market positions across several countries and a large number of firms, we aim to form a reliable picture of the technological contributions that FDI is making to local economies, and the role that they occupy in international industrial networks.

Our Conceptual Approach

In our research, we have tried to overcome the limits of the aggregate econometric approach, and also the weaknesses of case studies, in pursuing the analysis at the meso level. We collected data on several hundred firms in several countries. The sample is large enough to permit econometric analysis, but at the same time, we have maintained the advantages of working with information collected directly at the firm level.

Our focus is explicitly on the local subsidiary as the mechanism through which FDI affects productivity growth in the host economy. The role of the subsidiary determines the mechanisms by which linkages between the domestic and global economies and mechanisms of control of these linkages are generated. In that respect, we combine growth and international business studies perspectives. MNC networks are viewed as differentiated networks in which each subsidiary is controlled through a specific mechanism according to its role in the MNC. The large sample enables us to generate insights on countries and sectoral differences regarding the position of subsidiaries and their relationship to other organizations.

The literature on subsidiary development is of recent origin. It focuses on the process by which MNC subsidiaries enhance their resources and capabilities, and in so doing add value *to the MNC as a whole* (for a review and conceptual analysis of subsidiary evolution, see Birkinshaw and Hood, 1998). The literature on subsidiary strategy has advanced our understanding of how MNCs operate. The contributions of White and Poynter (1984), Bartlett and Ghoshal (1989), Young, Hood and Dunlop (1988), and Birkinshaw and Hood (1998) have generated a much more realistic understanding of that process. Systematic study of the heterogeneity of the role of subsidiaries has helped us to understand MNCs as differentiated networks of subsidiaries (Bartlett and Ghoshal, 1989) 'which operate as "quasi firms" (Tavares, 1999), while MNCs can be treated as "interorganizational networks" (Roth and Morrison, 1992, p. 141)' (Tavares, 2001).

Our focus in this chapter is on the position of CEE subsidiaries within these networks, and on changes in *their* resources and capabilities and on the implications thereof for the *host economy*. We are concerned above all with the productivity effects on the host economy of upgrading of local subsidiaries. In that respect, our focus is different from that of the international business literature, which looks at the MNE network for its own sake. We are interested in the micro basis of growth, and hence our perspective could be defined as Porterian (Porter *et al.*, 2002). The closest to it in the literature is the 'developmental subsidiaries' approach in the regional development context, as developed by Young, Hood and Dunlop (1988). As noted above, our research is based on large-scale questionnaire surveys rather than on case studies. This reflects our primary interest in indicators of autonomous behavior on the part of the subsidiary, i.e., in outcomes rather than the process of building up autonomous behavior or internal, corporate venturing as researched by Burgelman (1983). We have to abstract from some of the drivers of subsidiary evolution, for example, gaps between subsidiary capabilities and charters (Birkinshaw and Hood, 1998). We assume, following the literature on subsidiary development, that 'the subsidiary is a semi-autonomous entity capable of making its own decisions, but constrained in its actions by the demands of head office managers and by the opportunities in the local environment' (Birkinshaw and Hood, 1998, p. 780).

On the empirical level, our objective is to:

1. Map the existing strategic position or level of autonomy of local subsidiaries and the evolution of their mandate.
2. Map the scope of control of individual business functions at the subsidiary level, and how these functions have been distributed between the subsidiary and other entities of the MNC.

Specifically, we try to explore the following four research questions:

1. What are the roles that CEE subsidiaries initially play within MNC networks?
2. What are the relationships of CEE subsidiaries with headquarters, and with other subsidiaries?
3. What are the relationships with local companies and the local environment?
4. How does the role and activities of subsidiaries change over time in terms of the scope and scale of value added?

Our conceptual model is based on two forms of upgrading of the position of subsidiaries, and on several dimensions of integration of the subsidiary into the MNC network.

The subsidiary can upgrade its position through:

- Functional extension (sales, manufacturing, finance), i.e. by adding new mandates or functions.
- Lines of business extension (for example, color TV and AV equipment), i.e., by extending the scale of the existing mandate through home sales and exports or new lines of business (products).

The upgrading of the subsidiary proceeds on several dimensions, each of which captures a different aspect of upgrading. The dimensions of upgrading and integration are[9]:

- Product flows (export, import or local sales or purchases within total sales).
- Knowledge flows (changes in the pattern of control of the R&D, patents and licenses functions).
- Capital flows (changes in equity).

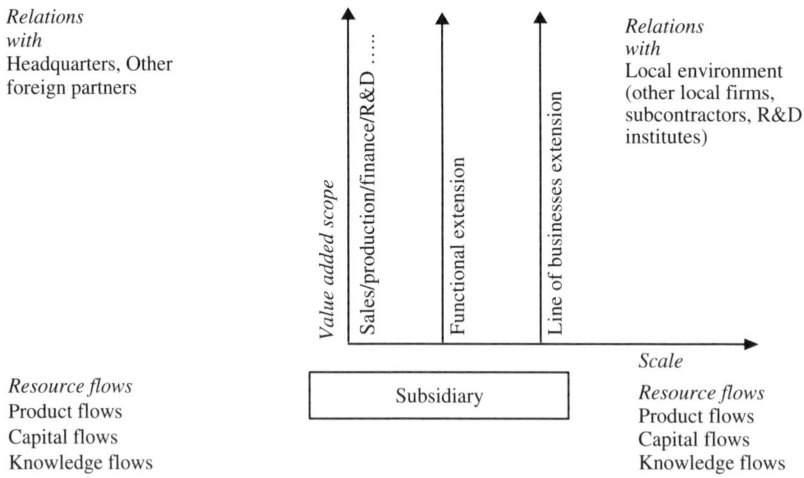

Fig. 3.1. Mechanisms of productivity growth via FDI: A conceptual model.

[9]Randay and Li (1998) show that each flow is to a degree independent of the others.

These dimensions can be analyzed in terms of (1) their intensity and, (2) direction (from HQ to subsidiary; from subsidiary to HQ; from subsidiary to subsidiary, etc.).

In continuation, we discuss the relevance of this model for productivity growth in CEE, and propose several hypotheses. First, following Szalavetz (2000), we distinguish between *static* and *dynamic* modernization effects of FDI. *Static* modernization effects are those designated by the parent company as necessary for the subsidiary to achieve basic production capability. This entails autonomy over operational functions, and should result in similar levels of efficiency as in the parent company. As long as there is no change in the level of autonomy of other functional areas, the increase in sales and exports is interpreted as expansion within a basically unchanged mandate. *Dynamic* effects accrue when the subsidiary expands the range of functions under its control (functional upgrading). Subsidiaries take on responsibility for additional corporate functions and increase local value added (Szalavetz, 2000, p. 358). Note that, in this context, an increase in the number of lines of businesses (product diversification) cannot be interpreted unambiguously. In the case of local-market-oriented FDI, an increased number of lines of business/products denotes *diversification* with no increase in functional autonomy.

Second, differences between countries and sectors in the level of autonomy of subsidiaries reflect differences in capabilities inherited from the socialist period as well as differences in the tasks designated to them by the parent company. CEE countries differed in the extent to which their enterprises were genuine business organizations, as opposed to simply production units. It is clear that the more subsidiaries have to be specialized within the MNC network, the narrower will be the range of business functions that they control. Equally, however, the range of inherited capabilities could be a key factor determining the degree of functional control.

Third, increased autonomy of the subsidiary within the corporate function portfolio develops from operational to marketing and then to strategic autonomy, which shows the dynamic effect of industrial integration. As Szalavetz (2000) stresses, '*the quality of the transferred technology depends not only on the recipient's absorption capabilities but also* (or maybe even more) *on its marketing capabilities*' (p. 369). Success in this transition depends greatly on the market orientation of the subsidiary. For exporters, the shift from the status of production-only subsidiary to that of subsidiary with autonomous control of marketing functions is very difficult. Marketing for exporting involves significant upfront expenditure — but also much larger profit margins. For local-market-seeking FDI, the marketing function is essentially part of the mandate. For exporters, on the other hand, production is commonly the only corporate function acquired. Thus CEE subsidiaries, like local firms from emerging markets (Craig and Douglas, 1997), generally enjoy partial participation or production-only participation in transnational value chains. Marketing capabilities are linkage capabilities and thus are crucial for breaking dependence on the parent company.

Fourth, responsibility for strategic functions, especially product development and strategic management, is even more difficult to acquire. Autonomy in this area means that subsidiaries become largely independent, and can potentially operate as centers of excellence within the MNC network. Given this hierarchy of functions, we may expect that subsidiaries will be least likely to initiate changes in the organization of business function and most likely in the sales or product portfolio.

Methodology and Sample

The above conceptual framework was tested via a two-page 'Questionnaire for foreign investment enterprises'. Questionnaires were sent to 2,203 FIEs in Estonia, Hungary, Poland, Slovakia and Slovenia. Of the total, 433 were returned, which gives a 19.7% response rate. The response rate was highest in Slovenia (34.4%), followed by Slovakia (30.2%), Estonia (30.0%), Poland (18.8%) and Hungary (10.6%). Obviously, it was easier to practice a more targeted, proactive approach to the respondents in the smaller countries than in Poland and Hungary, where the number of FIEs is much higher. The sample of 433 respondent FIEs is presented in Tables 3.1–3.11. The major characteristics of the sample are:

(1) Poland has the highest share of FIEs in the sample in terms of the number of FIEs, as well as in terms of employment;
(2) significant differences exist among the analyzed countries as far as sectoral distribution of FIEs is concerned;
(3) representativeness of the sample in terms of the number of firms is relatively low, but it is quite high in terms of employment; representativeness by country is rather good;
(4) most of the FIEs included in the sample are medium-sized; the share of larger firms is higher in the case of Poland and Hungary, which is due to bigger country size;
(5) most of the sample FIEs were established in 1993 or before;

(6) majority-foreign-owned companies are heavily prevalent; and
(7) the share of FIEs producing intermediate products is much higher than that of firms producing final products.

We present a more detailed presentation of the sample FIEs below.

Distribution of sample FIEs: Out of 433 FIEs, 135 (35.5%) are from Poland, 80 (18.5%) from Hungary, 78 (18.0%) from Slovakia, 72 (16.6%) from Slovenia and 50 (11.5%) from Estonia (see Table 3.1). All 2-digit NACE manufacturing sectors are represented in the sample. The highest proportion of sample FIEs is in DL — electrical and optical equipment (16.4%) and DJ — basic metals and products (14.1%), followed by DA — food, beverages and tobacco (10.2%), DI — non-metal mineral products (9.0%), DG — chemicals and man-made fibers (8.5%), and DH — rubber and plastic products (6.9%). There are significant differences among the countries as far as sectoral distribution of sample FIEs is concerned (see Table 3.2).

Distribution of employment of sample FIEs: In terms of employment, FIEs from Poland dominate, with 70.3% of total employment in the sample FIEs. The share of Hungarian sample FIEs in total sample employment is 13.7%, of Slovenian sample FIEs 8.1% and of Estonian sample FIEs 7.8%. Comparison of the shares of individual countries in terms of employment and in terms of the number of FIEs is biased by the lack of data on FIE employment for Slovakia. It is nevertheless clear that (in terms of employment) sample FIEs from Poland are much larger in size than sample FIEs from other countries (see Table 3.3). The highest proportion of sample FIE employment is in DJ — basic metals and products (37.9%), followed by DL — electrical and optical equipment (13.6%), DG — chemicals and man-made fibers (8.6%), DM — transport equipment (8.4%), DA — food, beverages and tobacco (7.8%) etc. As in the case of number of FIEs, the sectoral distribution of FIE employment differs substantially among the countries (see Table 3.4).

Representativeness of the sample: Adequate representativeness of the sample is an important factor in the relevance of the results of any empirical analysis. In the present case, sample FIEs represent only 4.9% of all FIEs in the analyzed countries, the highest proportion of 23.8% being in Slovenia, followed by Estonia with 12.4%, Poland with 3.5% and Hungary

Table 3.1. Distribution of sample firms by country; by 2-digit NACE rev. 1 manufacturing sector and total.

NACE 2	Estonia*		Hungary		Poland		Slovakia		Slovenia		Total	
	Number	%	Number	%	Number	%	Number	%	Number	%	Number	%
DA	9	20.5	14	31.8	16	36.4	3	6.8	2	4.5	44	100.0
DB	7	25.0	8	28.6	5	17.9	5	17.9	3	10.7	28	100.0
DC	0	0.0	2	33.3	0	0.0	2	33.3	2	33.3	6	100.0
DD	5	38.5	2	15.4	1	7.7	4	30.8	1	7.7	13	100.0
DE	4	28.6	1	7.1	3	21.4	4	28.6	2	14.3	14	100.0
DF	4	80.0	1	20.0	0	0.0	0	0.0	0	0.0	5	100.0
DG		0.0	7	18.9	16	43.2	6	16.2	8	21.6	37	100.0
DH	2	6.7	9	30.0	10	33.3	4	13.3	5	16.7	30	100.0
DI	4	10.3	4	10.3	20	51.3	6	15.4	5	12.8	39	100.0
DJ	5	8.2	6	9.8	21	34.4	13	21.3	16	26.2	61	100.0
DK	1	2.7	5	13.5	12	32.4	8	21.6	11	29.7	37	100.0
DL	5	7.0	16	22.5	29	40.8	10	14.1	11	15.5	71	100.0
DM	0	0.0	4	16.7	14	58.3	1	4.2	5	20.8	24	100.0
DN	4	33.3	1	8.3	6	50.0		0.0	1	8.3	12	100.0
Unknown		0.0		0.0		0.0	12	100.0		0.0	12	100.0
D — total	50	11.5	80	18.5	153	35.3	78	18.0	72	16.6	433	100.0

*DF + DG together.

Table 3.2. Distribution of sample firms by 2-digit NACE rev. 1 manufacturing sector; for individual countries and total.

NACE 2	Estonia*		Hungary		Poland		Slovakia		Slovenia		Total	
	Number	%	Number	%	Number	%	Number	%	Number	%	Number	%
DA	9	18.0	14	17.5	16	10.5	3	3.8	2	2.8	44	10.2
DB	7	14.0	8	10.0	5	3.3	5	6.4	3	4.2	28	6.5
DC	0	0.0	2	2.5	0	0.0	2	2.6	2	2.8	6	1.4
DD	5	10.0	2	2.5	1	0.7	4	5.1	1	1.4	13	3.0
DE	4	8.0	1	1.3	3	2.0	4	5.1	2	2.8	14	3.2
DF	4	8.0	1	1.3	0	0.0	0	0.0	0	0.0	5	1.2
DG		0.0	7	8.8	16	10.5	6	7.7	8	11.1	37	8.5
DH	2	4.0	9	11.3	10	6.5	4	5.1	5	6.9	30	6.9
DI	4	8.0	4	5.0	20	13.1	6	7.7	5	6.9	39	9.0
DJ	5	10.0	6	7.5	21	13.7	13	16.7	16	22.2	61	14.1
DK	1	2.0	5	6.3	12	7.8	8	10.3	11	15.3	37	8.5
DL	5	10.0	16	20.0	29	19.0	10	12.8	11	15.3	71	16.4
DM	0	0.0	4	5.0	14	9.2	1	1.3	5	6.9	24	5.5
DN	4	8.0	1	1.3	6	3.9		0.0	1	1.4	12	2.8
Unknown		0.0		0.0		0.0	12	15.4		0.0	12	2.8
D — total	50	100.0	80	100.0	153	100.0	78	100.0	72	100.0	433	100.0

*DF + DG together.

Table 3.3. Distribution of employment of sample firms by country; by 2-digit NACE rev. 1 manufacturing sector and total.

NACE 2	Estonia*		Hungary		Poland		Slovakia		Slovenia		Total	
	Number	%	Number	%	Number	%	Number	%	Number	%	Number	%
DA	2093	12.2	4500	26.3	10153	59.3	n.a.	0.0	362	2.1	17108	100.0
DB	6520	56.1	3100	26.7	1172	10.1	n.a.	0.0	822	7.1	11614	100.0
DC	0	0.0	1600	57.6	0	0.0	n.a.	0.0	1177	42.4	2777	100.0
DD	1710	73.8	300	12.9	30	1.3	n.a.	0.0	277	12.0	2317	100.0
DE	1114	28.1	200	5.0	2302	58.0	n.a.	0.0	355	8.9	3971	100.0
DF	275	23.4	900	76.6	0	0.0	n.a.	0.0	0	0.0	1175	100.0
DG		0.0	5500	29.1	12633	66.8	n.a.	0.0	771	4.1	18904	100.0
DH	1071	14.5	2400	32.5	1736	23.5	n.a.	0.0	2185	29.6	7392	100.0
DI	249	2.4	1300	12.3	8655	82.0	n.a.	0.0	348	3.3	10552	100.0
DJ	996	1.2	1600	1.9	78610	94.2	n.a.	0.0	2225	2.7	83431	100.0
DK	9	0.1	800	8.4	5993	63.3	n.a.	0.0	2667	28.2	9469	100.0
DL	2465	8.3	5600	18.8	17855	59.9	n.a.	0.0	3910	13.1	29830	100.0
DM	0	0.0	2100	11.3	13963	75.2	n.a.	0.0	2505	13.5	18568	100.0
DN	704	24.0	500	17.0	1530	52.1	n.a.	0.0	204	6.9	2938	100.0
D — total	17206	7.8	30200	13.7	154632	70.3	n.a.	0.0	17808	8.1	219846	100.0

*DF + DG together.

Table 3.4. Distribution of employment of sample firms by 2-digit NACE rev. 1 manufacturing sector; for individual countries and total.

NACE 2	Estonia*		Hungary		Poland		Slovakia		Slovenia		Total	
	Number	%	Number	%	Number	%	Number	%	Number	%	Number	%
DA	2093	12.2	4500	14.9	10153	6.6	n.a.	—	362	2.0	17108	7.8
DB	6520	37.9	3100	10.3	1172	0.8	n.a.	—	822	4.6	11614	5.3
DC	0	0.0	1600	5.3	0	0.0	n.a.	—	1177	6.6	2777	1.3
DD	1710	9.9	300	1.0	30	0.0	n.a.	—	277	1.6	2317	1.1
DE	1114	6.5	200	0.7	2302	1.5	n.a.	—	355	2.0	3971	1.8
DF	275	1.6	900	3.0	0	0.0	n.a.	—	0	0.0	1175	0.5
DG		0.0	5500	18.2	12633	8.2	n.a.	—	771	4.3	18904	8.6
DH	1071	6.2	2400	7.9	1736	1.1	n.a.	—	2185	12.3	7392	3.4
DI	249	1.4	1300	4.3	8655	5.6	n.a.	—	348	2.0	10552	4.8
DJ	996	5.8	1600	5.3	78610	50.8	n.a.	—	2225	12.5	83431	37.9
DK	9	0.1	800	2.6	5993	3.9	n.a.	—	2667	15.0	9469	4.3
DL	2465	14.3	5600	18.5	17855	11.5	n.a.	—	3910	22.0	29830	13.6
DM	0	0.0	2100	7.0	13963	9.0	n.a.	—	2505	14.1	18568	8.4
DN	704	4.1	500	1.7	1530	1.0	n.a.	—	204	1.1	2938	1.3
D — total	17206	100.0	30200	100.0	154632	100.0	n.a.	—	17808	100.0	219846	100.0

*DF + DG together.

with 2.1%. At the same time, employment in sample FIEs represents no less than 22.6% of total FIE employment in the analyzed countries — as much as 53.3% in Estonia and 50.8% in Slovenia, and 29.5% and 7.9% in Poland and Hungary respectively. The data on representativeness offer the following conclusions:

1. Although overall representativeness of the sample in terms of the number of FIEs may not seem high, representativeness in terms of employment is quite high.
2. Representativeness by country varies considerably; representativeness in Slovenia and Estonia is generally rather high, especially in terms of employment, which it is around 50%, while it is much lower in Poland and especially Hungary.
3. Representativeness by manufacturing sector varies less than by country, but still ranges over a broad interval (see Tables 3.5 and 3.6).

Distribution of sample FIEs by number of employees is a proxy for the *distribution of FIEs by size*. Sample FIEs range from very small firms with less than ten employees to large firms with more than 1000 employees, with most of them being small and medium-sized firms. As much as 39.6% of sample FIEs have 100 or less employees, 40.0% between 101 and 500

Table 3.5. Share of sample FIEs in all FIEs — number of firms, by country and by 2-digit NACE rev. 1 manufacturing sector.

NACE 2	Estonia*	Hungary	Poland	Slovakia	Slovenia	Total
DA	36.0	3.2	3.4	n.a.	13.3	4.7
DB	8.9	2.0	1.2	n.a.	17.6	3.1
DC	0.0	1.8	0.0	n.a.	33.3	3.6
DD	11.9	1.1	0.4	n.a.	11.1	2.5
DE	11.8	0.3	0.9	n.a.	6.7	1.8
DF	33.3	33.3	0.0	n.a.	0.0	20.0
DG	0.0	4.7	7.3	n.a.	36.4	9.5
DH	7.7	3.5	2.5	n.a.	19.2	4.2
DI	17.4	2.4	6.0	n.a.	25.0	7.2
DJ	16.7	1.1	3.6	n.a.	29.6	5.1
DK	3.6	1.3	3.2	n.a.	33.3	4.5
DL	11.9	3.7	7.6	n.a.	25.0	7.9
DM	0.0	3.9	5.7	n.a.	29.4	6.4
DN	10.0	0.5	1.7	n.a.	11.1	2.1
D	12.4	2.1	3.5	n.a.	23.8	4.9

*DF + DG together.

Table 3.6. Share of sample FIEs in all FIEs — employment, by country and by 2-digit NACE rev. 1 manufacturing sector.

NACE 2	Estonia*	Hungary	Poland	Slovakia	Slovenia	Total
DA	85.2	8.8	12.8	n.a.	23.0	12.7
DB	74.6	7.9	2.8	n.a.	46.8	12.8
DC	0.0	12.3	0.0	n.a.	47.2	13.2
DD	63.9	6.0	0.2	n.a.	77.6	8.3
DE	62.6	1.7	6.8	n.a.	14.9	7.9
DF	22.3	6.9	0.0	n.a.	0.0	5.4
DG	0.0	19.6	42.0	n.a.	39.0	31.5
DH	n.a.	15.0	5.5	n.a.	61.2	12.4
DI	14.4	9.3	22.9	n.a.	32.3	19.3
DJ	n.a.	4.2	n.a.	n.a.	48.9	9.0
DK	1.2	2.4	20.0	n.a.	50.7	13.5
DL	38.1	6.3	27.5	n.a.	65.8	17.9
DM	0.0	9.5	20.8	n.a.	64.3	19.7
DN	22.8	6.3	3.4	n.a.	80.3	5.3
D	49.2	7.9	15.5	n.a.	50.8	14.8

*DF + DG together.

employees, while just 20.6% have more than 500 employees. As expected, the share of sample FIEs with more than 500 employees is much higher in Poland and Hungary than in the other three countries. It is equally unsurprising that the share of sample FIEs with 100 or less employees is much higher in Estonia, Slovakia and Slovenia than in Hungary or Poland (see Table 3.7). Comparison of mean rankings of the number of employees in sample FIEs using the Mann–Whitney test show, however, statistically significant divergences of individual countries from the total sample average in the cases of Slovenia and Hungary. Slovenian sample FIEs are significantly smaller and Hungarian sample FIEs significantly larger than the average total sample FIE. Comparison of manufacturing sectors shows significantly higher than average number of employees per company only in DA — food, beverages and tobacco, and DM — transport equipment. In all the other manufacturing sectors, there are no statistically significant differences in the number of employees.

Age of sample FIEs: Table 3.8 exhibits the distribution of sample FIEs by the year of their establishment. Most of the sample FIEs were established in 1993 or before; the respective percentage for the total sample is 61.3% (31.0% were established before 1990), for Slovenia 59.4%, for Slovakia

Table 3.7. Distribution of sample FIEs by number of employees; %.

No. of Employees	Total	Slovenia	Slovakia	Hungary	Poland	Estonia
up to 10	6.5	9.72	7.89	1.18	7.84	4.26
11–50	19.9	29.17	26.32	12.94	16.34	19.15
51–100	13.2	12.50	17.11	10.59	10.46	21.28
101–200	16.4	19.44	13.16	16.47	14.38	23.40
201–500	23.6	15.28	19.74	34.12	26.14	14.89
501–1000	10.2	8.33	7.89	15.29	9.80	8.51
more than 1000	10.4	5.56	7.89	9.41	15.03	8.51

Table 3.8. Distribution of sample FIEs by year of establishment.

Year of Establishment	Share (%)					
	Total	Slovenia	Slovakia	Hungary	Poland	Estonia
1990 or before	31.0	39.9	39.5	47.1	34.6	25.0
1991	6.7	9.7	9.6	8.2	5.9	4.2
1992	11.2	5.6	5.5	8.2	11.1	16.7
1993	12.4	4.2	4.1	14.1	8.5	29.2
1994	7.3	11.1	11.0	2.4	4.6	14.6
1995	6.9	6.9	6.9	2.4	5.2	4.2
1996	6.0	8.3	8.2	3.5	7.2	4.2
1997	7.1	4.2	4.1	8.2	9.2	0.0
1998	4.6	9.7	9.6	2.4	4.6	0.0
1999	2.8	0.0	0.0	2.4	4.6	0.0
2000	3.9	1.4	1.4	1.2	4.6	2.1
2001	0.2	0.0	0.0	0.0	0.0	0.0
Total	100.0	100.0	100.0	100.0	100.0	100.0

58.7%, for Hungary 77.6%, for Poland 60.1% and for Estonia 75.1%. The Mann–Whitney test shows statistically significant differences among countries as far as their age is concerned. Slovakian FIEs are on average older, while Hungarian ones are generally younger than the average total sample FIE. No such statistically significant differences were found for different manufacturing sectors.

The picture with regard to the distribution of sample FIEs according to the *year of their establishment as FIEs* is rather different. This demonstrates that a number of sample FIEs were created via acquisitions of firms by strategic foreign investors, or via joint ventures of firms with strategic foreign investors. In total, 12.8% of sample firms were established as FIEs in

1990 or before, the respective percentages being 27.1% in Hungary, 15.3% in Slovenia, 10.5% in Estonia, 7.7% in Poland and zero in Slovakia. More than half of sample firms were established as FIEs before 1995. The share of such FIEs is highest in Hungary (69.4%) and Estonia (79.2%) (see Table 3.9). There are statistically significant differences among countries as far as age as FIE is concerned. Polish sample firms have been established as FIEs on average longer than total sample firms, while the opposite is true for Hungarian, Estonian and Slovenian FIEs. As far as the various manufacturing sectors are concerned, a statistically significant difference was found only for DC — leather and leather products — where sample firms have been on average established as FIEs for a shorter time than the average firm from the total sample.

Foreign equity shares in FIEs: Majority foreign-owned FIEs, with more than 50% foreign equity share, strongly prevail in the sample. Of all sample FIEs, only 14.5% are 50% or less foreign-owned. It does not seem that there are any important differences in this regard among the countries concerned (see Table 3.10). The Mann–Whitney test of mean ranks shows a statistically significant and lower average foreign equity share vis-à-vis the total sample only for Slovenia. As far as differences among manufacturing sectors are concerned, sample FIEs in DE — paper, publishing and printing — prove on average to have a statistically significant, higher foreign equity share than

Table 3.9. Distribution of sample FIEs by year of establishment as FIE.

Year of Establishment	Share (%)					
	Total	Slovenia	Slovakia	Hungary	Poland	Estonia
1990 or before	12.8	15.3	0.0	27.0	7.7	10.4
1991	6.0	2.8	6.4	9.4	5.8	4.2
1992	11.0	6.9	10.3	11.8	11.5	16.7
1993	15.5	6.9	16.7	14.1	11.5	33.3
1994	9.6	11.1	7.7	7.1	9.6	14.6
1995	11.9	13.9	17.9	7.1	11.5	8.3
1996	8.4	11.1	9.0	8.2	5.8	6.3
1997	8.4	11.1	10.3	9.4	7.7	0.0
1998	5.7	9.7	6.4	2.4	9.6	0.0
1999	4.8	5.6	3.8	2.4	11.5	2.1
2000	5.4	4.2	11.5	1.2	5.8	4.2
2001	0.6	1.4	0.0	0.0	1.9	0.0
Total	100.0	100.0	100.0	100.0	100.0	100.0

Table 3.10. Distribution of sample FIEs by foreign equity share.

Foreign Equity Share (%)	Share (%)					
	Total	Slovenia	Slovakia	Hungary	Poland	Estonia
10–50	14.5	14.5	10.3	16.5	15.2	6.3
51–99	29.0	29.0	20.5	20.0	35.1	27.1
100	56.5	56.5	69.2	63.5	49.7	66.7
Total	100.0	100.0	100.0	100.0	100.0	100.0

Table 3.11. Distribution of sample FIEs by type of product.

Type of Product	Share (%)					
	Total	Slovenia	Slovakia	Hungary	Poland	Estonia
Intermediate good	48.2	50.0	43.8	40.0	54.4	47.9
Final product	14.3	23.6	19.2	22.4	5.4	6.3
Both	37.5	26.4	37.0	37.6	40.3	45.8
Total	100.0	100.0	100.0	100.0	100.0	100.0

the total sample. The opposite is true for DG — chemicals and man-made fibers.

Type of product produced by sample FIEs: The questionnaire distinguishes between intermediate goods and final products. FIEs may also produce both. Intermediate goods prevail in all the countries. Just 14.3% of total sample FIEs produce only final products, the respective share in Slovenia (23.6%), Hungary (22.4%) and Slovakia (19.2%) being much higher than in Poland (5.4%) and Estonia (6.3%) (see Table 3.11). These differences do not seem to be confirmed by the Mann–Whitney test, which shows statistically significant different average structure of FIEs products only for Slovenian FIEs. Manufacturing sectors with statistically significant different average product structure include DA — food, beverages and tobacco, DB — textiles and textile products, and DD — wood and wood products.

Descriptive Analysis

Autonomy of subsidiaries

The data enable us to find out whether individual business functions are undertaken only/mainly by the subsidiary or only/mainly by the foreign parent company. Autonomy of business functions of subsidiaries is then broken down into operational, marketing or strategic autonomy. Table 3.12 shows the average degree of control of individual functions by subsidiaries across the five countries, in aggregate, and by specific function.

Table 3.12 shows that subsidiaries have the greatest degree of autonomy in operational functions (accounting and finance, supply and logistics, operational management and process engineering) and the least in strategic functions (determining product price, investment finance, product development and strategic management). Levels of marketing autonomy come in between. Analysis of autonomy of business functions shows that the highest level of autonomy in all countries is in accounting and finance. Within operational-management-related functions, process engineering is the least autonomous in all countries. This is perhaps to be expected, given that process engineering involves technological improvements, and thus a certain degree of technological mastery. Autonomy in product development is even less in all countries than in process engineering. In

Table 3.12. Autonomy of business functions of FIEs.

Business Functions	Autonomy Indicator*					
	Total**	Slovenia	Slovakia	Hungary	Poland	Estonia
Operational management	0.253	0.111	0.199	0.212	0.370	0.262
Process engineering	0.353	0.278	0.245	0.396	0.426	0.338
Supply and logistics	0.247	0.194	0.278	0.237	0.268	0.232
Account. & financ. operations	0.145	0.083	0.140	0.124	0.165	0.220
Operational autonomy	*0.250*	*0.167*	*0.216*	*0.242*	*0.307*	*0.263*
Distribution, sales	0.306	0.319	0.454	0.323	0.201	0.366
Advertising	0.336	0.333	0.460	0.340	0.282	0.310
After-sales services	0.256	0.305	0.362	0.270	0.181	0.232
Marketing	0.373	0.403	0.515	0.352	0.295	0.379
Market research	0.391	0.463	0.563	0.376	0.287	0.352
Marketing autonomy	*0.332*	*0.365*	*0.471*	*0.332*	*0.249*	*0.328*
Determining product price	0.363	0.315	0.490	0.335	0.355	0.310
Investment finance	0.389	0.269	0.475	0.307	0.412	0.506
Product development	0.501	0.454	0.643	0.490	0.475	0.447
Strategic management and planning	0.500	0.398	0.580	0.468	0.532	0.482
Strategic autonomy	*0.438*	*0.359*	*0.547*	*0.400*	*0.444*	*0.436*

*Indicators are calculated by giving individual answers the following weights: 0 = only FIE, 0.33 = mainly FIE, 0.66 = mainly foreign parent, 1 = only foreign parent. The nearer the indicator is to 0, the higher is the autonomy of FIEs, and *vice versa*.
**Weighted average.

fact, product development is the least autonomous of all functions. Among marketing functions, after-sales services and distribution activities are the most autonomous, while market research is the least.

There are some statistically significant differences across countries for all business functions except supply and logistics. The usual ordering of FIE functional autonomy, with the highest being in operational functions, the lowest in strategic functions and marketing functions in between, is present in three of the analyzed countries (Slovakia, Hungary and Estonia). For Poland, marketing autonomy is more frequent than operational autonomy. This may result from the size of the Polish market and the market-seeking nature of FDI in Poland. The pattern is confirmed by the Mann–Whitney test. Thus in all marketing functions except advertising, Polish FIEs show a statistically significant, higher level of autonomy than does the average firm in the total sample; in some operational functions (operational management and process engineering), the situation is the opposite. By contrast, Slovakian FIEs show statistically significant and lower autonomy in all marketing functions.

It thus seems that market orientation also influences levels of autonomy of subsidiaries. The more the subsidiary is oriented towards the local market, the more we may expect that it will have greater autonomy in terms of marketing functions, and to some extent in terms of operational autonomy. Poland seems to fit quite well into this pattern. The more export-oriented is the subsidiary, the more we may expect that it will have a lower level of strategic and marketing autonomy. Again, Slovakia pretty well reflects this situation. Indeed, when we look at data on FIE sales structure, Slovakian FIEs have the most clearly delineated export orientation, while Polish FIEs are the most local-market-oriented. The Mann–Whitney test tends to support this interpretation. However, the factors singled out — market-orientation and autonomy — operate in interdependence and only econometric testing can confirm our hypotheses.

For Slovenia, strategic autonomy is at more or less the same level as marketing autonomy. Indeed, in investment finance and strategic management and planning, Slovenian FIEs show statistically significant higher levels of autonomy than the total sample average. Slovenian FIEs also have significantly greater than total sample average autonomy in some operational functions (operational management, accounting and financial operations). This is true for Slovakia, too, in operational management and process engineering. However, marketing and strategic autonomy is lowest of all in

Slovakian FIEs, which exhibit statistically significant lower levels of autonomy than the total sample average in all marketing and strategic functions. All this may suggest that Slovenian subsidiaries are the most autonomous while Slovakian are the least autonomous.

How do we interpret these differences in functional autonomy across five CE countries? Differences may be explained by the nature of inherited capabilities and by the market orientation of subsidiaries. The more developed are a given subsidiary's capabilities, the more autonomous we may expect it to be. If we take as proxy for subsidiary technological capabilities the importance of own R&D and patenting activities, then Slovenian subsidiaries certainly attach significantly higher importance to own R&D activities than Slovakian. And Slovakian subsidiaries ascribe higher importance to quality control assistance by parent companies than Slovenian, which suggests that they are dependent and strongly production-oriented subsidiaries.

When control of functions is compared across manufacturing sectors, the following main features appear.

1. There are no statistically significant differences among sectors as far as operational functions is concerned.
2. There are only four sectors which show any statistically really significant differences from total sample averages.
3. Practically all the sectors which prove to be significantly different from the total sample average in terms of marketing functions are also significantly different in relation to strategic functions.
4. Where there are differences, they always go in the same direction. Sectors which have significantly higher than average autonomy in marketing functions also have significantly higher than average autonomy in strategic functions, and *vice versa*. Sectors with significantly lower than average autonomy in marketing and strategic functions are DC — leather and leather products, DD — wood and wood products and DM — transport equipment. The only sector with significantly higher than average autonomy in marketing and strategic functions is DA — food, beverages and tobacco. This suggests that levels of autonomy in marketing and strategic functions are linked, and that market orientation of subsidiaries is very much industry-specific as well as country-specific. Food, beverages and tobacco industries in CEE are in the main much more local-market- oriented, and higher than average autonomy in market and strategic functions corresponds to that orientation.

The transport equipment industry i.e., mainly the automotive industry, has very low marketing and strategic autonomy, which suggests that the CEE subsidiaries in this industry are predominantly production-oriented subsidiaries.

Market orientation and structure of suppliers

Market orientation of subsidiaries is a very important element for the understanding of the development of autonomy of business functions, and of patterns of upgrading. It is also a good indicator of the degree of integration of FIEs within their foreign parent company networks. Overall, sample FIEs export 51.8% of their sales. However, there are big country differences in this respect. We have three countries with distinctively export-oriented FIEs — Slovenia with a 72.9% exports-to-sales ratio, Slovakia with 64.4% and Estonia with 59.8%. At the other end of the spectrum, we have Poland, where 67.1% of sales is sold on domestic markets. Hungary, with a 52.1% exports-to-sales ratio, is somewhere in between. Export orientation is closely tied in with sales to the foreign parent company. Slovenian, and even much more so Slovakian, FIEs sell most of their total sales to their foreign parent companies (Slovenian FIEs 37.1% and Slovakian FIEs 47.5%). Slovakian FIEs export almost three times as much to foreign parent companies than to other foreign buyers. This confirms that Slovakian, and also Slovenian, subsidiaries are in most cases production-oriented, dependent subsidiaries. In the case of Poland, Hungary and especially Estonia, a much lower proportion of exports goes to foreign parent companies. In the case of Estonian FIEs, 30.6% of sales go directly to other foreign buyers and only 29.2% to foreign parent companies themselves. The orientation of Polish subsidiaries towards the local market is consistent with the high level of marketing autonomy of Polish subsidiaries. In all countries, sales to other local subsidiaries of the foreign parent are very limited. In Slovenia and Slovakia, they are almost non-existent (see Table 3.13). It is, of course, fairly improbable that MNCs would have more than one subsidiary in small countries like Slovenia, Slovakia or Estonia.

Application of the Mann–Whitney test confirms some of the above differences among countries as far as FIE marketing orientation is concerned. Slovakian FIEs show statistically significant, higher than total sample average, sales orientation to foreign parent companies, and lower sales orientation to domestic buyers. Similarly, Slovenian FIEs show a statistically significant higher orientation to other foreign buyers (but not to foreign

Table 3.13. FIE sales structure, %.

Country	Sales to			
	Other domestic buyers	Foreign parent	Other foreign buyers	Other domestic subs. of foreign parent
Total*	44.6	30.5	21.3	3.3
Slovakia	31.7	47.5	16.9	2.5
Slovenia	28.1	37.1	35.8	0.5
Hungary	43.3	27.7	24.4	3.5
Poland	62.6	20.8	12.0	4.5
Estonia	35.9	29.2	30.6	4.4

*Weighted average.

parent companies), and weaker sales orientation to domestic buyers. Quite the opposite is true of Polish FIEs, which show a statistically significant, weaker sales orientation to foreign parent companies and other foreign buyers, but a stronger sales orientation to domestic buyers. All of this confirms that Slovakian and Slovenian FIEs are significantly more export-oriented, while Polish FIEs are significantly more local-market-oriented.

There are also statistically significant differences in marketing orientation among FIEs in different manufacturing sectors. Export- and local-market-oriented sectors can be easily identified. Sectors DB — textiles and textile products, DC — leather and leather products and DM — transport equipment, are significantly more oriented to sales to their foreign parent companies, while sectors DA — food, beverages and tobacco, DE — paper, publishing and printing and DI — non-metal mineral products are significantly more highly oriented than the total sample average to local market sales.

Structure of suppliers is another variable for understanding patterns of autonomy of business functions of FIEs, and of FIE integration into their foreign parent companies networks and local economies. Contrary to the situation on the sales side, where foreign parent companies predominate, other domestic suppliers take the lead on the supply side, with 34.4% of total supplies, followed by other foreign suppliers with 28% and foreign parent companies with just 27.6%. It seems that FIEs have more autonomy in supplies than in sales. All in all, FIEs purchase more supplies from abroad (55.6%) than at home. Of course, there are substantial differences among individual countries. The share of imported supplies is lowest in FIEs from Hungary (49.9%) and Poland (51.8%), and highest in Estonia

Table 3.14. FIE purchases structure, %.

Country	Purchases from			
	Other domestic suppliers	Other foreign suppliers	Foreign owner	Other domestic subsidiaries of foreign owner
Total*	34.44	28.0	27.6	7.2
Slovakia	1.62	36.08	32.70	23.01
Poland	40.47	17.83	33.98	6.66
Estonia	36.57	30.10	24.84	5.43
Slovenia	41.3	34.6	23.5	0.5
Hungary	45.29	32.03	17.88	1.18

*Weighted average.

(54.9%), Slovenia (58.1%) and Slovakia (68.8%). The share of foreign parent companies in aggregate supplies is highest in Poland and Slovakia (see Table 3.14). The unavoidable conclusion is that FIEs from countries where sales are most local-market oriented (Poland and Hungary), are also more local-market-oriented as far as supplies is concerned. More exports are obviously linked to more imported supplies, and *vice versa*. Also, the size of the country is relevant here. Smaller countries offer more limited possibilities not only for sales, but also for supplies. The Mann–Whitney test seems to confirm these differences among countries. Thus, Slovenian and Slovakian FIEs source significantly more supplies than the total sample average from other foreign suppliers (Slovenia) or from foreign parent companies (Slovakia), and significantly less from domestic sources (Slovakia). By contrast, Polish FIEs source significantly less from other foreign suppliers, and Hungarian FIEs significantly less from foreign parent companies, and (in both cases) more from domestic suppliers. The only surprise in this pattern might be that Slovenian FIEs source significantly more from domestic suppliers.

As far as differences in supplier structure among manufacturing sectors are concerned, the Mann–Whitney test produces results which in part reflect the pattern in sales structure. Sectors which export significantly more to foreign parent companies or other foreign buyers (DB — textiles and textile products, DC — leather and leather products, DM — transport equipment), source significantly less locally — this is the classic outward processing pattern; sectors, which export significantly less to foreign parent companies or other foreign buyers (DA — food beverages and tobacco) source significantly more locally. Other sectors which source significantly more from foreign parent companies and significantly less locally are DL — electrical and optical equipment and DN — furniture and other manufacturing, while sector DH — rubber and plastic products — sources significantly more locally and significantly less abroad.

Effects of industrial integration on local subsidiaries

The questionnaire results enable us to get some idea of the magnitude and types of changes that have occurred in local subsidiaries since they became FIEs. The changes were classified into five categories: changes in the value of sales, changes in exports, changes in productivity levels, changes in technology levels and changes in quality. The analysis generated two main insights (see Table 3.15).

First, FIEs estimate that the intensity of change is very similar for productivity, technology and quality. Moreover, differences in patterns of improvement in these three categories are statistically not significant across the five countries (with the exception of Slovenian FIEs, where the magnitude of change with respect to quality has been significantly lower than for the total sample average). This general lack of differentiation in the magnitude of change suggests that technological improvements in CE are still very much focused on quality, training and organizational improvements, i.e., around production capability. Nevertheless, there are some statistically significant differences across manufacturing sectors. The magnitude of productivity change in DB — textiles and textile products — has been significantly higher than for the total sample average, while the opposite

Table 3.15. Magnitude of changes since the registration of companies as FIEs*.

Country	Value of total sales	Share of exports	Level of productivity	Level of technology	Level of quality
Total**	0.50	0.45	0.56	0.55	0.56
Slovenia	0.61	*0.57*	0.57	0.51	0.46
Hungary	0.59	0.39	*0.61*	0.56	0.56
Poland	0.46	0.35	0.54	*0.58*	0.58
Estonia	*0.69*	0.46	0.56	0.56	0.56
Slovakia	0.26	*0.57*	0.54	0.51	*0.60*

*Magnitude of changes ranges from −1 = considerable reduction, through −0.5 = reduction, 0 = no change and 0.5 = increase, to +1 = considerable increase.
**Weighted average.

is true for DG — chemicals and man-made fibers. DD — wood and wood products and DG — chemicals and man-made fibers have experienced significantly lower than average magnitude of change in relation to quality.

Second, changes in sales and exports are slightly lower in intensity, especially as far as exports are concerned. The lower magnitude of change in exporting suggests that, in many cases, FIEs may have already been exporters before take-over. A higher increase of sales than of exports may also suggest that subsidiaries have actually strengthened their local market orientation. The Mann–Whitney test suggests a significantly higher than total sample average magnitude of change in sales for Hungary and Estonia, and a significantly lower one for Slovakia. Slovakian FIEs are the only ones to have recorded a significantly higher than average magnitude of change in exports. There are no significant differences among manufacturing sectors as far as magnitude of change in sales is concerned. The magnitude of change in exports has been significantly higher than total sample average in DJ — basic metals and products, and significantly lower in DA — food, beverages and tobacco, and DI — non-metal mineral products.

Competence profile of subsidiaries

Key sources of competitiveness of subsidiaries are quality control (a sample average of 0.836 on a scale of 0 = not important to 1 = extremely important) and management capabilities (0.778), followed by trained labor force (0.698), and, bringing up the rear, R&D and licenses (0.532). This further reinforces the view that CEE subsidiaries base their market position on developed production, and much less on technological capabilities. This is most visibly the case in Hungary, where the difference between quality and R&D as a source of competitiveness is biggest. Among the analyzed countries, Poland and Slovenia are the ones whose subsidiaries attribute the greatest importance to R&D/licenses as a source of competitiveness (see Table 3.16). In the Polish case, this is hardly surprising, given the local market orientation of Polish subsidiaries. In the Slovenian case, it may be linked to the relatively high level of autonomy of Slovenian FIEs in strategic management and planning and product development. This pattern seems to be confirmed by the Mann–Whitney test, which shows R&D/licenses to be a significantly more important area of competitiveness in the case of Polish FIEs than for the total sample average. The opposite is the case for Hungarian FIEs. For those, quality control is an area of competitiveness of

Table 3.16. Areas of competitiveness of FIEs.

Areas of Competitiveness	Importance*					
	Estonia	Slovenia	Poland	Slovakia	Hungary	Total**
Quality control	0.801	0.861	0.811	0.822	0.895	0.836
Management	0.765	0.767	0.791	0.770	0.780	0.778
People and training	0.791	0.726	0.676	0.679	0.675	0.698
Patents, licenses, R&D	0.536	0.576	0.579	0.520	0.419	0.532

*Importance of areas of competitiveness ranges from 0 = not important, 0.25 = of little importance, 0.50 = important, 0.75 = very important, 1 = extremely important.
**Weighted average.

significantly above-average importance, while for Estonian FIEs, the same is true for trained labor force.

Statistically significant sectoral differences in the various areas of FIE competitiveness are quite few. There are no statistically significant differences in quality control, probably because it is very important for all the sectors. For DB — textiles and textile products and DN — furniture and other manufacturing, R&D/licensing is a significantly less important area of competitiveness than on average for the sample, which is to be expected for these 'low-tech' sectors. On the other hand, training for DE — paper, publishing and printing, and management for DH — rubber and plastic products and DI — non-metal mineral products are significantly more important areas of competitiveness than for the total sample average.

Internal and external sources of competitiveness

Levels of competitiveness of subsidiaries may stem from their own activities, or may reflect reliance on foreign parent or other external organizations. The data allow us to trace whether key sources of competitiveness are internal or external to the subsidiary. Table 3.17 shows areas of competitiveness by source. If we take 0.5 (on a scale ranging from 0 = not important to 1 = extremely important) as the threshold level of importance of a given source, a few conclusions can be drawn.

1. The subsidiary's (FIE's) own activities and relationship to the foreign parent company are the most important sources of competitiveness in all four areas (quality control, management, training, R&D/licenses).

Table 3.17. Sources of individual areas of competitiveness of FIEs*.

Sources	Quality control assistance	Management	People and training	Patents, licenses, R&D
*Total — all countries***				
Own company	*0.82*	*0.79*	*0.72*	*0.50*
Foreign parent	*0.61*	*0.66*	*0.5*	*0.57*
Other foreign buyers	*0.55*	0.35	0.29	0.31
Other foreign suppliers	*0.51*	0.3	0.26	0.3
Other local subsidiaries	0.23	0.21	0.19	0.16
Other local buyers	*0.52*	0.36	0.3	0.28
Other local suppliers	*0.52*	0.32	0.29	0.28
Other organizations	0.35	0.32	0.35	0.31
Slovenia				
Own company	*0.83*	*0.77*	*0.75*	*0.60*
Foreign parent	*0.62*	0.47	*0.62*	*0.63*
Other foreign buyers	*0.64*	0.30	0.33	0.38
Other foreign suppliers	*0.60*	0.25	0.28	0.35
Other local subsidiaries	0.11	0.06	0.09	0.09
Other local buyers	*0.50*	0.30	0.31	0.30
Other local suppliers	*0.55*	0.25	0.27	0.30
Other organizations	0.33	0.41	0.36	0.32
Slovakia				
Own company	*0.81*	*0.76*	*0.72*	0.43
Foreign parent	*0.72*	*0.73*	*0.57*	*0.60*
Other foreign buyers	*0.63*	*0.53*	0.35	0.27
Other foreign suppliers	*0.61*	0.49	0.38	0.31
Other local subsidiaries	0.35	0.31	0.27	0.18
Other local buyers	*0.56*	0.44	0.32	0.23
Other local suppliers	*0.62*	0.47	0.40	0.27
Other organizations	0.40	0.42	0.38	0.37
Hungary				
Own company	*0.91*	*0.81*	*0.73*	0.40
Foreign parent	0.49	*0.61*	0.37	0.48
Other foreign buyers	*0.52*	0.21	0.16	0.20
Other foreign suppliers	0.45	0.16	0.11	0.18
Other local subsidiaries	0.13	0.11	0.08	0.07
Other local buyers	0.48	0.25	0.14	0.15
Other local suppliers	0.47	0.20	0.15	0.17
Other organizations	0.26	0.28	0.31	0.23
Poland				
Own company	*0.81*	*0.78*	*0.68*	*0.56*
Foreign parent	*0.70*	*0.61*	*0.55*	*0.60*
Other foreign buyers	0.33	0.45	0.30	0.33
Other foreign suppliers	0.30	0.39	0.26	0.30

Table 3.17. (*Continued*).

Sources	Quality control assistance	Management	People and training	Patents, licenses, R&D
Other local subsidiaries	0.31	0.33	0.31	0.26
Other local buyers	0.38	0.55	0.35	0.36
Other local suppliers	0.32	0.49	0.33	0.33
Other organizations	0.27	0.42	0.35	0.36
Estonia				
Own company	*0.77*	*0.77*	*0.75*	0.39
Foreign parent	*0.61*	*0.51*	*0.55*	0.44
Other foreign buyers	*0.62*	0.36	0.44	0.34
Other foreign suppliers	*0.66*	0.33	0.35	0.38
Other local subsidiaries	0.15	0.09	0.14	0.05
Other local buyers	*0.52*	0.40	0.42	0.26
Other local suppliers	*0.55*	0.33	0.37	0.26
Other organizations	0.24	0.28	0.28	0.18

*Degrees of importance of sources ranges from 0 = not important, through 0.25 = of little importance, 0.50 = important and 0.75 = very important, up to 1 = extremely important.
**Weighted average.

2. Only in relation to quality control are subsidiaries significantly dependent on value chain partners (local and foreign suppliers and buyers).
3. Other local subsidiaries of the foreign parent company and other organizations are not important sources of competitiveness for subsidiaries in any area. Thus the determinants of productivity at subsidiary level are strongly dyadic, with an important value-chain-driven sub-dimension.

Country-specific patterns of sources of competitiveness show two main variations from the average aggregate pattern.

1. The Slovenian, Slovakian and Estonian patterns are the most similar to the aggregate one. We should remember that subsidiaries from those countries are the most export-intensive, which makes them dependent in quality control on foreign parent companies, but also on foreign suppliers and buyers. But these companies are also relatively strongly dependent in relation to quality control on local buyers and suppliers. This dependence is not as strong as in the case of foreign partners, but is still above 0.5. This may in fact also be due to the strong export orientation of the subsidiaries in question, inasmuch as pressure to meet export quality

requirements makes them more dependent on the quality performance of their partners.

2. Poland and Hungary are the least dependent on their value chain partners. The more local-market-oriented nature of these subsidiaries has led to a situation where they are more dependent in relation to quality control on local suppliers/buyers than on foreign. Unlike Hungarian ones, Polish subsidiaries are strongly dependent on foreign parent companies in all areas of competitiveness. Hungarian subsidiaries are relatively less dependent on foreign parents, and consider their own quality control as by far their most important source of competitiveness.

Country differences are important in terms of the balance between external and internal sources of competitiveness. Moreover, we can observe country-specific patterns of variation in the degree to which companies are dependent on external or internal sources of competitiveness. The Mann–Whitney test shows statistically significant differences from total sample averages for Hungary in 22 out of 32 possible pairs of areas and sources of competitiveness, for Estonia in 10, for Poland and Slovakia in 9 and for Slovenia in 7.

Hungary obviously stands out as rather specific in terms of sources of competitiveness. The pattern for Hungary is that FIEs themselves are significantly more important for quality control, but less so for R&D/licenses. Foreign parents are significantly less important in quality control and training. Other foreign buyers from and sellers to Hungarian FIEs are significantly less important sources in all areas of competitiveness, except in quality control. The same is true for domestic buyers and sellers from/to FIEs. In Hungary, FIEs themselves seem generally to be even more important for quality control than on average for the sample, while the opposite is true for foreign parents. This has to do with the greater importance of the local market in the case of Hungarian FIEs. Hungarian FIEs also lean more on their buyers and sellers than the overall sample average FIE as far as quality control is concerned.

In Poland, FIEs themselves are a less important source of quality control and training than the average sample FIE. Contrary to the situation in Hungary, foreign buyers and sellers are a less important source of quality control, but domestic buyers and sellers are significantly more important than for the total sample average. Obviously, the high predominance of the local market in the sales structure of Polish FIEs makes the actors on that market the main arbiters of quality.

The Mann–Whitney test does not provide a clear common pattern of significant differences in sources of competitiveness for FIEs from the smaller three countries — Estonia, Slovakia and Slovenia. The only real difference is that foreign buyers and sellers seem to be a significantly more important source of competitiveness for them than on average for the total sample of FIEs. This obviously has to do with the higher level of export orientation of FIEs from these three countries.

Differences among manufacturing sectors in their sources of competitiveness are very few. The Mann–Whitney test shows some statistically significant differences from total sample averages only in:

1. DA — food, beverages and tobacco, where foreign parent companies are a significantly less important source in all areas of competitiveness;
2. DB — textiles and textile products, where domestic buyers and sellers are a significantly less important source;
3. DI — non-metal mineral products, where FIEs themselves are a significantly more important source of competitiveness.

Financial integration

As with competence flows, CEE subsidiaries are dependent for financial flows on their own resources (average mark 0.692 on a scale ranging from 0 = not important to 1 = extremely important) and on foreign parent companies (0.618). While there are significant country differences, retained earnings and foreign parent companies are the two most important sources of finance for all of them. The situation is somewhat different only in Hungary, where domestic sources, either banks or other firms, are a more important source than the foreign parent company (see Table 3.18). This echoes the relatively lower level of reliance of Hungarian subsidiaries on foreign parent companies as a source of competitiveness. Some correspondence between competence flows and financial flows can also be observed in the pattern of correlation between reliance on foreign parent company as a source of quality control and foreign parent company as source of finance. The correlation coefficient between these two variables for our five CEE countries is 0.77. The incidence of reliance of subsidiaries on foreign sources other than the foreign parent company is highest in Poland. This may reflect the relatively high costs of local finance for Polish firms.

The Mann–Whitney test sheds some additional light on country differences in terms of sources of finance for FIEs. For Hungarian FIEs, other

Table 3.18. The importance of different sources of finance to FIEs*.

Country	Retained Earnings	Foreign parent Company	Other Domestic Sources (Banks, Other Firms, etc.)	Other Foreign Sources (Banks, Other Firms)	Other Domestic Subsidiaries of Foreign Owner
Slovakia	0.801	0.632	0.395	0.247	0.088
Hungary	0.732	0.528	0.627	0.168	0.048
Slovenia	0.699	0.562	0.462	0.285	0.035
Estonia	0.681	0.656	0.468	0.287	0.041
Poland	0.613	0.672	0.478	0.324	0.215
Total**	0.692	0.618	0.488	0.270	0.112

*The importance of sources ranges from 0 = not important through 0.25 = of little importance, 0.50 = important and 0.75 = very important, up to 1 = extremely important.
**Weighted average.

domestic sources are significantly more important sources of finance than on average, and other foreign sources significantly less. For Slovakian FIEs, retained earnings are significantly more important sources of finance than for the average sample company, while the opposite is true for other domestic sources. For Polish FIEs, retained earnings are significantly less important and other foreign sources significantly more important than the average.

There are very few statistically significant sectoral differences in FIE sources of finance. Retained earnings are a significantly more important source than average in DH — rubber and plastic products; foreign parent companies are a significantly more important source than average in DE — paper, publishing and printing; other domestic sources are significantly more important than average in DA — food, beverages and tobacco; and other foreign sources are significantly less important than average in DA — food, beverages and tobacco.

Upgrading activities

In this section, we ask two questions:

Who initiates changes in FIEs?

How will the future mandate of FIEs evolve?

We distinguish between functional upgrading (organization and business functions), product diversification (number of lines of businesses) and sale upgrading (sales and exports).

Table 3.19. Who takes the initiative for change?*

Country	Organization and business functions	Number of lines of business	Sales and exports
Total**	0.38	0.48	0.43
Slovenia	0.37	0.43	0.43
Slovakia	0.38	0.61	0.54
Hungary	*0.30*	0.46	0.46
Poland	0.44	0.50	0.39
Estonia	0.33	*0.31*	*0.31*

*Indicators are calculated by giving individual answers the following weights: 0 = only FIE, 0.33 = mainly FIE, 0.66 = mainly foreign parent, 1 = only foreign parent. Thus the nearer the indicator is to 0, the more initiatives have been undertaken by the FIEs themselves and *vice versa*.
**Weighted average.

Table 3.19 suggests several conclusions.

1. In all three aspects (organization and business functions, number of lines of business and sales and exports), FIEs themselves are more frequent initiators of changes than foreign parent companies. Overall, local subsidiaries thus seem to have a high degree of autonomy within their charter; the initiatives indicator ranges from 0.31 (lines of businesses in Estonia) to 0.61 (lines of businesses in Slovakia).
2. In all the countries except Slovakia, FIEs are a more important initiator of change than foreign parent companies. On average, foreign owners are relatively the most frequent initiator of change in Slovakia and the least frequent in Estonia. The Mann–Whitney test confirms these divergences on the part of Slovakia and Estonia from the total sample average as statistically significant. It is difficult to interpret these; they may reflect industry differences, which are certainly significant for sales and number of lines of businesses.
3. Foreign parents most frequently initiate changes relating to product diversification (number of lines of business) and are also prominent in terms of decisions regarding sales and exports. They are least involved as initiators of changes regarding organization and business functions. This latter point suggests that subsidiaries have a certain degree of autonomy to expand on their mandate, irrespective of their current charter. However, as foreign parents tend to take a bigger role in terms of changes

regarding products and sales/exports, changes in organization and business functions are always more likely to be changes within the limits of the existing charter of the subsidiary.

4. There are only very few statistically significant differences among manufacturing sectors in terms of who is the initiator of changes. These differences are as a rule in sales and exports, and are present in DA — food, beverages and tobacco, where foreign parents take significantly fewer initiatives for change than on average for the total sample, while the situation in DC — leather and leather products and DM — transport equipment is the opposite. This may have to do with the market orientation of these sectors.

Table 3.20 reveals the directions in which FIEs expect their future mandate will evolve. On average, FIEs from all the countries in all the areas expect that their future mandate will increase; the highest increase is expected in the number of business lines (0.506), followed by sales and exports (0.414), and finally by the number of business functions to be undertaken independently by FIEs (0.383). There are significant country differences in terms of the expected expansion of current mandate. On average, Hungarian and Estonian FIEs expect a more modest increase in their mandate than FIEs from the other three countries. The smallest increase of mandate is expected by Hungarian FIEs in business functions (0.205) and in lines of business (0.238), and by Estonian FIEs in business functions (0.279). The highest increase is expected by Polish FIEs in number of business lines (0.704) and business functions (0.503), by Slovenian FIEs in sales

Table 3.20. Expectations of development of future mandate of FIEs*.

Country	Sales and exports	Number of other business functions undertaken independently	Number of lines of businesses
Total**	0.414	0.383	0.506
Slovenia	*0.667*	0.319	0.472
Slovakia	0.474	0.455	*0.500*
Hungary	0.321	0.205	0.238
Poland	0.331	*0.503*	*0.704*
Estonia	0.349	0.279	0.395

*Indicators are calculated by giving individual answers the following weights: +1 = increased mandate of FIE, 0 = unchanged mandate, −1 = decreased mandate of FIE. Thus the nearer the indicator is to +1, the more the mandate of FIE is expected to increase, and *vice versa*.
**Weighted average.

and exports (0.667) and by Slovakian FIEs in number of business lines (0.500). The Mann–Whitney test confirms the above country differences and shows statistically significant differences from the total sample average for Slovenian FIEs in sales and exports (higher than average increase of mandate), for Poland and Hungary in organization and business functions and in lines of business (higher than average for Poland and lower for Hungary), and for Estonia in lines of businesses (lower than average). However, these differences are not significant across industries, which suggests that perhaps market orientation of subsidiaries, which is a country-specific variable, is the key intervening variable regarding prospects for changes in mandate.

It is difficult to interpret these differences, and why Hungarian and Estonian FIEs expect a more modest increase of their mandate than those from Slovakia, Poland and Slovenia. It seems that Slovenian subsidiaries will continue to evolve as exporters capable of functional upgrading. Given that Slovenian subsidiaries rank the best in terms of the role of R&D, this proposition seems plausible. Polish subsidiaries tend to expect increases in terms of number of lines of businesses. They do have a predominantly local market orientation, and such further product diversification may be consistent with that orientation.

Conclusions

In this chapter, we have examined the key features of industrial integration in CEE at subsidiary level. On the basis of our four research questions, we examined the process of integration of local subsidiaries and patterns of upgrading thereof by exploring degrees of autonomy, market orientation, competence profile, sources of finance and effects and patterns of management of change.

Subsidiaries have the highest level of autonomy in operational functions (accounting and finance, supply and logistics, operations, and process engineering) and the lowest in strategic functions (determining product price, investment finance, product development and strategic management). Operational and strategic autonomy is highest in Slovenia while operational autonomy is lowest in Slovakia. There are some indications that levels of autonomy in marketing and strategic functions are linked. We explain differences in functional autonomy across the five CEECs in terms of the nature of their inherited capabilities and the market orientation of the subsidiaries.

In terms of market relationships, the CE subsidiaries are in essentially dyadic relationships, with very limited local networking. These dyadic relationships are confirmed by the data on sources of purchases from other domestic subsidiaries of the foreign parent company. However, local purchases of inputs as well as local sales are strong, on account of the frequently local-market-seeking nature of FDI.

Industrial integration through FDI has led to big improvements in productivity, technology and quality. Moreover, differences in the extent of improvement in these three categories are statistically not significant across the five countries.

The key sources of competitiveness of subsidiaries are quality control and management capabilities, followed by the level of training of the labor force and, further behind, by R&D and licenses. This confirms the view that CEE subsidiaries base their market position on developed production, and much less on technological capabilities. The most important sources of competitiveness for subsidiaries are their own activities, their foreign parent company, and, in relation to quality control, value chain partners.

Local subsidiaries seem to have a high degree of autonomy within their charter, as it is they that most often initiate changes in the way the business is run. However, within that pattern, Slovakian, Hungarian and Estonian subsidiaries tend not to expect changes in their mandates, while Polish and Slovenian companies do expect changes calculated further to reinforce their market orientations.

References

Bartlett, C.A. and S. Ghoshal, *Managing Across Borders: The Transnational Solution*, Boston, HBS Press (1989).

Birkinshaw, J. and N. Hood, *Multinational Corporate Evolution and Subsidiary Development*, London, Macmillan (1998).

Burgelman, R.A., "A process mode of internal corporate venturing in the diversified major firm." *Admin. Sci. Quart.* **28**, 223–244 (1983).

Craig, C.S. and S.P. Douglas, "Managing the transnational value chain — strategies for firms from emerging markets." *J. Int. Marketing* **5**, 3, 74–84 (1997).

Ozawa, T. and S. Castello, "Multinational companies and endogenous growth: An eclectic – paradigmatic approach." Economics series, East–West Center, Honolulu, Working Paper No. 27, May (2001).

Porter, M.E., J.D. Sachs, P.K. Cornelius, J.W. McArthur and K. Schwab, *World Competitiveness Report 2001–2002*, New York, Oxford University Press (2002).

Randay, T. and Jiatao Li, "Global resource flows and MNE network integration." In J. Birkinshaw and N. Hood (eds.), *Multinational Corporate Evolution and Subsidiary Development*, London, Macmillan (1998).

Roth, K. and J. Morrison, "Implementing global strategy: Characteristics of global subsidiary mandates." *J. Int. Bus. Stud.* **23**, 4, 715–735 (1992).

Szalavetz, A., "Adjustment of Hungarian engineering companies to the globalising corporate network." In Bara, Z. and L. Csaba, *Small Economies' Adjustment to Global Challenges*, Budapest, Aula Publishing Ltd (2000).

Tavares, A.T., "Modelling the impact of economic integration on multinational's strategies." University of Reading Discussion Papers in International Investment and Management No. 254 (1999).

Tavares, A.T., "Strategic management of multinational networks: A subsidiary evolution perspective." Paper presented at the 6th International Symposium on International Manufacturing, 9–11 September 2000, symposium proceedings published by the Institute for Manufacturing, University of Cambridge (2001).

Young, S., N. Hood and S. Dunlop, "Global strategies, multinational subsidiary roles and economic impact in Scotland." *Reg. Stud.* **22**, 6, 487–497 (1988).

White, R. and T. Poynter, "Strategies for foreign owned subsidiaries in Canada." *Bus. Quart.* (Summer), 59–69 (1984).

CHAPTER 4

ANALYZING FDI IN CENTRAL-EAST EUROPE THROUGH CASE STUDIES

David A. Dyker, Katie Higginbottom, Neils Kofoed and Cordula Stolberg

Methodology

In contrast to the research reported in Chapter, 3, we did not use formal sampling techniques in the case study section of the project. Rather we set up in-depth interviews with a small number of firms which are very active in the area of FDI in Central-East Europe. The general justification for this essentially inductive approach lies not just in the inherent interest of the anecdotal dimension of case studies, but also in the scope for building theory from the anecdotes.

> While systematic data create the foundation for our theories, it is the anecdotal data that enable us to do the building. Theory building seems to require rich description, the richness that comes from anecdote. We uncover all kinds of relationships in our hard data, but it is only through the use of this soft data that we are able to explain them (Mintzberg, 1979, p. 587).

In a nutshell, 'the explanation of quantitative findings and the construction of theory based on those findings will ultimately have to be based on qualitative understanding' (Meredith, 1998, Section 7.3).

At the more specific level, the justification for our approach lies in the experience and outcomes of research on international technology spillovers and linkages, as discussed above.

> Existing estimation techniques simply do not provide sufficient potential for detecting the fundamental relations (that is, whether foreign firms learn from domestic firms, whether domestic firms learn from foreign firms or whether there are mutual advantages from interaction), and should be supplemented with case studies which focus on imitation of technologies, engagement of workers trained by MNEs, the extent of innovation networks and co-operation projects between foreign and local firms, as well as spin-offs in the form of new domestic firms (Kvinge, 2004, pp. 3 and 59).

The results of the interviews have been analyzed on the basis of *replicative logic*, i.e. 'the logic of treating a series of cases as a series of experiments with each case serving to confirm or disconfirm the hypothesis' (Eisenhardt, 1989, p. 542). The case-study firms cannot be taken to be strictly *representative* of any larger group, but they can be taken as *benchmark firms*. Every one is at the leading edge of the technologies used in its sector, and every one is heavily committed, in human and financial terms, to investment in CEE. By studying what they do, we can obtain an understanding of what is *possible*, an understanding of what might be termed the state of the art in technology transfer through FDI to transition countries. We should add that a number of these firms are very large firms. In those cases, even if ultimately they are only representative of themselves, that in itself carries a good deal of significance.

While case studies are, in the first instance, by their very nature, stand-alone studies, there are strong arguments for seeking to establish points of comparison with other methodologies and other bodies of empirical evidence. The case-study approach has great merits, but it also involves serious pitfalls. On the one hand,

> The results of case research can have very high impact. Unconstrained by the rigid limits of questionnaires and models, it can lead to new and creative insights, development of new theory, and have high validity with practitioners — the ultimate user of research (Voss *et al.*, 2002, p. 195).

On the other hand,

> People are notoriously poor processors of information. They leap to conclusions based on limited data, they are overly influenced by the vividness or by more elite respondents, or they sometimes inadvertently drop disconfirming evidence (Eisenhardt, 1989, p. 540).

The best way to handle these problems is through a process of *triangulation*, i.e., 'the use and combination of different methods to study the same phenomenon. Such methods can include interviews, questionnaires, direct observations, content analysis of documents, and archival research' (Voss *et al.*, 2002, p. 206). Triangulation is essentially an extension of the primary principle of replication. The most basic form of triangulation is to check case-study insights against quantitative material and analysis which 'can indicate relationships which may not be salient to the researcher. It also can keep researchers from being carried away by vivid, but false, impressions in qualitative data, and it can bolster findings when it corroborates those findings from qualitative evidence' (Eisenhardt, 1989, p. 538). In the present context, the obvious way to pursue that form of triangulation was to check our findings against that of other elements within the *East–West Productivity Gap* project that used standard quantitative approaches. Another key method of triangulation is literature survey. Where case-study findings conflict with those of the established literature, the explanation may be that the findings are incorrect, or simply idiosyncratic. Either way, the new information generated by the triangulation process is vital. Where case-study findings are in harmony with those of the established literature, the new information is equally vital, because 'it ties together underlying similarities in phenomena normally not associated with each other. The result is often a theory with stronger internal validity, wider generalizability, and higher conceptual level' (Eisenhardt, 1989, p. 544).

As noted above, we are not solely interested in convergence between different studies. It is equally important to detect inconsistencies. Webb *et al.* (1966) comment that the occurrence of apparent inconsistencies merely serves to highlight the problematic nature of reliance on one method of investigation alone. This view can be seen as a critique of the discourse in mainstream economics, which prescribes the almost exclusive usage of quantitative methods for empirical investigation. Though modern econometric techniques are indeed powerful tools for predicting outcomes, we take the position that quantitative and qualitative methods of investigation are complementary, rather than substitutes for one another. However, it should be noted that some scholars do not consider such a process of triangulation desirable or even possible. They argue that quantitative and qualitative methods rest on different paradigms, and that as a consequence the results of such different methods are incommensurable (Bryman, 2004, p. 453). We dispute this view on the grounds that it is possible to *interpret* different forms of information in such a way as to reconcile paradigmatic differences. We follow Webb *et al.* (1966) in believing that 'once a proposition has been confirmed by two or more independent measurement processes, the uncertainty of its interpretation is greatly reduced. The most persuasive evidence comes through a triangulation of measurement processes'.

Triangulation as a concept has multiple applications. Denzin (1970) identifies four: *data triangulation, investigator triangulation, theoretical triangulation,* and *methodological triangulation.* We are primarily applying the second and the fourth of these types in our analysis. To specify further, the type of methodological triangulation we are using is *between-method* triangulation as opposed to *within-method* triangulation. The results of this triangulation process are discussed in Chapter 5.

In-depth interviews of the kind we targeted cannot be conducted with anybody, or with any firm. To be successful, they have to be based on an empathetic relationship between interviewer and interviewee, and it is virtually impossible to organize such interviews except on the basis of some initial personal contact with the organization concerned. Access is crucial, and is quite properly a major criterion for selection of the interview group (Voss *et al.*, 2002, p. 203). Even where a good initial contact does exist, 'grooming' the firm for interview can be a time-consuming business. It can be a frustrating one too, with connections sometimes going cold, and interview arrangements often falling through at the last moment. Over the period of the research project, we groomed some 25 firms for interview. Just eleven interviews actually took place. While this represents a rather high failure rate, the final number of successful interviews more or less corresponds to generally accepted notions of the replicative ideal. As case studies cumulate, the material can quickly reach unmanageable proportions, and returns in terms of fresh insights may start of diminish sharply. With these considerations in mind, Eisenhardt recommends the use of between four and ten case studies (Eisenhardt, 1989, p. 545). On that basis, our interview group is on the large side, but not critically so. The individual interviews have proved to be enormously useful, each generating transcripts of some 6000–7000 words. It is on these transcripts that the next section is based. All the quotes from the transcripts have been rendered in English. It should be noted, however, that every interview was conducted in the 'home' language of the company, and the master transcripts are set down in those home languages. Thus the responses of the interviewees were not filtered through the neutralizing medium of international business English.

To repeat, the interview group is in no sense a sample. All of the firms interviewed are German (5), Danish (3), or British (3). Three of the firms interviewed are in the automotive industry (all German firms), one is in heavy electrical engineering, two produce control mechanisms and pumps (both Danish), and one is in telecoms technology. Just two are in traditional sectors, namely wood processing (a British firm) and food processing. One is in food retailing and one in banking. (The last two firms are both British.) To a degree, of course, the group is self-selecting. In accordance with the general principles of case-study research as discussed above, we interviewed firms in which there were people who were prepared to give us a good deal of their time — under strict conditions of confidentiality. In most cases, that meant firms with which one of the research team had a personal connection. At the same time, the group is, perhaps, more representative than appears at first sight. Why is there no British firm from a manufacturing sector? Because British manufacturers generally do not invest in CEE. Why so many automotive firms? Because this is, indeed, one of the main sectors involved in FDI in CEE.

But we must take the specific make-up of the interview group into account when interpreting our results. Since so many of the firms are German, might not 'germanness' be one the factors conditioning these results? More generally, since the FDI target countries come from a very limited group of (neighboring) countries, should we not be looking to spot country-specific factors? Perhaps more important, we must recognize that six out of our eleven interview firms come from the middle-tech, engineering-based industries which emerged in the earlier part of the twentieth century, and in which tacit knowledge is the main form of embedded technology, and the transfer of tacit knowledge the main vehicle for technological upgrading.[10] In the words of one of our interviewees, 'there are two key levers — personnel and know-how transfer and transfer of production technology (*fertigungstechnologie*)'. As argued by Zysman and Schwartz (1997), there are other sectors, based on high technology and software engineering, in which tacit knowledge may be less important than formal intellectual property rights (IPRs), in terms of embodying the state of the art in the given sector. And it is these sectors — the electronics- and software-based sectors — which are the fastest growing in the world

[10] We found that tacit knowledge was a very important element in our low-tech case-studies as well.

economy at present. Clearly, in sectors in which FDI is not actually a necessary condition of effective technology transfer (as it must be wherever tacit knowledge is key), the whole picture of FDI and technology transfer is likely to change. We return to this issue below, and we will be looking particularly closely at our one high-tech interview firm in this connection. More generally, we use our high-tech and low-tech cases to perform a version of informal sensitivity analysis on our (predominantly middle-tech-inspired) conclusions.

The Questionnaire

Here are the questions that we set out to ask:

1. How do lead companies specify the kind of production/technological system they wish to install in a subsidiary? Is the basic model always the company's plants in the home country? How is the basic model adjusted for variables like wage rates in the putative host country?
2. How do lead companies formulate their training programs for management and line workers? How do they assess the existing levels of capability of actual and/or potential employees? Is there a training program for everyone? What categories of worker are sent back to head office for training? To what extent are local training facilities used?
3. Following on from point 2 above, how do lead companies assess local training facilities? How do they evaluate professional qualifications of the host country?
4. Do lead companies see in-house R&D activity as a crucial element in capability? If so, how do they rate different kinds of in-house R&D activity (basic research, adaptation, design, skin-deep/root and branch) as factors of capability-formation?
5. Do lead companies see extra-mural R&D activity in the host country as a crucial element of capability? If so, how do they rate different kinds of extra-mural R&D (research institutes, universities, consultancy companies, individual consultants) as factors of capability formation? Do they have strategic goals for extra-mural R&D?
6. To what extent do lead companies extend their policies for capability into their supply networks? Are there training programs for management and workers of first-tier suppliers? Are there policies on R&D activity and cooperation for suppliers? To the extent that there are policies, are

they short-run, opportunistic, or strategic? Do lead companies help suppliers to move up the supply hierarchy?
7. Where lead firms give preference to suppliers from the home country, do they do so on general grounds of technological culture and capability, or specific, quantifiable grounds, in terms of price, quality etc? Do lead firms make strategic choices about the balance of home suppliers and host-country suppliers, or do they judge each firm on its merits?
8. Are IPR policies for subsidiaries exactly the same as for main plants in the home country? What about first-tier suppliers?
9. Do MNCs set quantitative targets for productivity for their subsidiaries? If so, how are they calculated? What about first-tier suppliers?

Results of the Interviews

In this section, we follow our research agenda questions as listed above, but only loosely — some of the most interesting points to emerge from interviews were not in direct response to questions.[11]

Business strategy

One of the most striking features of the interviews was the emphasis on the *global* nature of the overarching strategy of the firm.

> The basic point is that XXX is a world firm. If you look at how many countries we are active in, then we must be one of the top global players. And on the competitiveness side, we recognize that this world-wide network is a real advantage, to be at the coal face in every region. If we think of Eastern Europe in this connection, when the Iron Curtain came down, then it was clear from the point of view of the firm's philosophy the direction we had to take. We had to get in there. The markets were open, we had to engage with a similar or identical concept to the one which had been used in the rest of the world, and had proved successful.

[11] Eisenhardt notes that 'although early identification of the research question and possible constructs is helpful, it is equally important to recognise that both are tentative in this type of research.... Also, the research question may shift during the research' (Eisenhardt, 1989, p. 536).

> If we had not gone into Eastern Europe, we would have seen our share of the global market fall.... But if you are not a world-class company to start off with, you will not become one in Eastern Europe.

This is the kind of reasoning we are used to hearing from international oil companies, for example, in justifying their investments in the former Soviet Union — we are global players, we are in every region of the world, and that is part of our competitive advantage. So when a new region opens up, we have to get in there. But while the argument is transparent enough in relation to a natural-resource-based sector in which international prices are very volatile, it is less obvious, if not necessarily less compelling, in relation to engineering-based sectors. Here, the implicit argument is that, in Dunning's (1981) terms, you maximize your firm-specific advantages by being global — and therefore, you maximize your scope for technology transfer by being global. Thus, it is crucially important not to assume that a German firm investing in the Czech Republic is pursuing a purely regional strategy. If you do, you risk misunderstanding the nature of the technology transfer process involved, and therefore, the pattern of productivity enhancement. Most seriously, you risk misunderstanding the pattern of supply networking that may flow from the initial investment, and therefore, the pattern of productivity spillovers. It is not only leading firms that have global strategies. It became clear from one of our other interviews that first-tier suppliers may also think of themselves as global players, seeking to build production complexes in particular regions (e.g., CEE), but with *global* objectives in view. As we discovered, if you only ask such firms questions about their relations with *local* firms (including foreign-owned local firms), you may come away with the (completely mistaken) idea that they are not interested in network-building (cf. discussion of market orientation and structure of suppliers in Chapter 3).

Note, however, that within this global framework, regional, specifically locational factors may be of critical importance in terms of simple cost minimization and managerial proximity.

> We run a regular shuttle between Berlin and [town in the Czech Republic]. And it's great that it only takes us $3\frac{1}{2}$–5 hours to get there, and that we don't lose 24–30 hours like an American traveling to his subsidiary in East Asia.

Cost considerations apart, these strictly geographical considerations may make it much easier for [in this case German] firms to transfer tacit knowledge on the regional dimension. To complicate the picture even further, some firms are global players in relation to some of their products, but only regional players in relation to others.

Is there a productivity gap or not?

A quick reading of the transcripts might incline one to think that there is really no productivity gap at all as far as CEE is concerned, or a least none that cannot be liquidated in two or three years through the injection of Western capital, technology and marketing.

> We started with a level of productivity of 1.7 in comparison with that of the main factory, that is, it took 1.7 times as long to make a given volume of value added as in the main factory. That was the initial position. And our goal is to get that down to one within 2–3 years.

> We quite quickly achieved Western productivity levels. But we did not reinvent the bicycle. We took something that we knew we could do and was a safe bet, transferred it and trained the people in it, so that they were able to handle it just like the people in the West.

> What was lacking was the business dimension.... But we took on the rest of the workforce one-for-one. From the point of view of qualifications, they were of the same standard as you meet in Western firms. Their education and their technical skills (*facharbeiterausbildungen*) were on a par with ours.

> In terms of productivity, the Polish workers have a productivity level of around 80% [of the Danish level] I suppose. In Lithuania, it is maybe 30%–40% of the Danish productivity level, but it is a learning process. Here, in Denmark, we have people who have cut fish for 20–25 years. In Lithuania, they have at most one year of experience — maybe only half a year. So our experience is that they will come relatively close to the Danish productivity level within a short period.

In some cases, these statements are qualified with respect to technology choice. So if a more labor-intensive technology is being used in the CEE

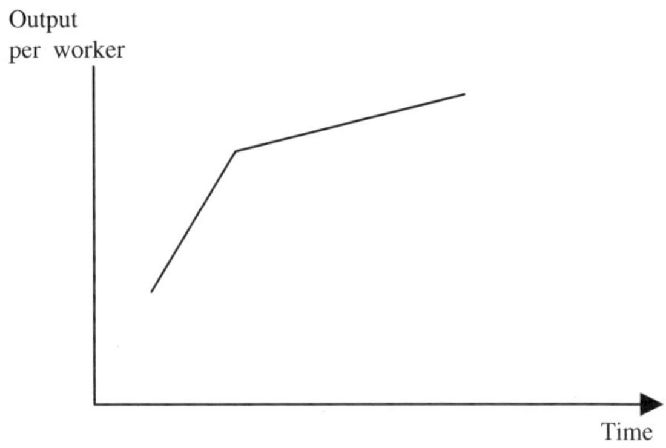

Fig. 4.1. Productivity over time in a foreign investment enterprise.

plant because wages are lower in CEE, productivity will converge to the levels of productivity that would be achieved *if you used a similar technology in the EU-15*. Even so, the general picture is a striking one. In terms of general growth theory, we are saying that CEE is on the path to *absolute convergence*, not just *conditional convergence*[12] — as indeed we would in principle expect, given that the basic endowment in human capital in the region is on a par with Western Europe. Whether the gap has been completely closed as of right now, the top firms in the FDI business *aim* to bring their CEE subsidiaries up to the productivity levels of Western Europe, or rather onto the dynamic path of those productivity levels, and foresee no serious difficulties in achieving that aim quite quickly. The vision of the managements of those firms with respect to future productivity trends in their subsidiaries in CEE is summed up in Fig. 4.1.

The picture is very different when we turn to transition countries outside CEE. In Romania, for instance, in a low-tech, labor-intensive traditional sector,

> There is a sort of catch-22 situation there. Because the labor is cheap, but the factories are fairly primitive, the price of the raw materials is actually higher than in countries like, say, France.

[12]The absolute convergence theorem posits that all economies will eventually reach the same steady state, where the rate of economic growth is given by the rate of technical progress and the rate of population growth. The conditional convergence theorem allows for different steady states, on the basis that human capital endowments may differ. (See Jones, 2002.)

This is the nightmare scenario for any foreign investor — where wages in the host country are low, but productivity is even lower. In this particular case, however, as we shall see later on, the problem did not prove to be insoluble.

The picture is also very different, even within CEE, when we start to talk about suppliers and supply networks, and here, the problem turns out to be less tractable.

> In some areas of supply, we simply cannot get the components to the quality and technical specifications that we require. So we have to bring these products largely from Western Europe. But not because we want to. We would like to get more involved in the local supply market...

What were the main reasons for getting rid of a local supplier — or for failing to take one on?

> Oh, quality, productivity, things like that ....
>
> The supplier base is certainly one of the biggest problems in Eastern Europe. We are always trying to solve the problem, for it makes little sense to move things from Western Europe to here and then back again — it's a long way....
>
> Nothing much has changed here, or very little, unfortunately. Suppliers are in any case international in our branch. I think we have taken on just one Czech supplier. I suppose we have neglected this a bit. But in the mechanical field, for instance, making mechanical parts for the housings, which accounts for some 10%–15% of our total costs — here, it would make sense to get them from Czech firms.

Thus, the globalization of supply networks theme is again clearly dominant, but it interacts with another theme, which we might tentatively dub the *lack of entrepreneurial vision* theme, with the *aversion to technological incongruity* syndrome, as discussed earlier, possibly lurking in the background. There are cases from more low-tech sectors where the experience with local supply network building has been more positive.

> In terms of third party suppliers, we use many, such as local advertising and design agencies, market research suppliers, accountancy firms, PR advisers, recruitment agencies, office suppliers etc.

> Regarding packing we use both local suppliers and foreign suppliers. It depends on costs — where can we get it most cheaply. Locals also do maintenance of the plants. We buy spare parts for the machines from two local companies. But, in general, we buy more and more in Poland and Lithuania because gradually they can produce as well as anyone else.

Even here, however, there are limits to the scope for local supply networking, and these limits are imposed less by lack of entrepreneurial vision as by the absence of the technological capability in the host countries to make a given key supply (in this latter case, a type of packaging — low-tech, but with very stringent quality requirements).

That last point brings out the key importance of quality in relation to supply networks. Even in cases where investor-companies have persevered with local suppliers, they are resigned to the persistence of a significant productivity gap, *if only because they have to impose (costly) quality inspections on their East European suppliers, whereas quality would be taken on trust in relation to West European suppliers.* And this sharp contrast between patterns of main activity productivity and those in ancillary production facilities is, indeed, what we would expect. Our case studies confirm the picture of CEE productivity patterns that we drew earlier on the basis of historical and *a priori* reasoning. The problem is not one of productivity or productivity potential in main industrial activities; it is a broader problem, a problem of *social* productivity rather than process productivity as such. We have seen what our leading companies can do, or believe they can do, about process productivity. Can they make any contribution to the solution of the broader problem?

FDI and human capital formation

Do leading companies help to build social capability through a process of (asset) creation? Each one of our interview companies stressed the importance of training, of upgrading the quality of the human capital stock within their subsidiaries. And they admitted that that human capital stock, once upgraded, was free to move to other companies. But the system of upgrading differs widely between individual companies. In some cases, it takes the form of a highly formalized, in-house education system. One company has a special department at head office which deals with all matters relating to the transfer of know-how and production technology (the key elements of tacit knowledge). But all interviewees stressed the importance of on-the-job training and personnel exchanges (between the lead factory and the subsidiary), and some were rather scathing about the role of formal training and retraining.

> We had to find work for 10,000 men. They had to make cars, cars that would sell. That's what you have to aim for — always better products, new markets, those are the things. I tell you, you cannot send 10,000 men back to school. That is simply not possible. And anyway, they would not learn what they need to learn there — assimilating new functions, learning about markets etc....

> We train locally and if there's anything that can't be trained locally, the staff will come over to the UK, We try and train people up locally because retailing is local business. And you have to understand your local customers — you're not going to be selling a Yorkshire pudding in Warsaw.

At the same time, the companies with more formal training systems stressed that these are available for all levels of personnel, and encompass the whole gamut of production operations.

> People from (the subsidiary in CEE) come and spend a period of time at the lead factory. And they don't just come to follow courses; they actually work in the factory as well. That includes assembly-line work, so that it includes blue-collar workers as well, right up to the management level — of course, with a different orientation.

> First comes skills training, then the emphasis shifts to management development.... During the set-up stage, a team of specialists is sent over from the UK to set up the business and recruit the core team. This team will stay in the country for a number of months in order to transfer knowledge and directly support the local management team. Once the core team is in place and up to speed, the set-up team returns to the UK. The UK continues to support the countries both remotely and with regular trips to the country as and when appropriate.

Thus, training programs are comprehensive, focusing primarily on the transfer of tacit knowledge, on the transfer of 'things that you cannot buy on the free market'. In some cases, the learning is 'collective', in the sense that personnel from the investing firm and personnel from the subsidiary are learning together about something exogenous that they need to know about — for example, EU food hygiene regulations. Even in a low-tech sector in low-wage Romania or low-wage Lithuania, you have to have a training program, *covering every job, even the humblest*, because otherwise, you cannot control the crucial productivity/wages relationship. And even on that scenario, you have to have a vision of the future, and a strategy for preparing your workers to face new challenges as the company climbs the technological ladder. So training programs must help to open up channels of asset creation which cannot be expected to develop spontaneously in the process of market-based transformation.

FDI and local educational and R&D facilities

Foreign firms can create assets, not just directly, through measures to upgrade their own human capital stock, but also indirectly, by helping to redevelop local educational and R&D facilities within the CEECs themselves. Clearly, these local facilities cannot play a role in the transfer of tacit, within-firm knowledge. Clearly, their role in human capital formation must be essentially ancillary. But the interviewees did stress the importance of local facilities, particularly with regard to the teaching of foreign languages (English and German) and the development of bespoke software. The first point hardly needs further discussion, the second is more interesting. Again, it is confirmed that software development, even for the very particular purposes of a given firm, is not a matter of tacit knowledge. Local suppliers are much cheaper as well as being closer, and their competitive advantage is clear-cut. But deep R&D cooperation between head office and CEE subsidiary does not occur in any of the *manufacturing* companies we interviewed. One interviewee stated bluntly that the local people simply did not at present have enough know-how for that. But in five years, he went one, it might be different.... Interestingly, but inconclusively, the only unequivocal confirmation among our interviews of the existence of two-way technology transfer came from service sector companies.

In some cases, firms have developed on-going relationships with particular host-country institutions, often universities. And these relationships tend to have a dual significance. On the one hand, much of the subcontracted software development work goes to university people. On the other hand, the companies use these on-going links as a basis for recruitment of local people into the organization. There are key individuals who play a central role in this dual process. Thus, in one case, a head of development within the subsidiary was eventually recruited by the local university as a full-time professor, on the basis of special lectures he had given while still working for the company. Thus, company involvement with local education and R&D organizations can lead to multiple forms of human capital enhancement. These effects remain, however, fundamentally peripheral to the main process of asset creation, which is within the firm. In a number of cases, given the kinds of technology involved, this pattern is perhaps inevitable. But one interviewee noted that his firm cooperated with local universities in the Far East on a large scale, but had not yet developed this in Eastern Europe. It would be dangerous to build too much on one interview, but one can speculate that Far Eastern universities might be seen as more effective partners than their East European counterparts.

Does FDI ever help local suppliers to raise their game?

Although all of the companies we interviewed had serious problems with their local suppliers, and all were anxious to resolve these problems, none integrated those suppliers into their own, within-company training and technology transfer programs. To a degree, the companies sought to solve local supply problems indirectly — by operating with a much smaller number of first-tier suppliers than would be normal within Western Europe, and thus effectively devolving the problem of productivity and quality control to a limited number of first-tier suppliers. More directly, some of the interviewed companies followed an active policy of helping local suppliers to find foreign partners. This policy was obviously based on the supposition that it is not possible for local CEE suppliers to make it as first-tier suppliers in global terms on their own, a supposition that is supported by other research (Dyker *et al.*, 2003). More specifically, one of the interviewees had a clear vision of their buying department as playing a kind of educational role vis-à-vis local suppliers.

> The subsidiary has its own buying department — relatively strong, with 25 people. The process always starts with the identification of suppliers, which are in general terms relevant for us, and which have the technological level we need for our products. So we have here in the buying department clear benchmarks on supplier qualifications, and we will continue to do this. We train people especially in this business of assessing suppliers....

So, here is a case of the multinational company setting up a system of *training the trainers*, enhancing its own human capital stock with a view to helping other firms do the same for their human capital stock — though without taking on any corporate commitment to ensuring the success of the second stage of the process.

All of this is very positive, yet in the end, perhaps a little inconsequential. The top firms in the FDI business do not have many ideas about raising the game of local suppliers beyond helping them to sell out to other foreign firms. So the whole cycle stays within the ambit of FDI, remains, in the terminology of the authors of Chapter 3, fundamentally dyadic. The key issue of linkages and spillovers *outside* the area of FDI remains unresolved. And it is that issue which is crucial in terms of considerations of overall social productivity.

Is the picture any different in the electronics sector?

We interviewed only one 'high-tech' company — from a hardware rather than a software sector. Here, the limitations of our methodology are starkly revealed. We found no evidence whatsoever to support the Zysman thesis, as outlined above. Rather, technology transfer in this case was implemented through 'close contact, and transfer of machines and production process documentation', suggesting that the underlying technology base was embodied primarily in tacit structures and in documentation which may well not have been IPR-protected. In that context, it is not surprising that cost-driven FDI in CEE has been an important strategic element for the firm in question. All that this proves in relation to the Zysman thesis is that the question remains open. And, indeed, we are unlikely to resolve it unless we interview some high-tech firms which have chosen *not* to engage in direct investment in the region.

Is the picture any different in the services sector?

With only two service-sector companies in the interview set, we must again be very cautious about generalization on that sector. It is nevertheless striking that both those companies laid particular stress on the long term in their strategic thinking. This is interesting, not only because they are in sectors which interface directly with the mass consumer, but also because both companies are British. Where systematic comparisons have been made between British firms investing in Eastern Europe and, say, German firms, a strong contrast between British short-termism and Rhenish long-termism has often been remarked (see Barz, 1999). We have certainly not disproved the proposition in the present project, but we have found no evidence to reinforce it.

In relation to training, the two service-sector companies show no significant divergences from the general picture — their commitment to training seems to be *at least* as strong as that of any of the manufacturing companies. But on local supply networking, the contrast is stark. Where manufacturing firms struggle to procure adequate supplies from local firms, one of our service-sector firms (a retailer) manages to procure over 90% of food supplies for its Polish subsidiary from Polish producers. This may simply be a sectoral peculiarity of the food sector, but in a part of the world where you are never far from an international border, food stores are not *compelled* to source everything from local producers. In the given case, the company is clearly perfectly happy with the quality of Polish supplies — in a sector where the kinds of technological congruence problems that bedevil manufacturing sectors simply do not arise.

Finally, in this section, as noted above, the two service-sector companies are the only ones that explicitly confirm the presence of two-way technology transfer. With one firm in retail and distribution and the other in financial services, there can be no argument that this reflects low levels of competence or know-how on the part of the lead firms. Rather it seems to reflect a high level of fluidity and dynamism in relation to the organization of these businesses. The two-way technology transfer is almost certainly strictly in the realm of soft technology, which is of overwhelming importance in service sectors. There is, nevertheless, a suspicion that manufacturing companies might learn something from the service sector in relation to cumulative technology transfer (see also Dyker, 1996).

The issue of country specificity

As noted in the last section, the interviews did not always confirm conventional views about the peculiarities of particular countries. More generally, however, country specificity did come through very strongly in our interviews as a factor affecting productivity trends, although we did not explicitly ask about it. As already noted, nearly half our interviewee firms were German. And the subsidiaries involved were mainly in Poland, the Czech Republic and Hungary, with a few also in Romania, Slovakia and the Baltic countries. A number of our interviewees expressed very strong views about differences between different transition countries. 'Since we set up in Poland and the Czech Republic we have been able to refine our new country entry model enormously, although it is a continuous learning curve as *no two countries are ever the same*'. One interviewee said quite emphatically that the process of unconditional convergence was clear-cut in the case of the Czech Republic alone. Another made the same point in relation to supply networks.

> In relation to the supplier problem, you have to differentiate clearly between countries. In the Czech Republic, they are making good progress here. There also we started off with mainly German suppliers, to make the transition as fast and smooth as possible. Since then, however, we have been able to bring in a number of Czech suppliers. The situation is much more problematic in Hungary. The Hungarian supplier industry is not so well developed. Our clients have very stringent requirements, and we still have difficulty in finding Hungarian suppliers who can come up to those requirements.

This statement is clear enough, yet it raises as many questions as it answers. While Hungary has a somewhat lower level of GDP per head than the Czech Republic, it has a well-developed engineering industry, and the emergence of Hungary as a major exporter of specialist supplier goods (admittedly largely on the basis of foreign capital) has been one of the notable achievements of transition. So, there is little basis at the aggregate level for putting the Czech Republic in a higher league than Hungary. Is the problem that the Hungarian economy is more dualistic than the Czech, so that the difference between the foreign- and domestically-owned sectors is greater? Or is it more of a cultural issue? Should we be looking, not just at country-specific factors, but also at country-pair-specific patterns? Is there something special, perhaps historically conditioned, about the relationship between Germany and the Czech lands, which impinges on the issues we are studying? Can it be argued that cultural congruence is an important element in technological congruence? And if there is, why is that German–Czech technological congruence seems to be so much stronger on main production lines than in component supply? And when one of our (German) interviewees says (à propos the Czechs) that 'it's still a planned economy: the managers are still different from over here', is he saying something specific about that ethnic/cultural group, or could that statement be applied to any transition country? These are questions which we cannot answer categorically. But we can propose some basic statements about the implications of all this for the convergence process which may serve as interim conclusions on our case studies.

Country specificity and convergence

Investing companies are aware of country differences, and adjust their strategic plans accordingly. That may mean slower convergence in the given economic activities for some countries. But it does not affect the basic trend towards convergence (see Fig. 4.2). In domestically-owned firms, we must presume that there are similar, or even greater inter-country differences in productivity levels. And here, there is no mechanism for ironing out those differences. The pattern that is likely to result from this is presented in Fig. 4.3. Under the impact of FDI, there is a strong tendency to convergence between East and West, and between CEE countries in sectors dominated by FIEs. In the domestically owned sector, by contrast, the productivity gaps between East and West, and between individual CEE countries, persist into the medium-to-long term. Because underlying social capability gaps are bound to narrow over time, and with progressive integration into the EU market, irrespective of the incidence of FDI, convergence in domestically-owned sectors is also ultimately inevitable. But the prospect

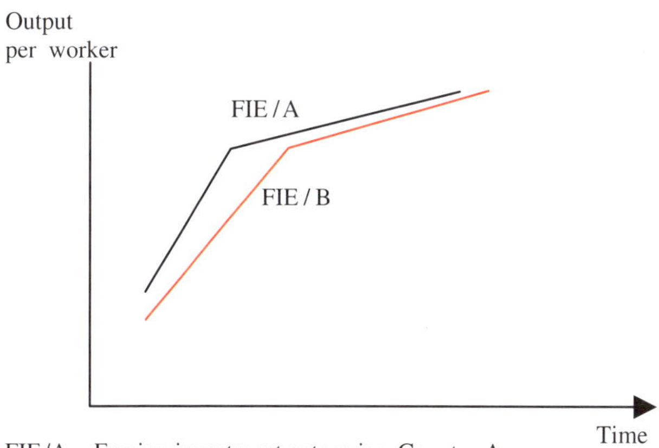

FIE/A = Foreign investment enterprise, Country A
FIE/B = Foreign investment enterprise, Country B

Fig. 4.2. Productivity over time with foreign investment and inter-country differences.

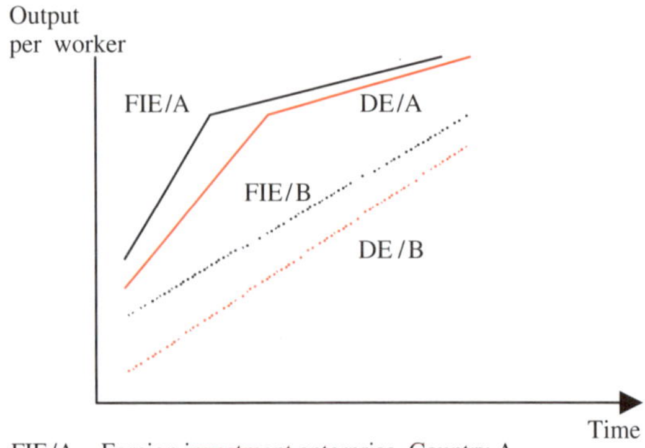

FIE/A = Foreign investment enterprise, Country A
FIE/B = Foreign investment enterprise, Country B
DE/A = Domestic enterprise, Country A
DE/B =Domestic enterprise, Country B

Fig. 4.3. Productivity over time, with and without foreign investment, with inter-country differences. The diagram portrays the case where initial levels of productivity are higher for FIEs than for DEs. This corresponds to the reality for most transition countries and most sectors. If we assume, however, that initial levels of productivity are the same in both sectors, or even higher in DEs, the basic analysis is not affected.

is banished to the very long run, well beyond the time horizons of business managers, politicians and citizens alike.

References

Barz, M., "British and German MNCs in Russia and the FSU: Evidence from the Western side." In D.A. Dyker (ed.) *Foreign Direct Investment and Technology Transfer in the Former Soviet Union*, Cheltenham, Edward Elgar (1999).

Bryman, A., *Social Research Methods*, 2nd edition, Oxford University Press (2004).

Denzin, N.K., *The Research Act in Sociology*, Chicago, Aldine (1970).

Dunning, J.H., *International Production and the Multinational Enterprise*, London, George Allen and Unwin (1981).

Dyker, D.A., "The computer and software industries in the East European economies — A bridgehead to the global economy?" *Europe-Asia Studies* **48**, 6, 915–930 (1996).

Dyker, D.A. *et al.*, "'East'-'West' networks and their alignment: Industrial networks in Hungary and Slovenia." *Technovation* **23**, pp. 603–616 (2003).

Eisenhardt, K.M., "Building theories from case study research." *Acad. Manage. Rev.* **14**, 4, October, 532–550 (1989).

Jones, C.I., *Introduction to Economic Growth*, 2nd edition, Norton, New York and London (2002).

Kvinge, T., "Knowledge diffusion through FDI — Established wisdom or wishful thinking?" Centre for Technology, Innovation and Culture, University of Oslo, Working Paper No. 31/2004 (2004).

Meredith, J., "Building operations management theory through case and field research." *J. Operations Manage.* **16**, 441–454 (1998).

Mintzberg, H., "An emerging strategy of direct research." *Admin. Sci. Quart.* **24**, 580–589 (1979).

Voss, C.A., N. Tsikriktsis and M. Frohlich, "Case research in operations management." *Int. J. Operations Production Manage.* **22**, 2, 195–219 (2002).

Webb, E.J., D.T. Campbell, R.D. Schwartz and L. Sechrest, *Unobtrusive Measures: Nonreactive Measures in the Social Sciences*, Chicago, Rand McNally (1966).

Zysman, J. and A. Schwartz, *Enlarging Europe: The Industrial Foundations of a New Political Reality*, Berkeley, University of California Press (1997).

CHAPTER 5

CHECKING THE RESULTS OF THE CASE STUDY INTERVIEWS — AN ESSAY IN TRIANGULATION

Leonardo Iacovone and Niels Kofoed

Introduction

This chapter is divided into three parts. In the first, the case-study material is triangulated against the quantitative research that has been done on FDI, technology transfer and productivity trends across the world. In the second, we present comparative analysis of some key case-studies from non-transition countries. In the third part, the case-study material is triangulated against some of the other pieces of research that have emerged from the *East–West Productivity Gap* project.

The Global Literature

Macro-econometric studies

This group of studies has come out of the development of the new growth theory. While useful in assessing general and macro trends linking FDI and growth, they are less useful in evaluating the impact of spillovers. Working at a very high degree of generality and aggregation, they tend to lump together the multiple dynamics unfolding at micro level.

In a comprehensive paper, Borensztein (1998) utilized data on FDI flows from industrialized countries to 69 developing countries to test the effect of FDI on growth in a cross-country regression framework. His findings are as follows. First, FDI contributes *more* to domestic growth than does domestic investment, suggesting that it may indeed be a vehicle of technology transfer. Second, FDI is more productive than domestic investment *only when the host country has a minimum threshold stock of human capital.* The latter finding is especially interesting since it clarifies under what precise conditions FDI should be expected to effect growth. These findings are supported by Keller (1996), who argues that mere *access* to foreign technologies may not increase growth rates of developing countries. The implication is that the notion of technological congruity is applicable at the macro as well as the micro level.

Using cross-section data from 46 developing countries, Balasubramanyam *et al.* (1996) also investigate the effect of FDI on growth in developing countries. They report two main findings. First, the growth-enhancing effects of FDI are stronger in countries that have pursued a policy of export promotion rather than one of import substitution, suggesting that trade policy regime is an important determinant of the effects of FDI. Second, they find that, in countries with export-promoting trade regimes, FDI has a stronger effect on growth than domestic investment. Both findings relate well to the results of Borensztein (1998). The second finding may be viewed as a confirmation of the hypothesis that FDI does, indeed, result in technology transfer.

Xu (2000) provides yet another confirmation of the argument that, in the absence of adequate human capital, technology transfer from FDI may fail to increase productivity growth in the host country. Using data on outward FDI from the United States to forty countries, Xu finds that technology transfers from FDI contribute to productivity growth in developed countries but *not* in less developed countries, because the latter lack adequate human capital endowment. Incidentally, as Xu notes, FDI may contribute to productivity growth for reasons other than technology transfer. Thus, a statistically significant coefficient on some measure of FDI in a productivity growth equation does not necessarily imply that technology transfer is the mechanism through which FDI contributes to productivity growth. Xu measures the technology transfer intensity of MNE affiliates on the basis of their spending on royalties and license fees as a share of their gross output. He measures pure R&D spillovers induced by the import of (superior) capital equipment on the basis of the subsequent increase in exports. In this way he estimates that, of the total effect of trade (via R&D spillovers) and FDI (via technology transfer) on productivity growth in developed countries, 41% is due to technology transfer.

Conclusions: Macro-econometric studies indicate that FDI has a positive impact on host country productivity, but conditional on favorable public policies (i.e. trade policies) and the existence of a sufficient level of initial human capital to absorb the 'knowledge benefits' conferred by the presence of MNCs. The importance of technological congruity is strongly confirmed.

Micro-econometric studies

To repeat, the principal problem of the macro-econometric studies is that they aggregate and lump together a variety of underlying dynamics at firm and sectoral level. On the other hand, the more disaggregated, micro approach has been seriously constrained by problems of data availability.

Cross-sectional studies

In a nutshell, this group of studies assesses the impact of FDI penetration on productivity in domestic firms, principally through technological spillovers, using cross-sectional firm-level data. It is important to underline what this implies: each firm is observed at just one point in time, which means that it is impossible to address causality as such, viz. — to determine whether it is FDI that is increasing productivity in domestic firms in that sector, or whether it is simply that FDI is entering a sector where productivity happens to be high (for some other reason independent of FDI). It is nevertheless significant that these studies have normally found evidence that FDI has a consistently positive impact on productivity in domestic firms.

Earlier cross-sectional studies focused on the relationship between FDI and productivity at sectoral level. Caves (1974) analyzed the impact on value added per worker in 23 Australian industrial sectors, using as a proxy for foreign presence the share of foreign firms in industry employment. He found confirmation of the 'spillovers hypothesis', viz. — that the higher the foreign subsidiary share in a given sector, the higher the productivity level in competing domestic firms from the same sector. Similar findings, based on data from Canadian firms, are presented by Globerman (1979).

Focusing on a key developing country, Blomström and Persson (1983) found positive evidence of sectoral (horizontal) spillovers, when testing the relationship between labor productivity and the share of employees in plants with FDI[13] (proxy for exposure to FDI) in a sample of 215 four-digit Mexican industries. Following up on this study, Blomström (1986) tested for the existence of spillovers using as productivity proxy an efficiency index defined as the ratio of average value added per employee in a given industry to that of best practice, and comparing that productivity proxy to a proxy for the entry of foreign firms,[14] namely the share of industry employees in foreign plants. He found that entry of foreign firms had a positive impact on average productivity, but no impact on the least productive firms, which he interpreted as evidence that entry of foreign firms increases efficiency through competition, rather than speeding up technology transfer. Still on Mexico, Blomström and Wolff (1989) tested for spillovers by trying to answer a slightly different question. They started off with the classical question on the impact on the productivity levels of domestic firms of the 'degree' of penetration of foreign firms. They then went on to look at the rate of catch-up of domestic firms with foreign-owned firms and US firms in particular. Their findings seem to confirm the existence of spillovers, and the hypothesis that 'foreign penetration' is positively correlated with catch-up.

Looking at the question from a slightly different angle, Blomström *et al.* (1995) analyzed how the characteristics of domestic industries are related to imports of technology by subsidiaries. Their hypothesis is that domestic competition and availability of skilled labor create an incentive for MNCs to transfer more technology to their subsidiaries. Again they focus on Mexico, and build an indicator for 'transfer of technology' based on technology payments to MNCs by their respective subsidiaries. The proxies for 'availability of skilled labor' are the share of white-collar workers in total labor force and in the total wage bill of foreign-owned firms, while the proxy for 'domestic competition' is given by the market share of domestically-owned companies and the growth rate of the share of domestic firms in total

[13]To avoid omitted variables bias, they also control for various other variables that could account for the level of labor productivity: capital intensity, labor quality measured by the ratio of white-collar to blue-collar workers, economies of scale measured by the ratio of average gross production in domestic firms to estimated minimum efficiency scales (MES), average effective work days during 1970, and the degree of competition measured by various concentration indices such as the Herfindahl index.

[14]He also controls for concentration, using the Herfindahl index, market growth variables, defined as the relative growth of employment of each industry in the period 1970–1975, and the rate of technological progress, defined as the rate of change in labor productivity in the best-practice plants within each industry.

capital stock.[15] Both hypotheses were strongly supported by the Mexican data for the period 1970–1975. Expanding on this line of enquiry, Kokko and Blomström (1995) looked at US MNCs' operations in 33 countries in 1982, and tested for the impact on their subsidiaries' technology imports (NB from all sources, including from parent companies)[16] of three principal variables:

(a) host country restrictions on FDI (e.g. local content requirements);
(b) level of domestic competition; and
(c) learning capacities.

They find that, while the two latter variables positively influence imports of technology, the opposite is true for the first variable.

Some of these cross-sectional studies focus on industry-level productivity (Blomström, 1986). The problem here is, again, that it is difficult to assess the causality unequivocally. It may well be that FDI raises productivity through spillovers; it may equally well be that the rise in productivity is due to the exit of inefficient domestic firms, or an increase in the market share of foreign, more productive, firms.

Lessons: This set of studies has been particularly important in terms of policy implications; the positive message that FDI generates spillovers has led the governments of nearly all the countries of the world to try to attract FDI and justify its subsidization. In strict methodological terms, however, the issue is not resolved by cross-sectional studies.

Panel data studies

The availability of better data bases, against the background of the unsolved question of causality, has more recently moved the empirical analysis on FDI towards the use of panel data; this has two fundamental advantages over cross-sectional analysis:

1. Since the panel allows us to observe the behavior of each plant over time, it is possible to control for the effect of fixed differences in productivity among different industries such as may influence the level of FDI in

[15] Based on the assumption that more investment means higher levels of labor productivity and higher competitiveness.
[16] Using payments of royalties and license fees as a proxy for import of technology.

that industry. It also allows us to follow the trend of productivity over a longer period, instead of just relying on one unique observation in time; this helps us to disentangle the pattern of causality between productivity and FDI.

2. The panel approach allows us to investigate the existence of spillovers while controlling other factors. (By contrast, cross-sectional data, especially when aggregated at industry level, has difficulty in controlling time-invariant differences in productivity that may be correlated with, but not caused by, foreign investment.)

It should be noted that this group of studies differs from the previous, not only in relation to the data used, but also because it has often made use of more sophisticated econometric techniques.

Panel data studies focusing on the own-plant effect: Here we look at the impact of FDI on the host firm. It is to be expected that recipients of FDI will show higher productivity as a result of the transmission of the firm-specific resources/capabilities that make MNCs more competitive despite their relative disadvantage as outsiders vis-à-vis domestic firms (Teece, 1977). This own-plant effect is generally assumed to be unequivocally positive. However, some interesting qualifications of this hypothesis have been proposed by recent literature using advanced econometric techniques.

Haddad and Harrison (1993) found, in analyzing the effect of FDI in Morocco, that plants with foreign participation are closer to 'best practice', and that the larger the firm, the higher the productivity level tends to be. However, they also found, as previously noted, that these tend to have slower productivity growth rate than their domestic counterparts.

Similarly, Aitken and Harrison (1999) found that FDI has a positive impact on subsidiary productivity. However, the causation is clear-cut only for smaller plants. For bigger plants, Aitken and Harrison find that plants with a higher level of productivity attract more FDI, rather than vice versa.

Moving the angle of the inquiry towards investigation of the determinants of technology transfer and productivity effects, Djankov and Hoekman (1999) confirm in their Czech study the existence of the own-plant effect, with MNC subsidiaries more productive than their domestic counterparts.[17] They find further that firms where the foreign share is 100%

---

[17]Note that this result is robust when controlled for the selection bias that prevails because foreign investments tend to go to firms with higher average productivity.

tend to have higher total factor productivity (TFP) growth than firms with joint ventures. They also find negative spillovers of FDI on domestic firms without foreign participation, but positive for other firms with foreign participation. *The authors observe that this may indicate that technological spillovers from FDI require a minimum level of technological capabilities and effort to be absorbed.* Consistent with other studies, they found that FDI is biased towards firms of larger size and with higher labor productivity.

Using data from a similar period, and still in the Czech Republic, Evenett and Voicu (2003) estimate the sign and magnitude of the direct effect of FDI on recipient firms. The innovative and interesting elements of their analysis are the use of more advanced econometric techniques for taking account of the bias introduced by the 'exit' of firms from the sample, and the estimations done at sector level, which allow the researchers to control for errors caused by pooling all the firms together. They find that, the publishing sector apart, recipients of FDI have larger capital stock and higher value added. But many firms exit the sample, and these tend to be lower-productivity firms, so it is important to take account of this. In estimating the effects of FDI, Evenett and Voicu's results vary, depending on whether they address the econometric concerns related to selection bias, pooling bias, or accounting for non-random exits. Once the selection bias is taken care of, the impact of FDI comes through as positive. But when the pooling bias is taken into account, the results change. Finally, controlling also for non-random exits, they manage to show that, except for one sector, FDI does, indeed, have a positive impact on recipient firms.

A very recent paper from Mariotti *et al.* (2003) analyses the Italian case, using data from the 1990s, and controlling for endogenous selection bias, size bias and technological progress bias.[18] Their 'empirical strategy' to

---

[18] The reader is reminded that these are defined as follows:

a *Endogenous selection bias*: Multinational entrants may be attracted to more productive and/or more profitable industries, thus leading to a spurious observed relationship between ownership changes and productivity levels of target firms in cross-sectional studies.
b *Size bias*: Since establishments experiencing a change of ownership are normally smaller than those characterized by stable ownership, one would expect the former to exhibit higher employment growth, even in the absence of any effect of ownership change on performance.
c *Technological progress bias*: Technological progress may significantly affect a given firm's performance and productivity over the period analysed. It is accordingly necessary to control the effect of time, in order to rule out idiosyncrasies in particular periods.

gauge the pure effects of foreign ownership on productivity is twofold. Firstly, they focus explicitly on the medium-term effect of foreign ownership. Secondly, they use a so-called 'like with like' procedure, which consists of comparing changes in productivity and employment of firms that have undergone foreign acquisition and firms that present a similar profile, but have remained domestically-owned over the same period. Their findings are the following:

(1) labor productivity was indeed increased by foreign acquisition (an increase of 60% over the medium term,[19] and was never lower than in the control group[20];
(2) when a domestic firm is taken over by another domestic firm, there is a positive differential in productivity growth between such 'domestically acquired' and 'foreign acquired' firms over the first three years, but this turns negative in the fourth year; overall, the relationship is statistically insignificant;
(3) in assessing whether there is a difference according to the country of origin of the acquiring firm, they found that the increase in productivity is higher when acquisition is by EU MNCs (always greater than 80%) than by US MNCs (never higher than 60%);
(4) the effect on employment growth of foreign acquisition is statistically significant only in the case of small firms (with less than 49 employees), or when the firms are acquired by EU MNCs.

Lessons: In general, the hypothesis that there is a positive own-plant effect and that domestic subsidiaries appear to be more productive than other similar companies without foreign participation is confirmed by the literature.

Panel data studies focusing on horizontal spillovers: Haddad and Harrison (1993), using a panel of firm-level data from Morocco for the period 1985–1989, found that (a) foreign firms tend to be more export-oriented and pay higher wages (but NB this may be because those firms are big, and not because they are foreign-owned); (b) foreign firms show a higher *level* of TFP, but lower rates of TFP *growth* than domestic firms, which may be consistent with the 'catch-up' hypothesis. However, when

[19]2–4 years.
[20]A group of domestically-owned firms with the same characteristics as the FIEs.

testing for spillovers, (c) the result is that, although domestic firms exhibit higher *levels* of productivity in sectors with a larger foreign presence, they do not exhibit higher productivity *growth* in those sectors. In order to control this last finding for the possibility that spillovers are absent because foreign firms are attracted to protected sectors, the authors looked at detailed data on quotas and tariffs. But they still did not find evidence of positive spillovers in either protected or unprotected sectors. What they did find is that (d) productivity growth rate differentials are partially due to the distortionary effects of protection, as productivity growth in foreign-owned firms in protected markets lags behind that of domestic firms in those same markets.[21] Perhaps the most interesting finding of this paper is that (e) the positive impact of FDI on the productivity of domestic firms appear to be driven more by increased competition (i.e. X-efficiency effects) than by technology spillovers.[22]

Aitken *et al.* (1997), analyzing a panel from Mexico in the aftermath of trade reforms (1986–1989), found that local concentrations of MNC exporting tend to increase the likelihood that domestic firms will also export, while no spillovers are found to emanate from domestic exporters. In this sense, they indicate that FDI imparts some sort of local 'information spillovers' with regard to export markets.

Aitken and Harrison (1999), using a panel from Venezuela covering the period 1976–1989 and more than 3,000 firms, found a 'negative spillover effect' from FDI to domestic firms, which tends to be bigger for smaller firms (likely because they are less prepared to face competition, and thus tend to lose market share). They confirm that the negative spillover is due to market-stealing effects, and that MNCs tend to invest in more productive sectors. They also test for local spillovers, but the results do not change — local spillovers are also negative. Finally, they calculate the net effect of FDI, weighing up the negative spillovers and the positive own-plant effect, which ranges from mildly positive to negative. The principal message for our research is that the positive impact of FDI appears to be confined to the subsidiaries, but also that investing MNCs are selective in their choice of subsidiaries at the level of industry and plant.

[21] This may suggest that the reason behind the FDI tends to influence the pattern of performance of subsidiaries; thus when the goal is 'market exploitation' behind protective walls, there is less focus on technological upgrading and innovation.

[22] Interestingly, no differences come through for firms with different degrees of foreign equity participation: firms with less than 50% equity participation behave much the same as majority-owned foreign firms.

In another paper, Djankov and Hoekman (1999) also found a negative spillover effect of FDI on domestically-owned firms in Czech industry. Interestingly, however, when joint ventures were excluded from the sample and attention was restricted to the impact of majority-owned foreign affiliates on *all* other firms in an industry (including joint ventures), the negative effect lost statistical significance. The authors report that survey questionnaires revealed that joint ventures invested significantly more in new technologies than purely domestic firms did. The authors suggest that purely domestic firms may have lacked the ability to absorb the technologies introduced by foreign firms (due to their lower R&D efforts). Once again, the importance of technological congruity is brought out.

In relation to developed countries, the findings appear to be more ambiguous; Chung *et al.* (1996) found no positive impact from Japanese FDI in the automotive sector on American component suppliers. By contrast, Girma and Wakelin (2001) found, for the electronics sector in UK, that FDI had a positive impact on domestic firms located in the same region. Similarly, Haskel *et al.* (2002) find positive evidence of horizontal spillovers from FDI in the UK, though these spillovers are considered to be of an order of magnitude substantially smaller than the subsidies given to attract the FDI in the first place.

It is suggestive that a recent paper comparing the cases of Estonia and Slovenia finds evidence of horizontal spillovers only in Estonia and not in Slovenia, once absorptive capabilities have been controlled for. This is explained by differences in privatization policy strategy, with Estonia more open to foreign acquisition, while Slovenia has tended to favor employee and manager buy-outs (Damijan and Knell, 2003).

The hypothesis that horizontal spillovers may be dependent upon the motives behind the FDI is empirically explored by Chung (2001). His assumption is that the motives of investing firms will be strongly influenced by the characteristics of the market which they are entering, in particular by the degree of competition. The hypothesis is that exploiting existing capabilities is suitable for less competitive markets, while sourcing new capabilities and knowledge is appropriate for markets with a higher degree of competition.[23] He finds that increased foreign presence in relatively uncompetitive industries is subsequently associated with productivity increase,

[23]The implicit assumption is that more competitive markets will produce knowledge that MNCs try to acquire through participating in them, while less competitive markets tend to be characterised by investment that exploits the firm-specific advantages of the MNC rather than country-specific advantages.

not attributable to competition change; while increased foreign presence in relatively competitive industries is subsequently associated with productivity stagnation, not attributable to competition change.

Still exploring the conditions and the determinants under which horizontal spillovers may occur, some papers have focused on the influence of local participation. A recent work analyzing a panel of Romanian firms in the period 1998–2000 showed consistent evidence that horizontal spillovers are more likely from fully-owned FDI than from joint domestic and foreign ownership (Javorcik and Spatareanu, 2003). The explanation, consistent with the theoretical conceptualization of the MNC as well as other empirical studies (Romero and Mansfield, 1980), is that MNCs are likely to transfer more technology to their wholly-owned subsidiaries than to partially-owned ones, because of fears of technology leakages.

Lessons: Summing up, these studies tend to find no significant and solid evidence of horizontal spillovers, and in certain cases they even find evidence of negative intra-sectoral spillovers. However, as the authors recognize, these findings must be handled with a certain care; two factors may be preventing an accurate gauging of the existence of positive spillovers. Firstly, the time span of the studies may be too short. While it must be expected that entry of foreign firms may negatively affect some domestic firms in the short run through market-stealing mechanisms, the process of adjustment and the dynamics of entry and exit can have, in the longer term, a positive impact on domestic productivity. Secondly, in focusing on horizontal knowledge spillovers, these studies may be leaving out other important channels through which FDI can enhance domestic productivity (this point will be brought out more clearly in the following sections on spillovers through labor markets and vertical spillovers). However, if it is true that panel data studies of horizontal spillovers do not, in general, imply positive intra-sectoral spillovers, it is equally true that they do pin-point such effects in specific circumstances, dependent upon: (1) MNC strategies, (2) market orientation, (3) ownership structure, (4) domestic policies.

Panel data studies focusing on vertical spillovers: Some recent studies have suggested that one of the problems with the analyses discussed in the previous section is that they may have been looking for spillovers in the wrong place. With this perspective in mind, these recent studies have concentrated on searching for vertical as well as horizontal spillovers.

Blalock (2001) used micro-plant data from Indonesia, jointly with interviews for qualitative evidence, and showed the existence of vertical backward spillovers, but not horizontal spillovers.[24] He tested these findings for 'possible external sources' of bias, viz.,

(1) *Scale effects*: selling to MNCs may allow the firm to operate at a more efficient scale.
(2) *Public goods*: the correlation between FDI and local plant productivity could be explained by the multinational's provision of public goods rather than by technology transfers.
(3) *Export market effect*: a correlation could exist between supplying multinationals and exporting, to the extent that firms exporting may be selected by MNCs as suppliers, and this would make them even more successful in exporting.

These tests, however, merely confirm his findings — in sectors where there is higher upstream demand from MNCs, productivity in the local companies is higher.

Smarzynska (2002), analyzing the case of Lithuania with an unbalanced panel covering the period 1996–2000, found evidence of positive spillovers through backward linkages (inter-sectoral), but not through horizontal linkages (intra-sectoral), showing that productivity is enhanced by contacts with multinational customers, but not by the presence of FDI in the same sector. The vertical spillovers are not geographically restricted, though they appear to be stronger locally. Interestingly, the productivity effect of backward linkages is stronger when FDI is oriented towards the domestic market than when the focus is mainly on exports. But the pattern of ownership (i.e. joint venture or totally foreign-owned) of foreign firms does not make any difference. The study is not able to disentangle the causes of these spillovers between competition effects, driven by increased upstream competition because of the higher stringency of MNCs and possible exit of less efficient firms, and knowledge spillovers.

The work of Damijan and Knell quoted earlier looked for backward as well as horizontal linkages in Estonia and Slovenia. In the event, they found evidence of spillovers through backward linkages only in the case of Estonia. This cautions us against assuming too readily the universality of

[24] Blalock's factory interviews in Indonesia with MNCs managers suggested that the 'horizontal' channels do not really work in reality. No movement of workers from MNCs to domestic companies in response to wage differentials was observed — the only movement tended to be between MNCs. There was, furthermore, no evidence of 'long-term' competition between MNCs and domestic companies.

vertical spillovers. Javorcik and Spatareanu (2003) look to see if 'local participation matters', and find consistently that this is the case. In particular, they find that vertical spillovers are more likely to happen in the case of partially-owned affiliates than in that of wholly-foreign owned ones, which is consistent with the hypothesis that foreign investors entering a country through green field investment are less likely to source domestically than in the case of joint ventures with domestic companies.

Lessons: The studies focusing on inter-sectoral spillovers tend to confirm the hypothesis that FDI may benefit domestic firms through the generation of vertical linkages (i.e. backward and forward linkages). However not even vertical spillovers are 'ubiquitous and universal'; some important determinants qualify and influence them, in particular: (1) ownership structure; (2) market orientation; (3) domestic policies.

Panel data studies focusing on labor-driven spillover: The relative importance of labor turnover is difficult to establish for obvious reasons: one needs to track individuals who have worked for multinationals regarding their subsequent job choices and *then* determine their impact on the productivity of their new employers. And there exist few empirical studies that attempt to measure the magnitude of labor turnover from multinationals to local firms.

A study of Kenyan industries by Gershenberg (1987) finds only limited evidence of labor turnover from multinationals to local Kenyan firms. The *World Investment Report* of 1992 discusses the case of Bangladesh's garment industry in some detail (see also Rhee, 1990). Korea's Daewoo supplied Desh (the first Bangladeshi firm to manufacture and export garments) with technology and credit. Eventually, 115 of the 130 original workers left Desh to set up their own firms, or to join other newly established, garment companies. The remarkable speed with which former Desh workers transmitted their know-how to other factories clearly demonstrates the role labor turnover can play in technology diffusion. Pack (1997) also discusses evidence of the role of labor turnover in disseminating the technologies of multinationals to local firms in Taiwan. For example, in the mid-1980s, almost 50% of all engineers and approximately 63% of all skilled workers that left multinationals left to join local Taiwanese firms.

One possible generalization here is that, in countries such as South Korea and Taiwan, local competitors are less disadvantaged relative to their counterparts in many African economies, thereby making labor turnover possible. Thus, the ability of local firms to absorb technologies introduced by multinationals may be a key determinant of whether or not labor turnover occurs as a means of technology diffusion in equilibrium. Another explanation may be a local investment climate that supports the creation of new companies. These two factors may, indeed, be mutually reinforcing. It is not clear, however, that they fully explain the Bangladeshi case.

An effective method of limiting technology diffusion is for the MNC to curtail labor turnover by offering higher wages than local rivals offer. Thus the wage premiums paid by a multinational can provide a rough estimate of the value it places on the knowledge it transfers to its workers. The more interesting point is that such a premium may either exceed or fall short of the benefit the local economy would enjoy, if the multinational were to sit back and allow its workers to leave. In this vein, Aitken, Harrison, and Lipsey (1996) sought to analyze the issue of spillovers on the basis that technology spillovers should increase the marginal product of labor, and that this should show up in wages for workers. The study employed data collected from surveys of manufacturing firms in Venezuela, Mexico, and the United States. For both Mexico and Venezuela, a higher share of foreign employment was found to be associated with higher overall wages for both skilled and unskilled workers. Furthermore, royalty payments were also found to be highly correlated with wages. Most importantly, there was *no positive impact* of FDI on wages of workers employed by domestic firms. In fact, the authors report a small negative effect. Finally, they found that the overall effect (for the entire industry) was positive. These findings can be contrasted with those for the United States, where a larger share of foreign firms in employment was found to be associated with both a higher average wage and higher wages in domestic establishments. When the findings of the second study are put into the context of previous work, it is clear that wage spillovers (from foreign to domestic firms) are associated with higher productivity in domestic plants. Conversely, absence of wage spillovers appears to reflect the existence of productivity differentials between domestic and foreign firms.

Lessons: The evidence presented by the literature on labor-driven spillovers is very mixed. The most important detail to emerge from that literature in terms of the triangulation of our case studies is the suggestion that, once again, positive spillovers may only start to accrue where local workers have attained some critical basic level of human capital endowment.

Case Studies from a Global Perspective

Box 5.1: The Indian software industry: The path towards higher productivity[25]

The Indian software industry has its origin in the Indian government policy applied up to 1984. The policy aim was self-reliance in hardware capability. One major event was the exit of IBM from India, in protest against the Foreign Exchange Regulation Act,[26] which required the dilution of foreign equity.

After 1985, when hardware prices crashed worldwide, the demand for software accelerated globally as firms moved from mainframe to client server systems. India's subsequent development of an export industry addressing that demand can be explained, to a large extent, in terms of international contracts for low value-added work, including the search for codification errors and codification itself. The Indian software industry developed a strong advantage based on relative costs. Some Indian outsourcing software firms tried to follow an independent catching-up path, by moving from low added-value software to more innovative products. However, they did not succeed. The limited degree of competition in the internal market is considered to have been an important reason for this. In 1991 the leading firm, Tata Consultancy Services (TCS), held 40% of the total Indian market.

After the liberalization, there was a transitional period — roughly 1992–1999. The sharp depreciation of the rupee and the liberalization of financial flows resulted in large-scale entry by multinational firms coincident with a peaking of worldwide demand for software. During this period, there was a gradual erosion of Tata's market share by national companies and some multinational subsidiaries (See Table 5.1).

The operation of MNCs in the Indian sector was based on a new kind of business model — the off-shore model. MNC subsidiaries explored the scope for greater cost saving, doing most of the work in India and only doing the implementation work on site. The off-shore model is cited as a reason for the higher productivity reported by multinational enterprises by comparison with business house firms.[27] This model was imitated by leading local companies that had set up Development Centers dedicated to specific foreign clients. It faced the constraint that foreign customers only entrusted fairly small, specific and non-critical tasks to these companies, at least initially. Nevertheless, this model has had a growing impact on Indian understanding of international markets and vertical segmentation.

Recent years have seen a consolidation in the industry, after a decrease in demand. There is a tendency, once again, for leading firms to shift their resources and attention to particular segments with high profitability, and thus to move up the 'technological ladder'. As a result, the added value of their activities has grown significantly over the last few years.

Lessons: Government industrialization policies in favor of the hardware industry were unsuccessful. However, they did create a reserved market and developed the local capabilities which subsequently formed the basis of the development of the software industry.

During the reserved market period, India's 'national champion' failed to change its business model towards higher value-added activities. When that change did finally come, it was driven by the MNC off-shore model, and TCS has only caught up with this development in the last few years.

---

[25] Based on Arora (2004) and Athreye (2003).

[26] Act 46, 1973, ultimately repealed by Act 29, 1993.

[27] Leading local software development service providers not competing directly with MNCs in terms of product and/or client.

Box 5.2: The Brazilian telecoms sector: Impacts on local technological capabilities[28]

Considered a strategic area by the Brazilian government, the telecoms sector was initially in the hands of a public company, Telebras. In 1976, CPqD was created, a public R&D centre considered at the time to be the most important telecoms research centre in the Southern Hemisphere (Hobday, 1986). The research centre was crucial for the development of the sector in Brazil within the framework of a protected market.

However, the technological gap in the Brazilian telecoms sector worsened c. 1980–1995 on account of the limitations of the import substitution policy. In 1995, Brazil started a complete reorganization of the sector, including privatization of Telebras. The privatization programme was the third largest telecom privatisation in the world (after NTT Japan and BT in UK). Aligned to the reforms, CPqD was also privatized.

The Brazilian telecoms privatization has been a success in terms of infrastructural development. The high demand from service providers, in both fixed and mobile systems, made the domestic sector commercially promising. The largest global telecoms manufacturers devoted special attention in the Brazilian market. Some of them increased their local production facilities, while others set up subsidiaries in the country (See Table 5.2).

In recent years, multinational equipment suppliers have had a dominant presence in the sector. Local companies have been absorbed by multinationals. The old switcher cluster, mainly located in Campinas (CPqD), has lost out in terms of capabilities and competitiveness in the international market (Szapiro and Cassiolato, 2003). There has been a change from a Campinas-centered cluster towards a more decentralized structure based on subsidiary hardware suppliers and a large number of universities and private research institutes.

Tax incentives were introduced in 1993 to foster manufacturing and R&D activities among hardware producers. After ten years of indiscriminate tax incentives for R&D projects in subsidiaries and for partnerships with local R&D institutions, the results in terms of innovation in areas of competitive advantage remain controversial. Despite the large investments induced by the R&D tax incentives (more than $3 billion to the electronic industry), output indicators such as patents and publications point to an insignificant presence of Brazilian subsidiaries in MNC innovative activity. Just three subsidiaries — Siemens, Motorola and Ericsson — have achieved integration into Global Product Development in some niches (Galina, 2003; Galina and Plonski, 2002).

It has been argued that the capabilities developed in local R&D organizations are highly dispersed, and that there is no effective coordination that would constitute a Brazilian telecoms innovation system. Although there has been development within the subsidiaries, questions about its efficiency and sustainability, and about public policy for the sector, continue to arise. In a detailed case study of 73 initiatives inside one of these companies, it was observed that after initial technological accumulation, local managers' entrepreneurship shifts towards the internal outsourcing market. Thus R&D investments and advanced capability do not indicate local innovative dynamics. Increasing R&D investment does not necessarily promote spillover to the local market. In fact, the opposite flow — from the subsidiary to the global R&D complex — may be much more important.

(Continued)

[28]Main source: Perini (2004).

(*Continued*)

Lessons: The capabilities developed by MNC subsidiaries are less and less linked with CPqD.

Tax incentives have promoted subsidiary absorptive capacity and created significant spillovers in terms of labor mobility and institutions formed.

Sectoral policies have also promoted the internal initiatives of subsidiary managers, and the evolution of subsidiary capabilities and the role of the subsidiary inside the MNC network.

However, innovation based on internal market demand is not linked to vertical and horizontal spillovers or increasing own-plant productivity.

Box 5.3: The Portuguese auto industry: Learning and upgrading within the supply chain[29]

Links between companies in the value chain create a complex network of relations within a sectoral structure. This network is particularly highly developed in the automotive industry. Hierarchical organization gives way to more blurred types of inter-firm linkages related to production, technology and marketing. The number of automakers declines (based on merger and acquisition), as does that of first-tier suppliers (mainly based on strategic alliances). The number of second-, third-, and fourth-tier suppliers grows, with increasing pressures for integration in cases where learning — upstream, downstream, and horizontally — is essential. Automakers have outsourced complete systems and components. The worldwide expansion of supply chains is replicated in different locations. To incorporate flexibly with local tastes, standard platforms are used to respond actively to global concentration forces.

In the 1960s, the Portuguese automotive industry was characterized by a multiplicity of small assembling units, addressing the protected market. But protection did not foster a component industry. In the 1970s, the first component manufacturers were attracted to Portugal, as a result of a new mechanism that allowed compensating exports and imports of manufactures.

In the early 1980s, incentives and privileged access to the internal market attracted Renault to Portugal. The plant, with a capacity for 80,000 vehicles per year, was especially significant for the Portuguese automotive sector. Renault paid for privileged access to the Portuguese market by accepting local value-added objectives. It played a key role in the process of creating a technological and manufacturing base by developing professional training and technological information systems. The Renault project facilitated the upgrading of the capabilities of local firms. In some cases, the latter remained development partners even after the decision to close the plant in Portugal, following the accession of that country to the EU. One company established an engineering unit in France, and followed Renault plants to Slovenia and Brazil.

In the 1990s, European Regional Fund support brought the Auto-Europa project, (JV between Volkswagen and Ford) to Portugal. With a capacity for 180,000 vehicles per year, it was the largest foreign investment ever undertaken in Portugal. The Portuguese government saw the Auto-Europa project as the nucleus of a local cluster of upgraded local suppliers. However, the Auto-Europa plant enjoyed only a low level of autonomy, mostly limited to operational issues (manufacturing and logistics). Initial support was provided for the accreditation of Portuguese suppliers, but negotiations regarding most technical aspects of supply agreements had to be held with head office. In practice, the opportunities for enhancing and expanding supply relationships had to be set within the wider MNC network.

MNC subsidiaries established in Portugal with an established relationship with head offices have had a broader dialogue at the local and global level. For the Portuguese firms that had higher expectations inside the supplier network, the options were the establishment of direct dialogue (considered an intermediate stage) or the creation of a development unit near head office. Auto-Europa played a role as facilitator in this, confirming the technological and manufacturing capabilities of the suppliers. Portuguese firms are still, however, typically second-tier suppliers (Féria, 1999). Few companies have managed to upgrade their status in the network, though some have been able to extend into new areas. It has been observed that a good track record of performance is the best catalyst for further cooperation.

(Continued)

[29]Main source: Simöes, V.C. (2003).

(Continued)

Lessons: The sectoral global structure creates specific challenges to new firms, *and it is the position of the firm within that global structure that largely determines specific firm growth possibilities.* Government intervention and the Renault subsidiary played an important role in creating and supporting the infant car parts industry in Portugal.

In the Auto-Europa model (with comparatively less autonomy), local firms have had to create international linkages to absorb and learn inside the multinational.

Box 5.4: The electronics industry in South-East Asia (SEA): Gradual development of technological capabilities [30]

Through the 1980s and 1990s, electronics remained the largest, most dynamic export sector in the fast-growing East and South-East Asian economies. Within the NIEs, two groups can be picked out. The first one is the East Asian (South Korea and Taiwan are typical examples) in which export-led industrial growth was driven by local firms. Since the 1960s, there has been a gradual progression of latecomer firms from OEM activities (original equipment manufacture), to ODM (own design manufacture), and finally to OBM (own brand manufacture). The second group are the South-East Asian (SEA) countries (e.g. Singapore, Malaysia and Thailand), which, by contrast, have depended largely on TNCs. In these countries, TNC-led growth, like OEM, has proved, so far, to be a remarkably successful strategy, contributing to national economic growth, innovation, and technology absorption. On export indicators, Singapore and Malaysia have matched or even surpassed South Korea and Taiwan. Wafer fabrication in Singapore and Malaysia has established SEA as an important hub within the global electronics industry. It is expected that the MNCs may continue to increase the number of regional headquarters in Malaysia, as they have already done in Singapore. Feeling less welcome in Japan and South Korea, many MNCs would prefer to continue investing in SEA.

The dependence on FDI in SEA presents familiar problems. Research conducted on innovation patterns within twelve TNC subsidiaries shows that there is little long-term R&D, though most of them carried out substantial innovative activity on short-term production process improvements. Some firms employ large numbers of engineers and technicians (in the case of Sony, 1,300 or 16.2% of the workforce, and at MEMC, 120 or 18.8% of the workforce). These innovative activities are, however, carried on mainly by drawing the necessary technology from head office, rather than from own innovative capabilities (Ariffin, 2000). The reliance on FDI exposes SEA to international recession as well as changing global TNC strategies. In Malaysia, as in Singapore, the supply chain of locally-owned firms remains weak, and lags far behind the backward linkage industries of Hong Kong and Taiwan at similar stages of development. Poor backward linkage restricts the potential for further integration with the MNCs. Subsidiaries in SEA lack new product design and R&D capabilities, and depend on low-end products for their exports. Despite significant advances in manufacturing technology, they face competition from lower-cost countries in the region. Responding to higher domestic costs, some MNCs (and local OEM suppliers) have relocated production to those countries.

Firms and governments recognize the difficulties, and have responded with various strategies aimed at promoting innovation. Government is active in developing intermediary institutions, such as technology parks and development corporations (Dodgson, 2000). As complements to FDI as key element in technology policy, OEM arrangements and subcontracting of technology from foreign firms is also encouraged. A number of new organizations, such as the Kulim Hitech Industrial Park and the Malaysian Technology Development Corporation (MTDC) were created to commercialize local R&D results, introduce strategic technologies, and encourage the development of venture capital in Malaysia.

Lessons: Market orientation has been an important factor for transferring cutting-edge technology to SEA.

Stability and market openness may allow evolution in the role of the subsidiary towards the status of regional headquarters.

Intermediate institutions such as technology parks and development agencies have a role in defining and promoting partnerships and collaboration, with a specific focus on local suppliers' technological development.

---

[30] Main source: Hobday (2000).

Box 5.5: *The automotive industry in China and India*[31]

The last decade has witnessed a profound transformation in the automotive industry in China and India. In the early 1990s, both countries had a closed market for cars. At the beginning of the decade, there had been only very limited multinational involvement — an early joint venture by Chrysler to produce jeeps in China, and the Suzuki–Maruti joint venture in India. Despite the closed market, the latter company enjoyed relatively early success. It went on to capture 70% of total passenger car sales in India by the early 1990s, working with suppliers to establish international best practice and to achieve high levels of productivity and quality. From the early 1990s onwards, a wave of multinational firms entered both markets. In each case, these entrants were required to achieve a high level of domestic content within a specified period (typically, 70% within 3 years). By the end of the decade, in India, car production had increased by a factor of two and a half times compared to the early 1990s (from 209,000 units in 1991 to 564,000 in 2001). In China, six joint-ventures with local groups now account for 84% of total output, with an increase in production by a factor of almost nine (from 81,000 in 1991 to over 703,000 in 2001). The local content rules pushed the new arrivals towards the development of high-quality, domestically-based suppliers. Even after WTO entry (under which such restrictions are banned), the local supply chain has maintained its position, indicating that it has achieved a level of quality similar to international best practice among first-tier suppliers. The development of the local supply chain in both countries has in large part been driven by the presence of multinational car makers; however, component exports are driven equally by multinational and domestic firms. The challenge for both sets of companies now lies in moving towards higher-level capabilities. On top of relatively low wages, advanced capabilities are considered to be a key factor leading to increases in exports of components and sub-assemblies from domestically-based firms to overseas car-makers. One of the six Indian seat-makers included in the cited study is already operating at this level, using a team of 200 design engineers to provide new seat designs for the international market. The main weakness of the supply chain lies in the fact that best practice techniques have still not been established among second- and third-tier suppliers.

Lessons: Government intervention and regulation (i.e. local content policy) was successful in created a competitive automotive industry in both India and China.

The entrance mode though strategic alliances and joint ventures was successful in transferring technology and creating world-class car manufacturing plants and first-tier suppliers.

Innovative activities inside the subsidiaries and local companies are still very limited.

The strategy has been unable to guarantee international levels of productivity at second- and third-tier supplier level.

[31]Source: Sutton (2004).

Table 5.1. Market shares of the top 10 software firms in India, 1991–2001.

Firm	1991–1992	1994–1995	1995–1996	1996–1997	1999–2000	2000–2001
TCS	40	13.44	12.28	11.43	8.35	8.32
Wipro	3.68	5.01	5.64	4.44	4.41	5.21
Infosys	2.38	2.13	2.23	2.28	3.62	4.91
HCL	n.a.	7.63		4.68	2.60	3.38
Satyam	n.a.	1.31	1.20	2.54	2.78	3.38
IBM India	n.a.				1.22	2.20
Cognizant	n.a.			0.75	1.70	1.87
NIIT	n.a.	1.99		3.37	3.07	1.81
Silverline	n.a.	2.10	2.05	1.23	1.80	1.73
Pentasoft/Pentafour	n.a.	2.26	2.69	2.72	3.27	3.22

Table 5.2. MNCs supplying telecom equipment in Brazil.

Company	Country of Origin	Entered Brazilian Market in
Ericsson	Sweden	1924
Nokia	Finland	1997
Motorola	USA	1992
Nortel	Canada	1990
NEC	Japan	1968
Lucent	USA	1996
Siemens	Germany	1905
Alcatel	France	1989

Summary of principal lessons from case studies

Government-led and FDI-led industrialisation — national champions and intermediate institutions

The case of the software industry in India based on the national champion Tata Consulting Services highlights the risks associated with this industrialization policy. Government industrialization policies vis-à-vis the hardware industry created a reserved market, and developed local capabilities, that sustained software industry growth. However, the policy was unsuccessful in its objectives in terms of the hardware industry. During the period of the reserved market, TCS failed to change its business model towards higher-value-added activities. It is only now beginning to change, by adopting the off-shore model used by MNCs. The early failures of the national champions in the automotive industry in China and India highlight how difficult it is to creating leading-edge companies by government intervention.

The FDI-led development of the automotive industry in Portugal, China and India has also shown its limitations in terms of long-term development of innovative capabilities and interconnections with the local economy. Regulatory and trade reforms at key points in the development of the industry growth have, furthermore, had a significant impact in determining the extent of local learning and technology absorption. Government intervention in the case of the Renault project in Portugal created scope for considerable learning for suppliers. Local content promotion was successful in creating competitive automotive component suppliers in China and India.

Critically, in the long run, upgrading and learning may depend strongly on the formation of intermediate institutions (such as development agencies, venture capital organizations and technology parks) that can promote targeted spillover and industrial dynamics where needed. The successful development of the electronics industry in Malaysia shows the value of creating horizontally intermediate institutions that understand firm and sectoral characteristics.

Firm-level absorptive capacity — learning, innovation and path dependence

Firm-specific knowledge, learning and innovation create long-term path-dependence and may determine the pattern of industrial growth. The creation of internal absorptive capacity in MNC subsidiaries, however, is generally only weakly connected with existing local capabilities. The automotive industry cases — and also that of the electronics industry in Malaysia — show that innovative activities are still very much restricted to the subsidiaries themselves, and to their partnerships with local R&D institutions. R&D tax incentives have been used in the Brazilian telecommunications sector to promote directly the development of the absorptive capacity of local hardware producers (including subsidiaries). And, indeed, these measures have created significant spillovers in terms of labor and the creation of new R&D institutions. However, the capabilities developed by the subsidiaries are less and less linked to established public-sector R&D organizations. It seems that, in the long run, internal coordination mechanisms within the multinational may, in response to R&D tax incentives, have inverted the knowledge flow, reducing the expected inward knowledge flow in vertical and horizontal or even own plant productivity terms and increasing the outward knowledge flow.

Multinational strategy and subsidiary development

MNCs focusing on internalizing country-specific advantages create a wide range of possibilities in relation to the specific role that a subsidiary may play inside the multinational network. In terms of the long-term learning process inside the multinational network, effective management may promote better integration with the local economy. In South-East Asia, stability and market openness are considered essential to the progression of the subsidiary towards the status of regional headquarters. The limited evolution of Brazilian telecommunications subsidiaries shows how firm-specific qualities of management and entrepreneurial culture may have an important bearing on the scope of the learning process and the potential for development of long-term subsidiary capabilities.

Market orientation — local and export markets

The differences between a development-led and an export-oriented industry are illustrated in the software industry in different countries. In Brazil and China, internal-market-oriented companies have been able to create vertical spillovers, facilitating productivity increases in other sectors. But while exploitation of the internal market may generate some learning effects, it does not generate exporting possibilities and international experience. Export market orientation has clearly been an important factor in the transference of cutting-edge technology to South-East Asia, and of related experience to fast-growing local companies within that region.

Sectoral structure and technological trajectories

There is an increasing degree of interdependence within the globalized production system. The differences in the pattern of autonomy and interdependence between the Renault and Auto-Europa subsidiaries in the automotive industry in Portugal show how the role attributed to the subsidiary may constrain the learning possibilities within the supplier network as a whole. Given the degree of interdependence of activities inside the multinational network, the level of interaction of innovative firms with local subsidiaries is far from sufficient to guarantee a powerful trend to technology absorption. Subsidiaries need to broaden out their international linkages with headquarters to maximize the learning potential of those linkages.

Partnership and alliances — 'packaged' technologies, the OEM model, alliances and joint-ventures

The global sectoral structure creates specific challenges to new firms, and their position in that structure largely determines the opportunities of growth for the firm. The dynamic competences of the firm are not defined in terms of simple packaged technologies that can be easily transferred. The nature of tacit knowledge predicates complex learning from different sources of technology such as:

1. arm's-length interaction with international clients, as in the Indian software industry and the export-oriented subsidiaries of Portugal and Malaysia;
2. the interaction of local companies with multinationals based on the OEM model, like the Portuguese local automotive suppliers; or
3. the joint ventures that created the world-class car manufacturing plants and first-tier suppliers of the Chinese and Indian automotive sectors. Intermediate institutions such technology parks and development agencies have a role in defining and promoting partnerships and forms of collaboration, as well as a specific focus on the development of local supplier networks.

The Results of the Other Work Packages Within the East–West Productivity Gap Project

In implementing the third stage of the triangulation process, we have to proceed in a slightly different way from that employed in the previous two sections. There, we were focusing on the 'big picture', and it would have been inappropriate to try in any sense to force that big picture into the frame of our specific inquiry. In the present section, by contrast, we are looking at other elements within a research project in which all work packages have focused on the same basic questions — what are the origins of the East–West productivity gap, and how can it be closed. So the basic framework for our own research here is exactly the same as the basic framework for the pieces of research against which we are triangulating. For that reason, we take our own preliminary conclusions as a starting point for this stage in the enquiry — always bearing in mind that final conclusions have to await the results of the triangulation process itself. And before proceeding to comparisons of our results with the results of other work packages, we do some preliminary intra-work-package triangulation.

As we noted earlier, the bulk of our interviews (six out of eleven) were with companies operating in medium-tech manufacturing industries; as a consequence, our results may be biased towards this category of company. We therefore pause to comment on whether the interviewed companies from low- and high-tech industries (two and one case(s) respectively) diverge significantly from the main conclusions. This has the added benefit of overtly acknowledging the lack of parity between the firms interviewed, and avoiding any fallacious interpretation of findings that are not wholly comparable. It should be noted in passing that our case studies may facilitate the interpretation of some of the quantitative analyses carried out within the project. This can be particularly helpful in the case of quantitative studies where proper control for certain variables in regressions is hindered by lack of data or dubious data quality. In other words, triangulation is a two-way process.

Preliminary main conclusions of the case studies

Always bearing in mind the crucial distinction between social productivity and basic process productivity within MNC subsidiaries, our respondents have given us very clear statements about the latter. It is generally taken as given that productivity at the host enterprise level is increased when a foreign company takes over a company in a less developed country. Our interviews reveal that East and Central European subsidiaries are close to obtaining basic process productivity approaching EU-15 standards. Of course there is a period of assimilation, but the generally high levels of education in the countries concerned facilitate the process. Hence, our first result is:

R1 — Process Productivity at EU-15 standards is relatively easy to obtain in a CEE subsidiary.

There is equally striking evidence from the interviews to suggest, however, that a social productivity gap does exist which is more recalcitrant than the process productivity problem. This qualitative evidence is strongly reinforced by basic quantitative evidence. Figure 5.1, below, is taken from the *East–West Productivity Gap* project home page, where it is presented as part of the motivation behind the whole project.

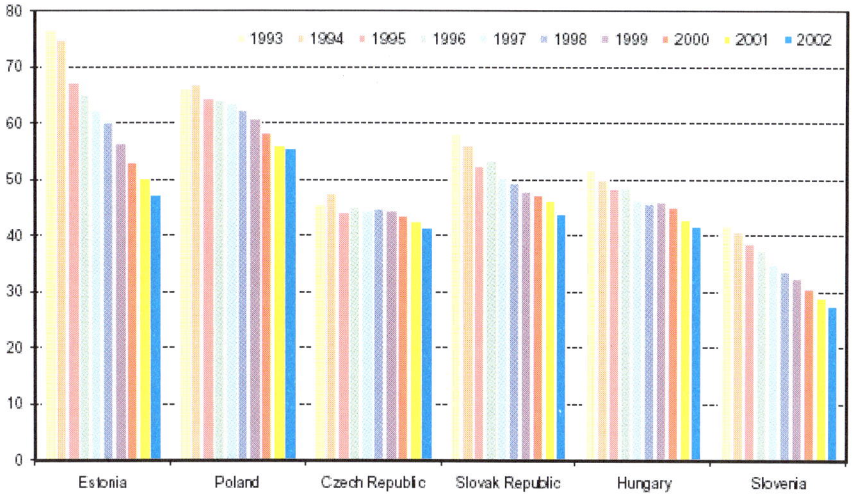

Fig. 5.1. PPP-productivity gaps for selected CEECs vis-à-vis the EU-15 average (% of GDP per head).

All the countries in the table except Slovenia (the most advanced transition economy) still exhibited a gap of more than 40% in social productivity (measured as GDP per head) relative to the EU-15 in 2002. In our introductory chapter, we presented an exegesis of the general failure of countries under communism to build efficient supply networks, such as are required in a fully-fledged market economy. We thereby arrived at the hypothesis that the legacy from the communist period — i.e. the lack of an efficient supply structure — is a reflection of a broader problem of low social productivity. The case studies are quite clear on this matter. Most interviewed firms identified the supplier base in CEECs as the biggest problem they face. The second result is accordingly:

R2 — The supply structure in CEE is deficient, and this may (partly) explain the stubbornness of the social productivity gap.

Continuing with this point, it was only logical to ask whether MNCs help local suppliers to raise their game. In terms of (vertical) spillovers, it would be a positive outcome if they did. Unfortunately, it seems that MNCs generally operate in a separate sphere from the host economy as a whole. Either they have a dominant global strategy that precludes local sourcing, or they invest minimal efforts to help suppliers improve quality. Support sometimes takes the form of assistance in selling up to other foreign firms. This would indicate that the FDI sphere of the economy will eventually absorb them, which is a preliminary signal of dualistic development. Stated in proposition form:

R3 — MNCs pursue global strategies and do not engage heavily in local supply networking, which limits the scope of vertical spillovers.

In terms of spillovers, training of local employees may be a more promising channel. This kind of spillover will typically be horizontal, depending on the extent to which MNCs train local employees, and to what degree the employees are free to move on to other companies. All our interviews confirmed that local employees go through training of some kind; on-the-job training is especially widespread. It is worth emphasizing that all levels of staff in companies from all the sectors covered in the interviews receive training. Moreover, the interviewed firms confirmed that there were no restrictions on trained staff leaving and taking up employment elsewhere, so the fourth result is summarized as:

R4 — MNCs have training programmes covering all jobs, and employees are free to move after having received training.

The last main conclusion emerging from the case studies concerns the role of FDI in the development of local R&D and training facilities. Apart from some language training and software development, our interviews indicated that there is no systematic cooperation with local human capital formation organizations; this is stated as result number five:

R5 — MNCs do not systematically cooperate with local R&D and training institutions to develop social capabilities.

R1–R5 have been essentially derived from the dominant middle-tech manufacturing group of interviews. The next step is briefly to discuss whether they are also representative of the case studies from low- and high-tech industries.

Do R1–R5 have to be adjusted for low and high-tech industry cases?

The two low-tech cases generally mirror the results outlined above. Particularly striking is that both companies seem to train their employees to the same extent as all the other companies interviewed. The question is, of course, whether this is a general feature of all low-tech MNCs, or whether it is specific to these two cases The two low-tech companies have one investment motive in common — they are both raw-material-seeking companies — fish and wood respectively. That is, the dominant factor has not been low labor costs (relative to labor quality) as for instance would be expected in the textile industry. It might therefore be expected that the companies, in placing priority on access to raw materials, would tend to take the existing or available labor force as a given, training and upgrading individuals as appropriate. We are not able to pursue this question further on the basis of just two interviews.

Obviously, conclusions about supply networking for these two companies are specific, on account of the raw-material-seeking motive. This is not a function of being low-tech as such, so we can hardly conclude that the two low-tech interviews confirm or challenge result R3 above (at least not on grounds of technological category). What is clear is that, no matter how close these two companies cooperate with their respective suppliers of materials and services, there is only limited scope for significant technology spillovers. Firstly, the two MNCs themselves are low-tech in terms of hard technology; and secondly, the very nature of the suppliers of the raw materials demanded may offer few prospects of moving up the supply hierarchy.

In terms of subsidiary process productivity, low-tech companies seem to experience quite rapid catch-up. In conclusion, the information gleaned from the low-tech company transcripts does not give rise to any doubts over our main conclusions, though we note that the supply network dimension here is inherently different.

As far as the high-tech company is concerned, the findings are generally consistent with R1–R5. Not one of the main conclusions is contradicted, or in need of modification. However, there is one particular feature worthy of comment. It relates to product demand. For middle-tech companies, accessing the local market is an important factor, since at the present stage of development their particular products tend to meet with high demand. The products of a high-tech company are not yet subject to such mass demand. What implications does this have for transfer of technology? This question is hard to answer, since the transfer of technology through forward linkages is difficult to track empirically (see above, pp. 27–28).

Selecting papers for triangulation

Having reviewed our case studies, and concluded that they are perfectly consistent with each other, we now proceed to the next step — to see if case-study conclusions R1–R5 are supported by other studies within the *East–West Productivity Gap* project. We will not set up any *a priori* expectations, but simply confront our results with those of the other studies. Of course, not all the other work packages of the project generate results that are directly comparable with ours. So we have to start off by selecting our comparator work packages.

The overall structure of the project is illustrated by Fig. 5.2, taken from the project home page. As our focus is primarily on technology transfer

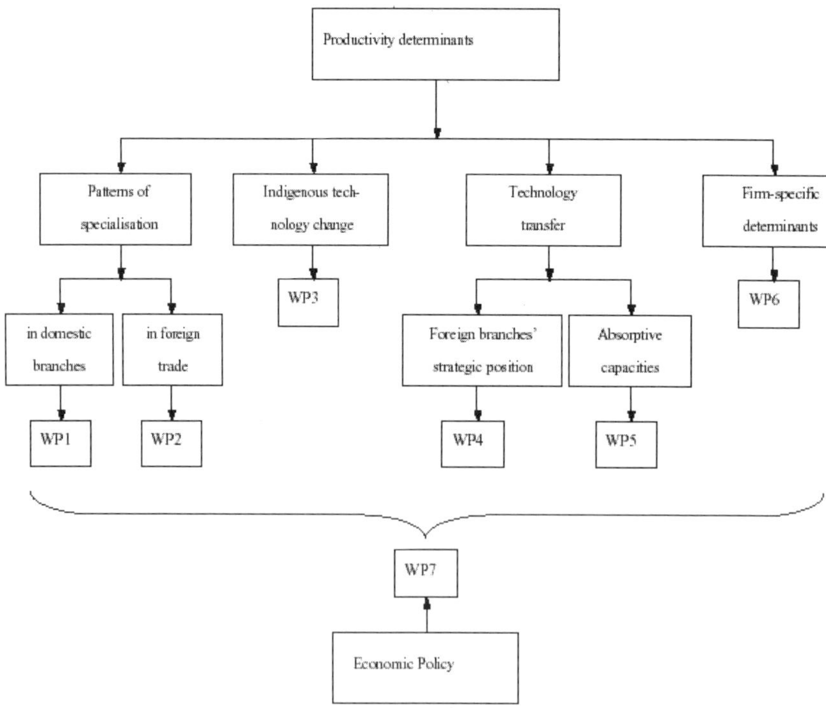

Fig. 5.2. Overall structure of the project.

(hard and soft), we should clearly make use of WP4. This is to see if we can reach a firmer conclusion about the role played by subsidiaries in CEECs, specifically in relation to the impact on productivity enhancement in the broader economy. The three papers by Majcen *et al.* (2003, 2004)[32] and the paper by Männik *et al.* (2004) will be used for this purpose. Aspects of R&D, innovation and their link to productivity are covered by WP3, and accordingly we will draw on these studies, conducted by Slavo Radošević (2002, 2003a, 2003b),[33] to see what can be inferred about the role of FDI in this context.

Analysis

The role of the subsidiary in the MNC network

The papers from WP4 mentioned above seek to analyze the role played by the CEEC subsidiary in the MNC network, and how this role may develop over time. A key question is: how much autonomy is given to the subsidiary and under what circumstances? The WP4 analysis of this subject is based on a questionnaire survey, so that there is an issue of subjectivity in respondents' answers, especially when it comes to perceptions of control over business functions. We regard this as an intrinsic drawback of questionnaire surveys, always to some extent present regardless of how carefully the questionnaire has been designed. But that in no way invalidates the results — rather it simply testifies to the importance of cross-checking through triangulation the results of *all* empirical research projects, not just ours.

Majcen *et al.* (2003b) run an ordered probit regression on the basis of their data, after constructing a set of relevant variables using factor analysis. The theoretical foundation is traditional growth accounting, and the aim is to see how various subsidiary-specific factors, such as the share of foreign ownership, influences productivity growth within subsidiaries. Thus we have a standard quantitative exercise which promises to complement the case studies. In their conceptual framework, the authors characterize subsidiary development in terms of three stages:

1. From the transfer of control to the subsidiary of operational functions
2. To marketing
3. Ending with strategic functions.

[32] A version of one of these is included as Chapter 3 in this book.
[33] A version of one of these is included as Chapter 6 in this book.

An interesting feature of their empirical analysis is that they essentially estimate two models. The first one includes the full set of explanatory variables, i.e. variables reflecting the three above-mentioned business functions. From this regression, they find that majority foreign equity share is associated with higher productivity growth relative to the alternative of minority foreign equity share. At the same time, however, they find that there is no statistically significant relationship between control over business functions and productivity growth. The authors present this as a puzzle: how can it be that majority foreign equity share (*a priori* a quite reliable proxy of control) is linked to productivity growth while parent-firm control over business functions is not (significantly) related to productivity growth? They propose that one explanation could be subjectivity, i.e. subsidiary managers are tempted to claim more control than they actually have.

To tackle this problem, Majcen *et al.* try an alternative approach. If business functions are classified as just operational or strategic, there should be less incentive, or less scope, for business managers to overstate the extent of their control over those functions. Majcen *et al.* estimate two versions of this second specification, one that includes a foreign equity share dummy and one that does not. The 'operational' variable enters both specifications negatively and significantly, whereas the 'strategic' variable enters significantly (and positively) only in the specification without the foreign equity share dummy. The interpretation is, firstly, that parent company's control over operational functions has a negative impact on productivity, and secondly, that the parent companies do not aim to control operational functions as the variable reflecting these enters significantly in both specifications. In contrast to this, the strategic variable enters significantly only in the specification without the foreign equity share dummy and with a positive sign. This tells us that the foreign parent actively wants to control strategic aspects of the business and that this has a positive impact on productivity growth. The implication is that it is optimal to leave operational tasks with the subsidiary and maintain strategic control at head office. Hamar (2003) arrives at similar results. The question for us is whether we can reconcile this result with our case study results.

Of the main results of the case studies reviewed in the first part of this section, the most relevant to this question is R3 — relating to global MNC strategies and supply networking. Most companies interviewed mentioned global strategy as the overall reason for being present in CEEC — without being explicitly asked. This we regard as a strong result from our case studies, though the usual warning about selection bias applies. To what extent can this global strategy motivation explain the findings of Majcen *et al.*? The answer seems to be that it provides a partial explanation. Thus if the MNC's strategy is global, it can plausibly be argued that, in order to maintain a coherent worldwide strategy, it will be anxious to remain in control of strategic functions — e.g. in relation to a large-scale (cost-minimizing) sourcing project for production inputs in geographically dispersed subsidiaries.[34]

There is at least one more possible explanation for Majcen *et al.*'s result. It may be the case that some MNCs pursue regional or even national strategies (this could be the case for a market-seeking, food-producing company engaged in horizontal FDI in, say, Poland), but retain control over strategic functions in the parent company on account of the immaturity of business management in CEECs. As managers mature, strategic functions will increasingly, if only partly, be undertaken in the CEE subsidiary. Because Majcen *et al.*'s regression is run on a cross-section of companies, it does not generate results that can shed light on the question of whether the pattern of control changes significantly over time.[35] Using a different method applied to the same data, however, Männik *et al.* (2004) conclude that 'more productive manufacturing industries have more autonomous subsidiaries only in the case of more developed countries (Slovenia and Hungary)', indicating that business management may be more mature in Slovenia and Hungary than, for instance, in Slovakia.

We certainly cannot claim that the study by Majcen *et al.* categorically confirms R3. On the other hand, we can say that the 'global strategy finding' makes sense in relation to their result. This makes our conclusion stronger, even if it does not completely validate it. The observation from the case studies that (most) MNCs pursue global strategies offers one credible explanation for Majcen *et al.*'s result. Thus the findings are mutually supportive.

We note, further, that Majcen *et al.* control for different aspects of competitiveness in their regression. The only significant competitiveness variable that appears in the regression is 'quality control', and it has a

---

[34]This will in turn have consequences for the observed pattern of supply networking of the CEEC subsidiary, and may explain why MNC managers may not be keen to build supply networks in the given CEEC.

[35]And, as noted in the first section of this chapter, we have a causality problem — we do not know whether a higher foreign equity share leads to higher productivity or rather higher productivity attracts more foreign investment.

positive sign, meaning that quality control spurs productivity growth. However, in one of our cases, the interviewee stated that the enforced introduction in their Hungarian subsidiary of quality controllers, in response to the immaturity of the workforce, had led to slightly lower (process) productivity levels than in the parent company, where quality control was internal to the producing unit itself. This does not, of course, disprove Majcen *et al.*'s result. Rather it simply shows that quality control may be a sign of low *levels* of productivity rather than the converse, which also makes sense in terms of our understanding of modern organizational structures, where the supreme form of quality control is *no control,* in the context of a high degree of inter-organizational trust (Ring, 1997). Hence, the lesson is not to be too mechanical in the directional interpretation of quantitative evidence — especially when the data lies under the suspicion of some degree of subjectivity.

Majcen *et al.* also look at 'people and training' as a competitiveness variable. However, it enters the regression insignificantly. We, on the other hand, concluded in R4 that all companies, from low-tech to high-tech, have training programs for their employees. How should this apparent contradiction be interpreted? Is it surprising that the people and training variable seems to be (statistically) insignificant as a competitiveness parameter? Our interpretation is that training of personnel, since it covers all jobs, is not really a parameter of competitiveness, but rather a requirement for remaining in business. That is, a training program, whatever form it takes, is indispensable in all types of companies. To the extent that it does impact on competitiveness, the impact may be indirect, and as such difficult to measure.

R&D, Innovation, and Productivity: what is the role of FDI?

Radošević (see Chapter 6; 2002; 2003a; 2003b) begins by arguing that productivity or efficiency gains in CEECs in the last ten years have been primarily due to reallocations from inefficient industries to more efficient ones. Moreover, inherited labor hoarding has been largely eliminated, and better management practices introduced, making enterprises far more productive than they were under communism. But the very success of these measures means that now new sources of productivity growth have to emerge, and R&D and innovation are obvious candidates. However, R&D and innovation have not automatically followed the relatively high rates of GDP growth reported in most advanced CEEC economies. There is a structural dimension to this, and Radošević points to the mismatch between demand and supply. The general recovery in demand has not been accompanied by an increased demand for technology, though indicators from business surveys (by Eurostat) show that demand-side difficulties have now been largely mitigated. Radošević argues that the key here is to be found in difficulties on the supply side, in particular a weak financial system, which in a market economy mediates between supply and demand. This conclusion is limited to R&D at the level of specialist institutions, since 'small and discontinuous R&D activities usually closely linked to production are not covered by R&D surveys.' Of course an enterprise is not an isolated entity, and accordingly does not innovate on its own. Figure 6.10 shows the relative importance of different sources of innovation in manufacturing in a selection of CEE countries.

Figure 6.10 shows that, in general, the immediate business environment is by far the most important source of innovation for companies, whereas 'external knowledge organizations' are less important (though there are variations by country). It is interesting also to observe that external sources of information are relatively more important in CEECs than on average in the EU, as can be seen from Radošević's next figure (Fig. 6.11).

By contrast, knowledge within the enterprise is less important in CEECs than in the EU-15, whereas suppliers and buyers — i.e. the value chain — play a similar role in both regions. This combination of observations can be interpreted in terms of local firms being poor innovators themselves, and therefore dependent on external knowledge, for instance via the value chain. The obvious vehicle by which this external knowledge can be acquired is through FDI. That is, new knowledge is brought in by MNCs and, it is hoped, disseminated to local firms in the host economy (spillover effects). This is obviously an interesting conclusion in relation to our case studies, and we will return to it in a moment. But Radošević himself warns of the fragility of that form of upgrading, arguing that 'exclusive reliance on knowledge from abroad as well as on a weak national system of innovation, coupled with very weak innovation capability of domestic firms, represents the most vulnerable aspect of the CEE economies.' It may be seen as a quick fix to rely too heavily on FDI for productivity enhancement, for two reasons. Firstly, the building of a strong national innovation system is crucial for continued growth as opposed to 'passive' reliance on foreign knowledge. Radošević discusses this in relation to the electronics industry, where he stresses that the dominant electronics companies in CEE are foreign-led. Hence, policies are needed to build a solid national innovation system which can make the economy less dependent on foreign knowledge. Secondly, FDI may fail to produce the spillover effects that are so important to spur productivity growth in local enterprises. This is the point at which our case studies may be particularly useful.

The business surveys on which Radošević bases his analysis seem to bring out the importance of interaction between local firms and the foreign subsidiaries of MNCs as a channel of knowledge creation for the former. R3 indicates, however, that MNCs do not engage heavily in networking via the value chain with local firms, even as a short-term measure. Thus FDI may be a poor means of facilitating this knowledge dissemination process. As mentioned before, this gives weight to the fear that a dualistic type of economy will emerge, with local firms stuck in their backward positions and productivity in foreign subsidiaries growing *pari passu* with their parent counterparts. What the Radošević research suggests is that we should not be too categorical in asserting that MNCs and their foreign subsidiaries do not *aim* to build supply networks in CEECs. Indeed, some of our respondents did express a desire to be more engaged in the local business environment. The problem is that, thus far, the price-quality relationship found with local suppliers has not been satisfactory. The big question is how and when competitiveness in relation to Western suppliers will be reached. In a sense, local firms are trapped in a vicious circle. Though subsidiaries would like to deal with the local suppliers, given a reasonable price-quality relationship, the latter need an initial opportunity to work together with the foreign subsidiaries in order to gain new knowledge, which can in turn increase productivity.

As far as R5 (relating to foreign subsidiary cooperation with local research institutions) is concerned, we reach a similar conclusion to Radošević, namely that enterprises do not cooperate on a systematic basis with local universities and the like. Of course, the reasons for this in the case of a foreign subsidiary may be specific, in that in many MNCs the bulk of R&D takes place at head office. Nevertheless both bodies of evidence give credence to the notion that national innovation systems are, in general, weak.

Conclusions

Considering the triangulation process thus far, we conclude that our results are generally supported, if not entirely confirmed, by reference to the results of other WPs. What we can say at this point without qualification is that our findings do make sense in relation to the results of other studies. So far there is nothing that actually questions our results.

Are there (vertical and/or horizontal) spillovers from FDI to local firms?

Our case studies do not shed light on the question of horizontal spillovers, apart from training spillovers. However, we do have evidence on vertical spillovers, suggesting that they are at best weak or erratic (R3 and R2). As discussed above, the global comparative/quantitative literature tends to support that conclusion, though there are significant differences between countries, and between methodologies, with panel-data studies generally giving a more pessimistic picture of the impact of spillovers than cross-sectional. What light do the other work packages within the project throw on this debate?

Vahter's (2004) study analyses the issue using panel data for Slovenia (1994–2000) and Estonia (1996–2001). The author tests for horizontal spillovers from foreign affiliates to domestic enterprises, and also to other foreign affiliates. For Slovenia, Vahter finds positive horizontal spillovers from FIEs to domestic enterprises, but negative ones from FIEs to other foreign affiliates. For Estonia, he finds the opposite to be the case. The conclusions appear to be solid, as they have been tested according to several approaches: fixed or random effects models, and a Heckman 2-step procedure. Vahter suggests that the explanation for these contrasting patterns is that in Estonia MNCs are mainly interested in low wages — i.e. broadly-based asset absorption which tends to squeeze out domestic firms, while in Slovenia they are attracted by high productivity, so that foreign firms end up competing for skilled labor. It is worth recalling at this point the study by Smarzynska (2002), who tests for both vertical and horizontal spillovers on a panel of Lithuanian firms. Here, the author detects the presence of vertical spillovers through backward linkages. This rather goes against the conclusions of our case studies. It should be borne in mind, however, that Smarzynska's conclusion does only apply to Lithuania. The general conclusion seems to be that it is very dangerous to generalize *any* results relating to vertical spillovers.

References

Aitken, B., A. Harrison and R.E. Lipsey, "Wages and foreign ownership: A comparative study of Mexico, Venezuela and the United States." *J. Int. Econ.* **40**, 3–4, 345–371 (1996).

Aitken, B., G. Hanson and A. Harrison, "Spillovers, foreign investments and export behaviour." *J. Int. Econ.* **43**, 1–2, 103–132 (1997).

Aitken, B. and A. Harrison, "Do domestic firms benefit from direct foreign investment? Evidence from Venezuela." *Amer. Econ. Rev.* **89**, 3, 605–618 (1999).

Ariffin, N., "The internationalisation of innovative capabilities: The Malaysian electronics industry." SPRU, University of Sussex, Brighton (2000).

Arora, A., "The globalisation of the software industry: Perspectives and opportunities for developed and developing countries." *Innovation Policy and the Economy*, Vol. 5, MIT Press (2004).

Athreye, S. S., "Multinational firms and the evolution of the Indian software industry." Working Paper No. 51, Economics Series, East-West Center, Honolulu, Hawaii (2003).

Balasubramanyam, V.N., M.A. Salisu and D. Sapsford, "Foreign direct investment, trade policy and economic growth." In V.N. Balasubramanyam and D. Greenaway (eds.), *Trade and Development: Essays in Honour of Jagdish Bhagwati*, p. 3–21, St Martin's Press, New York; Macmillan Press, London, (1996).

Blalock, G., "Technology from foreign direct investment: Strategic transfer through supply chains." Berkeley, University of California, Haas School of Business (2001).

Blomström, M. and H. Persson, "Foreign investment and spillover efficiency in an underdeveloped economy: Evidence from the Mexican manufacturing Industry." *World Development* **11**, 6, 493–501 (1983).

Blomström, M., "Foreign investment and productive efficiency: The case of Mexico." *J. Ind. Econ.* **15**, 97–110 (1986).

Blomström, M. and E.-N. Wolff, "Multinational corporations and productivity convergence in Mexico." Cambridge, Massachusetts, National Bureau of Economic Research (1989).

Blomström, M., A. Kokko and M. Zejan, "Host country competition and technology transfer by multinationals." Cambridge, Massachusetts, National Bureau of Economic Research (1995).

Borensztein, E., "How does foreign direct investment affect economic growth?" *J. Int. Econ.* **45**, 1, 115–135 (1998).

Caves, R.E., "Multinational firms, competition, and productivity in host-country markets." *Economica* **41**, 176–193 (1974).

Chung, W., W. Mitchell and B. Yeung, "Foreign direct investment and host industry productivity. The case of the American automotive parts industry." *Proceedings of the European International Business Association* (1996).

Chung, W., "Identifying technology transfer in foreign direct investment of industry conditions and investing firm motives." *J. Int. Bus. Stud.* **32**, 2, 211–229 (2001).

Damijan, J. and M. Knell, "How important is trade and foreign ownership in closing the technology gap? Evidence from Estonia and Slovenia." Mimeo, www.wiiw.ac.at/pdf/other knell paper.pdf (2003).

Djankov, S. and B. Hoekman, "Foreign direct investment and productivity growth in Czech enterprises." World Bank (1999).

Dodgson, M., "Policies for science, technology and innovation in Asian newly industrializing economics." In L. Kim and R.R. Nelson (eds.), *Technology Learning and Innovation: Experiences of Newly Industralizing Economics*, New York: CUP.

Dyker, D.A. *et al.*, " "East"-"West" networks and their alignment: Industrial networks in Hungary and Slovenia." *Technovation* **23**, 603–616 (2003).

Evenett, S. and A. Voicu, "Picking winners or creating them? Revisiting the benefits of FDI in the Czech Republic." Presented at ETSG (2003).

Féria, L.P., "A história do sector automóvel em Portugal, Lisbon." Gabinete de Estudos e Prospectiva Economica (Ministry of Economy), p 134, Working Paper (1999).

Galina, S.V.R., "Desenvolvimento global de produtos: o papel das subsidiárias Brasileiras de fornecedores de equipamentos do setor de telecomunicações," *Escola Politécnica.*, São Paulo: USP (2003).

Galina, S.V.R. and G.A. Plonski, "Global product development in the telecommunication Industry: An analysis of the Brazilian subsidiaries involvement." S. Antipolis, *9th International Product Development Management Conference*, Antibes, France (2002).

Gershenberg, I., "The training and spread of managerial know-how, a comparative analysis of multinational and other firms in Kenya." *World Development* **15**, 7, 931–939 (1987).

Girma, S. and K. Wakelin, "Regional Underdevelopment: Is FDI the Solution? A Semiparametric Analysis." London, CEPR Discussion Paper No. 2995 (2001).

Globerman, S., "Foreign direct investment and "spillover" efficiency benefits in Canadian manufacturing industries." *Can. J. Econ.* **12**, 42–56 (1979).

Hamar, J., "Mapping the technology structure of branch plants and technology integration of CEECs." http://www.iwh-halle.de/projects/productivity-gap/default.htm, November (2003).

Haddad, M. and A. Harrison, "Are there positive spillovers from direct foreign investment? Evidence from panel data for Morocco." *J. Devel. Econ.* **42**, 1, 51–74 (1993).

Haskel, J., S. Pereira and M. Slaughter, "Does inward foreign direct investment boost the productivity of domestic firms?" Cambridge, Massachusetts, NBER (2002).

Hobday, M., "Digital Telecommunications Technology and the Third World: The Theory, the Challenge, and the Evidence from Brazil." Brighton, SPRU, University of Sussex, Mimeo (1986).

Hobday, M., "East versus Southeast Asian innovation systems: Comparing OME- and TNC-led growth in electronics." In L. Kim and R.R. Nelson (eds.), *Technology, Learning and Innovation: Experiences of Newly Industrializing Economies*, Cambridge, New York, Cambridge University Press (2000).

Javorcik, B.S. and M. Spatareanu, "To share or not to share: Does local participation matter for spillovers from foreign direct investment?" Washington DC, World Bank (2003).

Keller, W., "Absorptive capacity: On the creation and acquisition of technology in development." *J. Devel. Econ.* **49**, 199–227 (1996).

Kokko, A. and M. Blomström, "Policies to encourage inflows of technology through foreign multinationals." *World Devel.* **23**, 3, 495–468 (1995).

Majcen, B., S. Radošević and M. Rojec, "FDI subsidiaries and industrial integration of Centra Europe: Conceptual and empirical results." http://www.iwh-halle.de/projects/ productivity-gap/default.htm [August, 2003a].

Majcen, B., S. Radošević and M. Rojec, "Strategic control and productivity growth of foreign subsidiaries in Central European countries." http://www.iwh-halle.de/projects/productivity-gap/default.htm [September/October, 2003].

Majcen, B., M. Rojec and S. Radošević, "Productivity growth and functional upgrading in foreign subsidiaries in the Slovenian manufacturing sector." http://www.iwh-halle.de/projects/productivity-gap/default.htm (2004).

Männik, K., H. Hannula and U. Varblane, "Country, industry and firm size effects on foreign subsidiary strategy. An example of five CEE countries." http://www.iwh-halle.de/projects/productivity-gap/default.htm, April (2004).

Mariotti, S., F. Onida and L. Piscitello, *Foreign Ownership: The Case of Italy*, Milan, CESPRI (2003).

Pack, H., *Productivity, Technology and Industrial Development*, New York, Oxford University Press (1997).

Perini, F., "Micro-dynamics of subsidiary development: Subsidiary initiatives, coordination mechanisms and technological capability accumulation in the Brazilian ICT Sector." Brighton, SPRU, University of Sussex, *PRIME Doctoral Conference* (2004).

Radošević, S., "Assessing innovation capacities of the Central and East European countries in the enlarged European innovation system." http://www.iwh-halle.de/projects/productivity-gap/default.htm [September, 2002].

Radošević, S., "Central and East European electronics industry between foreign- and domestic-led modernisation." http://www.iwh-halle.de/projects/productivity-gap/default.htm [June, 2003a].

Radošević, S., "What future for science and technology in Central and Eastern Europe in the 21st century?" http://www.iwh-halle.de/projects/productivity-gap/default.htm [June, 2003b].

Rhee, Y.W., "The catalyst model of development: Lessons from Bangladesh's suceess with garment exports." *World Development* **2**, 336–346 (1990).

Ring, P.S., "Processes facilitating reliance on trust in inter-organizational networks." In M. Ebers (ed.), *The Formation of Inter-Organizational Networks*, Oxford, CUP.

Romero, E. and A. Mansfield, "Technology transfer to overseas subsidiaries by U.S.-based firms." *Quart. J. Econ.* **95**, 4, 737–750 (1980).

Simöes, V.C., "Networks and learning processes: A case study on the automotive industry in Portugal." In J. Cantwell and J. Molero (eds.), *Multinational Enterprises, Innovative Strategies and Systems of Innovation*, Cheltenham, Edward Elgar (2003).

Smarzynska, B.K., "Does foreign direct investment increase the productivity of domestic firms? In search of spillovers through backward linkages." Washington, D.C., World Bank (2002).

Sutton, J., "The auto-component supply chain in China and India: A benchmarking study." Brussels, Annual Bank Conference on Development Economics — Europe (2004).

Szapiro, M. and J. Cassiolato, "Telecommunications system of innovation in Brazil: development and recent challenges." Rio de Janeiro, The First Globelics Conference: Innovation Systems and Development Strategies for the Third Millennium, Mimeo (2003).

Teece, D., "Technology transfer by multinational firms: The resource cost of transferring know-how." *Economic Journal* **87**, 346, 242–261 (1977).

Vahter, P., "The effects of foreign direct investments on productivity: Evidence from Estonia and Slovenia." http://www.iwh-halle.de/projects/productivity-gap/default.htm (2004).

Xu, Bin, "Multinational enterprises, technology diffusion and host country productivity growth source." *J. Devel. Econ.* **62**, 2, 477–493 (2000).

CHAPTER 6

DOMESTIC INNOVATION CAPACITY — CAN CEE GOVERNMENTS CORRECT FDI-DRIVEN TRENDS THROUGH R&D POLICY?

Slavo Radošević

Introduction

One of the key findings of the research reported in Chapters 3–5 is that the linkages between multinational activity, specifically FDI, in the CEECs and local R&D and educational sectors is weak. This poses a fundamental problem for the whole process of economic catch-up in those countries. It means that recovery and growth in CEE will not automatically be followed by recovery of demand for domestic R&D and innovation. In the worst case, some CEE countries may exhaust sources of growth coming from reallocation of resources, closures of inefficient companies and lay-offs of redundant workers, and face fundamental structural barriers to further upgrading. The result would be an extreme form of the scenario depicted in Fig. 4.3, in which the low-productivity side of the dual economy would predominate. Such obstacles to a sustained process of upgrading may, furthermore, appear even where the development of the institutional system of the market economy has been effectively addressed through transition-related policies. The weakness of the MNC/local R&D interface is a function of a quite specific institutional problem in the CEECs — the inadequacy of *national systems of innovation*, and of the mechanisms which integrate those systems with FDI. National systems of innovation are hybrids — based on public–private and local–global interfaces and interactions — but are at the same time an essential part of any market economy. It is a major challenge to policy-makers to facilitate the emergence of these public–private interfaces in the CEECs.

Innovation Policy in Central-East European Context

The patterns of transformation of the CEECs during the 1990s show that innovation does take place even with ineffective innovation policies. Slovenia, Poland and Hungary are clear examples of this. Does that mean that innovation policy is dispensable? Certainly, the impact of innovation policy should not be overestimated. However, we should bear in mind that the sources of growth in CEECs are changing. During most of the first ten years of transition, growth was unrelated to domestic technology accumulation. Large-scale reallocations of resources from unproductive parts of industry to services, and from less to more efficient firms, ensured growth over an extended period. However, there are signs that these sources of productivity growth are now drying up, and that the CEECs will in the future have to base growth on technology accumulation. Kubielas (2003), for example, argues that, in the case of Poland, the scope for Ricardian adjustment based on reallocations has been exhausted, and that Polish growth now depends on imported technology. Since Poland has lost the chance that it still had during the 1990s to strengthen the absorptive capacity of its R&D system, Kubielas argues, it now finds itself entirely dependent on FDI to ensure continuous technology accumulation.

It is possible that innovation will continue to develop in some CEECs based entirely on local or export demand. However, where growth depends on the strength of the national innovation system, innovation policy must be a key factor to facilitate domestic technology accumulation and diffusion. Certainly, innovation policy is no quick fix. In order to be successful, it requires a broad consensus of a wide range of stakeholders. As the experience of the CEECs shows, this kind of policy is easier to establish in periods of growth rather than in those of depression. Unfortunately, boom conditions also reduce pressure for the development of innovation policy. To make matters worse, the long-term nature of innovation policy does not offer clear benefits within the framework of four-year political cycles. All this suggests that demand for innovation policy is not easily articulated, and that we should not be too optimistic about its chances in CEECs.

When we look at the sectoral orientation of innovation policy in CEECs, we see immediately that high tech is the dominant paradigm, in the face of data which suggest that practical innovation in these countries is very much linked to equipment, often with a limited R&D component. As pointed out by Nauwelaers and Reid (2002), this leads to a narrow client base for innovation policy — just 50 large companies in the case of Estonia. In other countries, it means that attracting high tech through S&T parks actually functions as a *substitute* for innovation policy. In the best case, that route can create isolated pockets of competencies in new technology, leaving the majority of local firms untouched. This is not to argue that the science park route should not be pursued, but only that it should not serve as an excuse for not having an innovation policy.

The importance of this policy issue can best be seen if we compare the marginal relative position of CEECs in US or EPO patenting with the gradual increase in business enterprise R&D (BERD) in CEE reported in innovation surveys and R&D data. This suggests that innovative firms are increasingly involved in technology activities, but not necessarily in the area of high tech. That, in turn, points to a growing wedge between R&D policy and innovation policy, (see Kubielas, 2003 for discussion of the case of Poland). CEECs will have to close the gap which has emerged between dominant R&D policy and subordinate innovation policy. As CEECs increasingly try to emulate EU policies and to restructure towards knowledge-based activities, this gap will, indeed, become unsustainable. A shift towards the knowledge-based economy in CEECs will mean:

1. A reorientation towards diffusion-oriented activities within the R&D system.
2. A movement towards an enterprise-based R&D system.

As the interactive innovation model suggests, such a shift will not mean that R&D becomes irrelevant, but rather that R&D and innovation activities become integrated. While this may sound simple in conceptual terms, the change is very difficult to make in policy terms. The key problem is how to move from the current situation where 'science' and 'innovation' are seen in policy terms as a zero-sum game between the science establishment and a weak 'innovation community', towards a policy conception of a positive-sum game in which both elements can be a winner.

After ten years of implementation of transition-based policies, Central-East European economies have now finally started to introduce innovation policy measures. The emergence of such measures in these economies shows that important changes are taking place in their political philosophies. After being forced into a self-minimisation process which left only building the institutional framework of the 'open market economy' as a legitimate activity, the CEE state is now shifting towards a more proactive conception of its role. The challenge is to square innovation policy with the specific context in which it has to operate, viz.,

- Innovation surveys show that the market itself and the social environment of the enterprise are the main sources of information for innovation. Yet this aspect is not taken into account by innovation policy, which is rarely sector- or technology-specific. Innovation surveys show that specific measures could do much more for the innovativeness of enterprises than general measures like tax incentives or horizontal measures like innovation centers and S&T parks.
- As innovation surveys show, innovation links in CEE are value-chain-based, i.e., they are at their strongest, intra-firm links apart, with suppliers and buyers. This is the strength, but also the weakness, of innovation systems in the CEECs. Production integration through FDI-led value chains ensures high productivity, innovation linkages and regular sales to local firms. However, in the long term, product and technology upgrading does not necessarily follow value-chain logic, especially when value chains are changing or breaking up. Again, this means that innovation policy will have to strike a balance between supporting integration of local firms into global value chains (FDI, subcontracting), on the one hand and reinforcing domestic linkages with universities, S&T parks, cooperative centers, etc. on the other. Integration of local firms through value chains and FDI has been relatively undeveloped as a policy in CEECs. Hungary and the Czech Republic are the only two EU new member states which have developed elements of such a policy going beyond the simple marketing of the given country as a production location. There has been much more policy focus on linkage mechanisms like S&T parks, innovation centers, etc., i.e., on linkages for which weak and dependent local firms may not have immediate demand. This explains their irrelevance to local firms and their innovation activities, which are, primarily, value-chain driven. The challenge for CEECs, as we saw in Chapter 4, is to *integrate* FDI and innovation policy.

Innovation and R&D in Developmental Perspective

Growth, R&D and innovation

Economic recovery and growth in the CEECs during the 1990s was not linked to domestic R&D and technology efforts. Moreover, recovery in aggregate demand has not been accompanied by a recovery in the demand

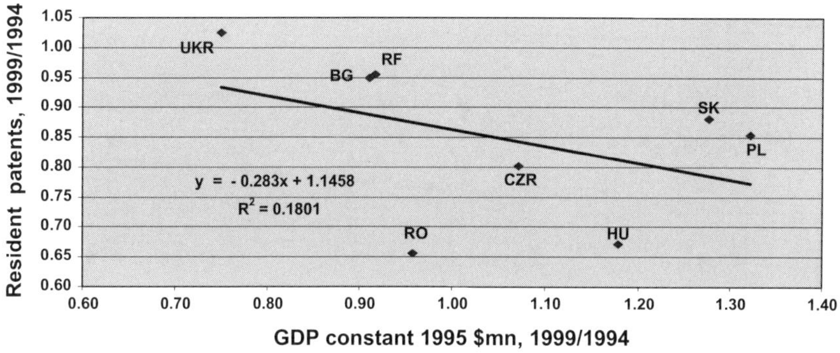

Fig. 6.1. Indices of GDP and resident patent applications 1999/1994.
Source: World Bank Development Indicators, CD ROM, 2002.

for technology. Figure 6.1 shows that the relationship between GDP growth and patenting as an indicator of R&D/innovation effort for eight CEECs over the initial transition period was slightly negative, with countries that grew faster in the period 1994–1999 recording a relatively sharper fall in resident patent applications than economies that continued to decline. Although the number of countries is far too limited to generalize the negative relationship, it is safe to conclude that there seems to have been no clear relationship between domestic technology activity and economic recovery in this period. This indicates that recovery of demand for local R&D and innovation may not emerge automatically with the return of growth.

The early to mid-1990s was clearly a period of transition-induced reallocations, where local S&T and innovation capabilities did not matter for growth. By contrast, we can observe from the late 1990s the emergence of a very moderate, statistically not significant, but nevertheless positive relationship between recovery and domestic innovative activity as proxied by resident patents (see Fig. 6.2). However, it would be unrealistic to argue that domestic innovative activity as reflected in patents lay behind economic growth in the late 1990s and early 2000s. In fact, the causation may be in the opposite direction — the recovery in GDP may have improved the financial position of the domestic R&D system — leading to an increase in domestic patenting, but without deeper structural changes in the role and functions of the domestic R&D system. This phenomenon is most visible in Russia, where high growth rates actually seem to have slowed down the restructuring of the national R&D system. Similarly, during the early-mid

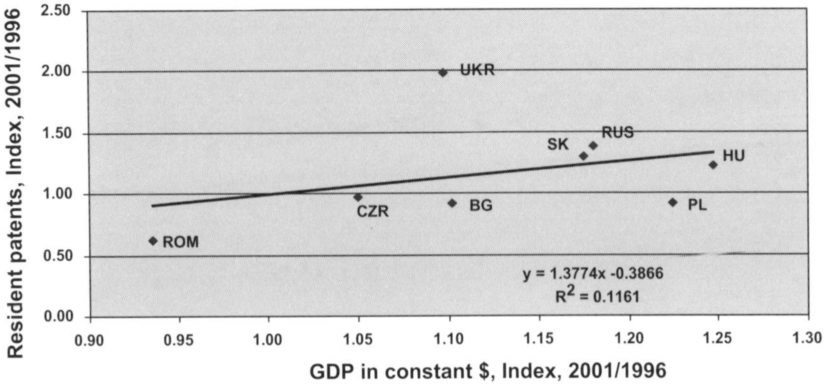

Fig. 6.2. Indices of GDP and resident patent applications 2001/1996.
Source: World Bank Development Indicators, CD ROM, 2004.

1990s, Poland did very little in terms of restructuring the R&D system; it is only with the subsequent slow-down in growth rates that it has been forced to take more proactive measures.

Business surveys suggest that there has been a clear easing of general demand-side difficulties in all CEECs for which survey data are available. Demand constraints were particularly onerous in the first half of the 1990s. Figure 6.3 shows that there was a significant decrease in demand-side difficulties for 'young' firms in CEECs around the turn of the century. We would expect, *a priori*, that demand-side improvements would be followed by an increased demand for technology.

However, this improvement in demand-side conditions has not been echoed by a commensurately strong improvement in supply-side conditions. Figure 6.4 shows a much more diversified picture regarding the supply side. It is noteworthy that one of the increasingly severe constraints for new firms has been lack of technology and limited access to trained workers. This has been coupled with a lack of funds and a worsening of the liquidity situation (non- or late-paying customers) in all countries except the Czech Republic.

A clear improvement in demand-side conditions confirms that the problems for innovators and entrepreneurs have now shifted to the supply side, especially to issues of access to credit, own funds and liquidity of clients, despite indications by companies that clients are now less

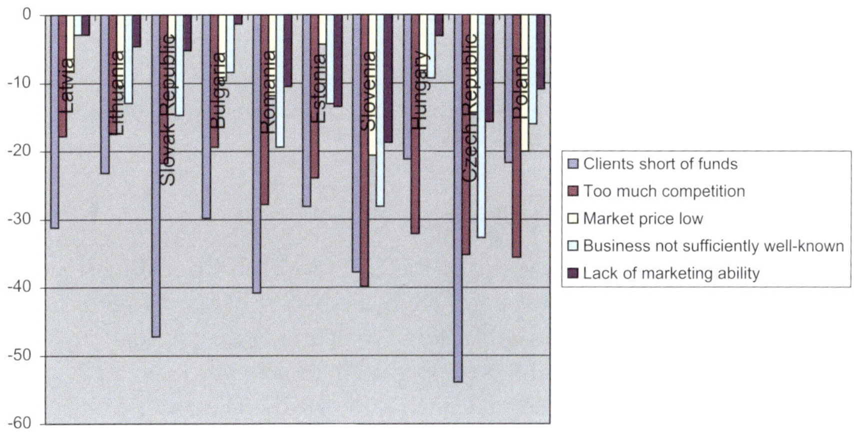

Fig. 6.3. Percentage change in demand-side difficulties facing enterprises between 1998 (start-up) and 2001.
Source: Based on Eurostat, New Enterprises in Candidate Countries, 2003.

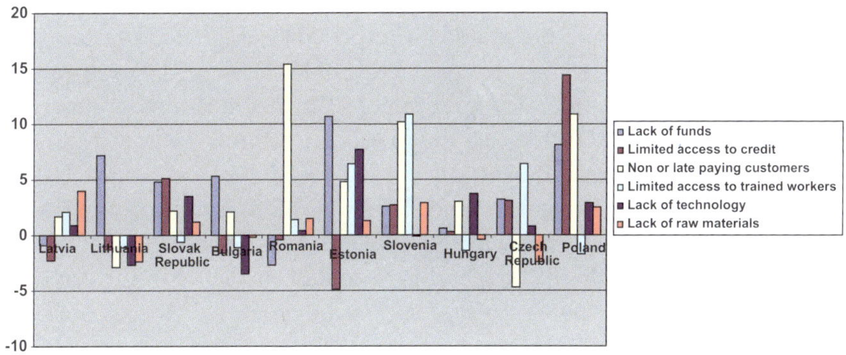

Fig. 6.4. Percentage change in supply-side difficulties facing enterprises between 1998 (start-up) and 2001.
Source: Based on Eurostat, New Enterprises in Candidate Countries, 2003.

financially constrained (see Fig. 6.3). This suggests that the problem is not a general lack of liquidity, but rather a mismatch between liquid supply and demand. Other supply-side problems like trained workforce bottlenecks and lack of technology represent quite a new phenomenon, and suggest that the CEECs are entering a new stage of entrepreneurship where requirements for growth have become more variegated and related less to finance by itself, but increasingly to the quality of supply and matching of supply and demand. From the policy perspective, this points to the problem of weak financial systems, which are failing to mediate between supply and demand, and to the importance of the national innovation system.

R&D in the post-socialist period

Given their income levels, some of the CEECs still have relatively large numbers of research scientists and engineers (RSE), while many of them report a relatively favorable educational structure of the population. Both these factors should, according to new growth theory, produce much more robust growth than we observed during the 1990s. The fact is, however, that economic recovery of the CEECs during the 1990s was unrelated to R&D, as it was unrelated to broader measures of innovative activity. Simple correlation coefficients between growth of GDP and share of GERD (gross expenditure on research and development) in GDP for 1992–1999 period are negative for six out of nine CEE economies.

Of course, we should not assess the importance of the R&D system just on the basis of its current role. Restructuring of R&D is one the key preconditions for further industrial upgrading. As Fig. 6.4 indicates, companies in the CEECs are now facing, for the first time, technology constraints as a limiting factor for growth. But during the 1990s, R&D was not felt as a constraint to growth. Hence demand for local R&D was quite limited. As a result, we have seen a radical shrinking of R&D systems in all the CEECs. Figure 6.5 shows the share of expenditure on R&D in GDP for thirteen East European countries.

R&D expenditures as a proportion of GDP in the East European countries fell from a high of 1%–2.5% at the end of the socialist period in the late 1980s to a range of 0.5%–1.5% of GDP in 2003. This downward trend can be disaggregated into three distinct periods. First, in the period between 1990 and 1993/94, with falling levels of GDP, the share of expenditure on R&D also declined sharply, with very high absolute declines in funding of large R&D systems. This was followed by a period of stabilization (1993/94–1996) in which the process of decline continued, but at a significantly lower rate. From 1996, signs of recovery have emerged, in some economies, in terms of both absolute and relative levels of funding of R&D. However, in a few CEECs, like Romania, the R&D decline has continued unabated. Overall, after an average annual decrease of 13% in 1991–1996,

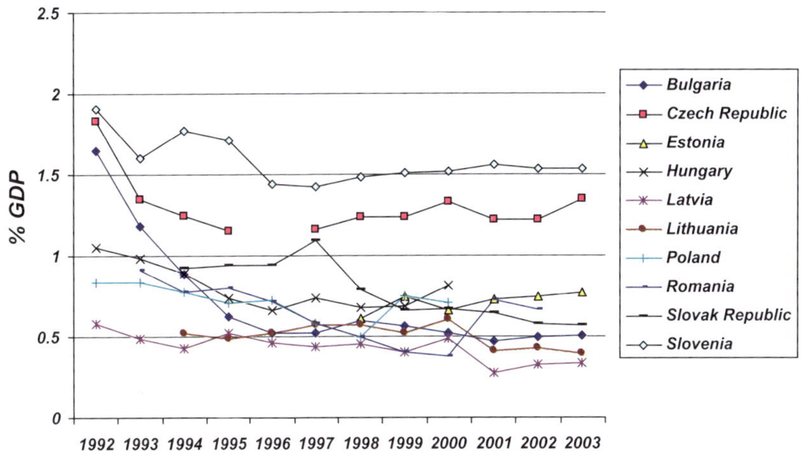

Fig. 6.5. Gross expenditure on R&D (GERD) as % of GDP, 1992–2003.
Sources: EU, R&D and Innovation Statistics in Candidate Countries and the Russian Federation, Data 1997–1999, EC, Theme 9, R&D, Luxembourg, Eurostat, 2002; for Moldova and Belarus, data bank of the CIS Statistical Committee (data are not comparable to OECD data in terms of definition); for 1999–2003 Eurostat.

the share of R&D in GDP in the East European countries decreased on average by just 1.67% annually in the 1997–2003 period. This came as result of a process of polarization among CEECs whereby relative shares increased in the Czech Republic, Hungary, Estonia and Slovenia, while decreasing in the other countries (see Fig. 6.5). This is mainly due to country differences in the status of public policy towards R&D aimed at counteracting the fall in demand for R&D from the private sector.

From the perspective of growth and restructuring, it is important to see what has happened specifically to R&D carried on in the business enterprise sector. The data show that that the share of BERD in GERD in the East European countries has remained relatively stable over the whole period. In other words, the business enterprise R&D sector has shared the fate, in absolute and relative terms, of the R&D sector as a whole (see Figs. 6.6 and 6.7).

National differences in the share of R&D funded by the business sector have remained, suggesting that the transition has not changed deep-seated structural and nationally-specific features in R&D systems (see Fig. 6.7). The high shares of R&D funding by the business sector in the Czech Republic

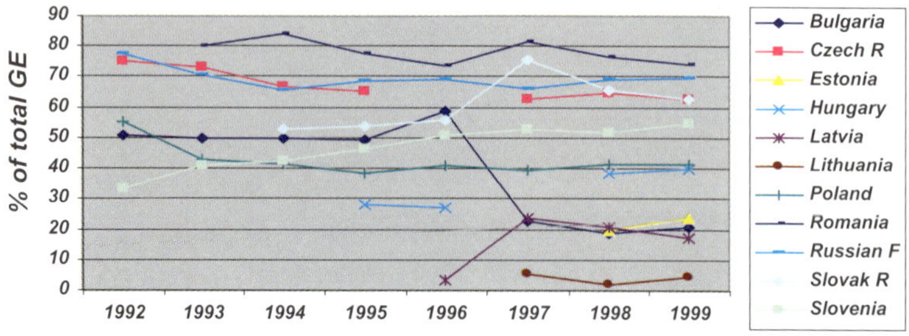

Fig. 6.6. Share of R&D performed by the business enterprise sector (BERD) in gross expenditure on R&D (GERD), 1992–1999.
Source: EU, R&D and Innovation Statistics in Candidate Countries and the Russian Federation, Data 1997–1999, EC, Theme 9, R&D, Luxembourg, Eurostat, 2002 and Eurostat Internet Database.

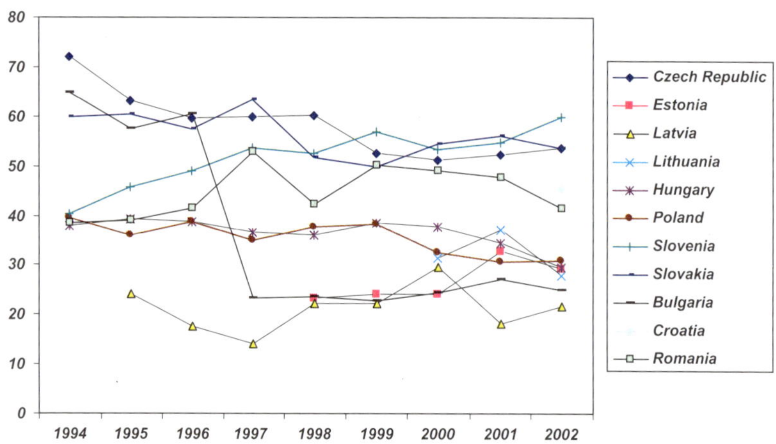

Fig. 6.7. Share of R&D funded by the business enterprise sector, 1994–2002.
Source: EU, R&D and Innovation Statistics in Candidate Countries and the Russian Federation, Data 1997–1999, EC, Theme 9, R&D, Luxembourg, Eurostat, 2002 and Eurostat Internet Database.

and Slovakia and very low shares in the Baltic states are the result of differences in industrial structure, especially in terms of the role of large firms, and also of neglect of R&D in the Baltic states during the early 1990s. The relatively high share of R&D performed by the business enterprise sector in Russia and Romania (see Fig. 6.8) indicates primarily unreformed R&D sectors dominated by extra-mural industrial R&D institutes, rather than strong in-house R&D. At the same time, the share of R&D funding

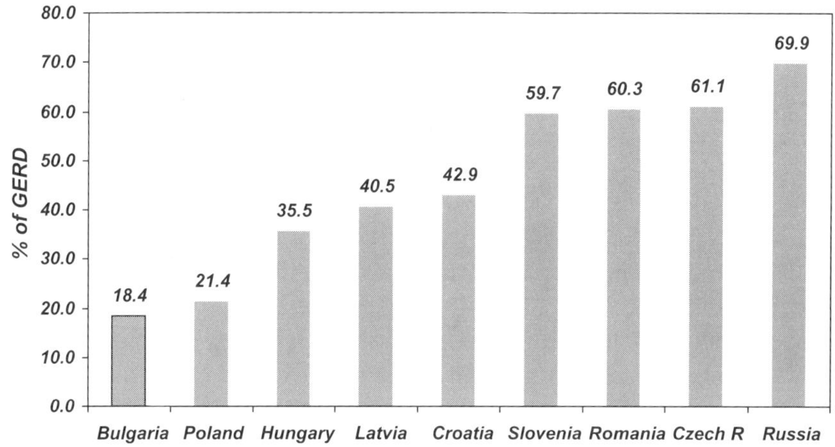

Fig. 6.8. Share of R&D performed by the business enterprise sector, 2002.
Sources: EU, R&D and Innovation Statistics in Candidate Countries and the Russian Federation, Data 1997–1999, EC, Theme 9, R&D, Luxembourg, Eurostat, 2002; for Moldova and Belarus, data bank of the CIS Statistical Committee (data are not comparable to OECD data in terms of definition); for 1999–2003 Eurostat.

by industry is low (in Russia 33%, in Romania 41% in 2002) and the share of government funding of business sector R&D correspondingly high in both countries.[36] This situation is generally rare in market economies, and can be taken as an indicator of slow restructuring in R&D. Our research (Radošević, 1999) suggests that the Russian innovation system is moving towards a situation where the in-house R&D activities of enterprises play a more important role than extra-mural R&D activities. However, the role of extra-mural R&D activities still continues to be significant, suggesting that some elements of the Soviet R&D model as described by Gokhberg (1997) are still present.

A simultaneous fall in government funding and weak demand for R&D from industry have blocked sectoral structural change within R&D systems, which have adjusted to deficient demand by simply shrinking across the board. Downsizing of R&D systems in CEE was not systematically linked to any specific individual factor on the demand or supply side (Radošević and Auriol, 1999). It is probably the combination of demand-side factors (changes in GDP and investment) and supply-side policies (budgetary policy for R&D) that in the end have shaped trends in

[36]Data are from OECD, *Main S&T Indicators* (2004).

R&D spending. Neither government nor market demand for R&D could buffer this fall. However, that does not mean that there was no change at micro level in R&D systems, as is shown very clearly in the Russian case (Radošević, 2003).

Business R&D and innovation

The supply of R&D is only a part of the overall process of innovation that leads to a finished product being placed on the market, or to economic growth at national level. The fall in aggregate R&D spending hides the changing nature of innovation and its sources. So if we want to understand why there has been a decrease in the demand for R&D, we should look beyond the R&D sector to the nature of the innovation process as a whole.

Research and development data measure the size of institutionalized knowledge-generating activities. Small and discontinuous R&D activities, usually closely linked to production, are not covered by R&D surveys (Sirilli, 1998). Moreover, continuous and institutionalized research activities are not necessarily used as inputs into the innovation process. This is especially apparent in 'catching-up' economies, where behind-the-frontier R&D work is usually much less integrated with innovation activities than in economies at the world technology frontier.

Variations in the structure of innovation expenditures should indicate differences in the main types of innovation activity. Taking into account differences in developmental levels between the EU and the CEE, we would expect that the structure of innovation expenditures should diverge significantly. Countries that are behind the technology frontier should spend relatively more on embodied technologies and on downstream innovation activities like reverse engineering, product and process imitation, than on R&D *per se*.

The analysis of innovation expenditures by Evangelista *et al.* (1996) shows that, first, the distribution of innovation costs is relatively consistent over all EU countries. Thus if innovation costs reflect the scope of different innovation activities, then the mix of innovative activities appears rather uniform across the EU. The second conclusion, based on the EU innovation survey, is that the industrial innovative process consists, first and foremost, of the purchase and use of 'embodied' technologies (innovative machinery and plants), which account for 50% of total expenditures on innovation. Third, among 'intangible' innovation expenditures, R&D activities are confirmed as a central component of the technological activities of firms (see also Evangelista *et al.*, 1997, Fig. 2, p. 529). Fourth, in terms of expenditure, the acquisition of 'disembodied' technology through patents and licenses emerges as a secondary innovation component when compared to embodied technological sources across all European countries.

A comparison of the structure of innovation expenditures for the group of new member-states and non-EU countries (including Turkey) presented in Fig. 6.9 shows that there are significant differences as compared with the EU-15 costs structure. R&D costs amount to a smaller share of innovation expenditures than in the EU-15. Only Slovenia, which is the most developed of the CEECs, has a share of R&D similar to the EU. Acquisition of machinery and equipment generally amounts to the biggest item among innovation expenditures. In Romania, in particular, innovation activity is essentially about installing new equipment. This cost structure reflects the nature of innovation in CEECs, which is primarily based around new equipment, most often imported.

Enterprises do not innovate on their own. Technological upgrading is dependent on the supply chain (suppliers and buyers) within which enterprises operate, on the degree of competition, and on the 'social networks' on which they can rely. Figure 6.10 shows the main sources of information for innovation in four CEECs. The data confirm the importance of the immediate business environment of firms as the main source of knowledge for innovation. Universities, consultants and R&D institutes are at best only secondary sources of direct knowledge. This is not surprising, and

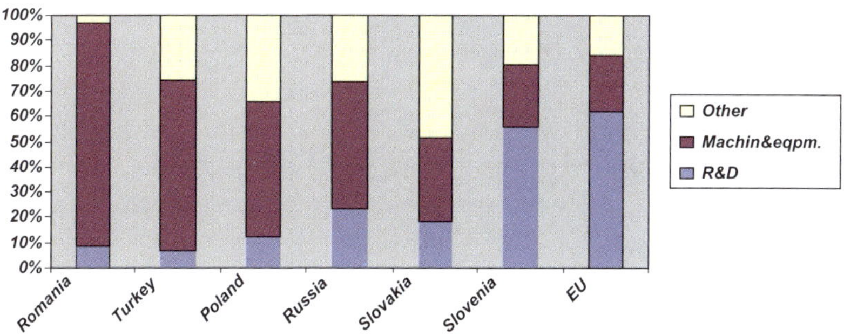

Fig. 6.9. Innovation expenditures in manufacturing, percentage structure, 2000.
Note: Data for Russia is for 1997.
Sources: EU, R&D and Innovation Statistics in Candidate Countries and the Russian Federation, Data 1997–1999, EC, Theme 9, R&D, Luxembourg, Eurostat, 2002; Statistics of Innovation in Europe, Luxembourg, Eurostat, 2000; for Slovakia, Slovak Statistical Office; for Turkey, Turkish Statistics Institute.

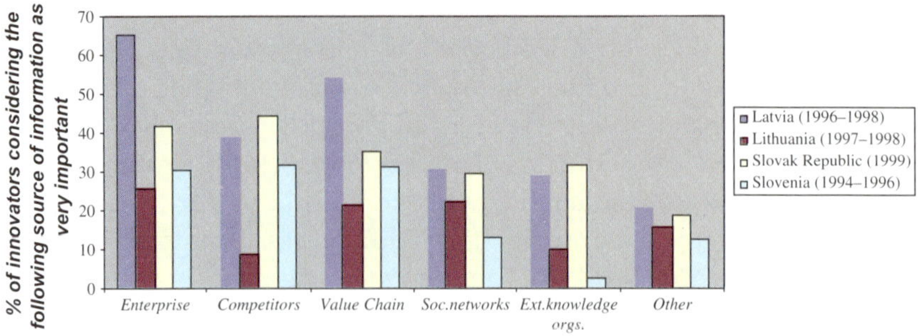

Fig. 6.10. Sources of information for innovation in manufacturing.
Notes: 1. *External knowledge organizations* = average importance of universities, consultants and R&D institutes; 2. *Value chain* = average importance of clients and suppliers; 3. *Social networks* = average importance of professional conferences, meetings, fairs, exhibitions, electronic networks; 4. *Other* = patents.
Sources: EU, R&D and Innovation Statistics in Candidate Countries and the Russian Federation, Data 1997–1999, EC, Theme 9, R&D, Luxembourg, Eurostat, 2002; for Moldova and Belarus, data bank of the CIS Statistical Committee (data are not comparable to OECD data in terms of definition); for 1999–2003 Eurostat.

corresponds to the findings of EU innovation surveys. Universities serve as sources of skilled professionals i.e., as indirect knowledge providers, rather than as direct sources of knowledge for information. On the other hand, when we compare the importance of external and internal sources of information of innovation for the EU-15 on the one hand and the average of four CEECs and Turkey on the other, we observe that in the less developed economies, external sources of knowledge are more important than knowledge coming from within the enterprise (see Fig. 6.11).[37]

Figure 6.11 shows that competitors, social networks and external knowledge organizations all play a more important role for innovators in the four CEECs plus Turkey than in the EU, while own sources of knowledge for innovation are more important in the more developed context than in the less developed CEECs and Turkey. Value chains (suppliers and buyers) play a similarly important role in both groups of countries.

These findings have important policy implications. First, they point to the relatively greater importance of national systems of innovation (competitors, social networks, external knowledge organizations) for

[37] We compare the weighted EU-15 average with the unweighted average of the five countries. This makes sense to the extent that our EU indicator is therefore biased towards bigger and technologically more developed countries like Germany, France and the UK. The data required to calculate a weighted average for the CEECs and Turkey is in any case unavailable.

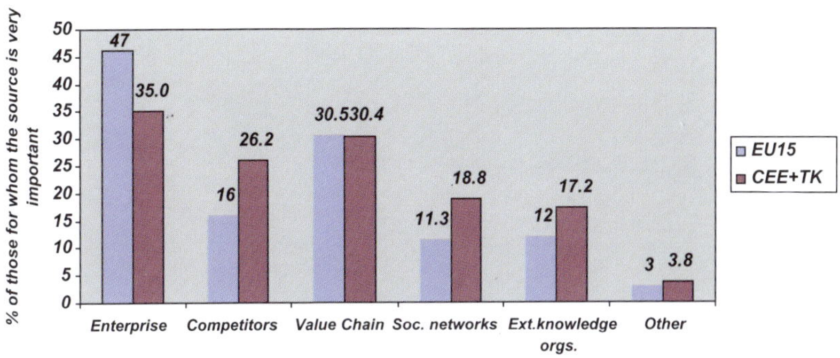

Fig. 6.11. External and internal sources of information for innovation in manufacturing for the EU-15 and four CEECs plus Turkey, 2000.
Notes: See Fig. 6.10: the four CEECs are Latvia, Lithuania, Slovakia and Slovenia.
Sources: EU, R&D and Innovation Statistics in Candidate Countries and the Russian Federation, Data 1997–1999, EC, Theme 9, R&D, Luxembourg, Eurostat, 2002; Turkish National Statistical Office, 2003 (mimeo).

innovators in the CEECs. The innovation capabilities of those companies are more dependent on systemic features of the external environment in which they operate. Second, the weakness of the innovation capabilities of local firms unable to generate new knowledge within their own R&D activities points to a need to support firm-level R&D or to induce demand for internal knowledge.

The relatively higher degree of dependence on external sources of knowledge in less developed environments suggests that CEECs may be dependent on FDI for new knowledge. Weak innovation capabilities of local firms and the gap between the 'old' S&T system and new sources of knowledge for enterprises may have led to increasing reliance on foreign technologies. Limited data for the CEECs suggest that FDI is, indeed, an important channel of inflow of new knowledge as expressed through payments for licenses. The correlation coefficient between payments for licenses and FDI inflows for the seven CEECs for which data are available is positive and high (0.706)[38, 39] (Fig. 6.12).

[38]In view of the small number of countries in the sample, this should be taken as a very tentative, but nevertheless indicative, result.
[39]NB while transfer of licenses is certainly not a necessary condition of the effective transfer of tacit knowledge (see Chapter 4), the two do in practice often go hand in hand. Note also that the corresponding correlation coefficient for 10 'catch-up' economies (China, India, South Africa, plus selected East Asian and Latin American economies) is low (0.122), suggesting that FDI is not the only channel of technology inflow.

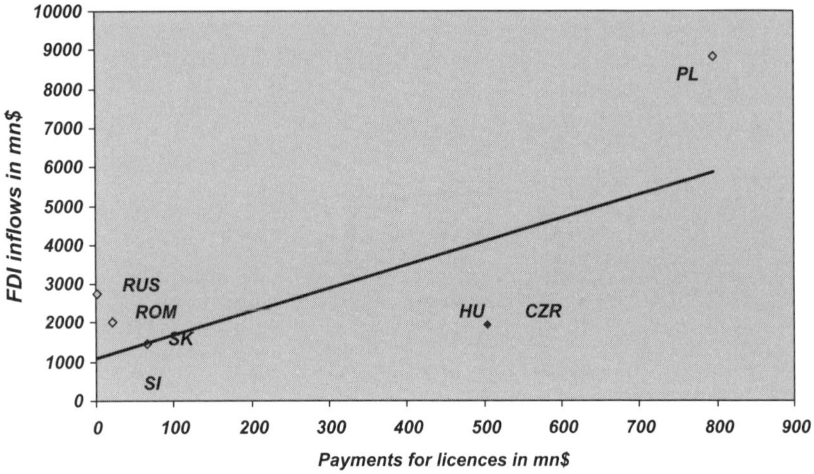

Fig. 6.12. Payments for licenses and FDI inflows, various years, $ m.
Note: Data for Slovenia, Russia and Romania are for 1998, for Hungary 1999, for Slovakia and Poland 2001, and for the Czech Republic 2003.
Source: UNCTAD, World Investment Reports 2000–2005, Geneva, UN, and Paris, OECD, Main S&T Indicators, 2004.

Conclusions

The evidence presented in this chapter strongly reinforces one of the key conclusions of Chapters 3, 4 and 5 — that local firms in CEE generally have to rely on FDI in order to gain new knowledge. This is the strength but also the weakness of the innovation process in the CEECs. Exclusive reliance on knowledge from abroad and on weak national systems of innovation, coupled with the very weak innovation capabilities of domestic firms themselves, represents the most vulnerable aspect of the CEE economies. As we saw from the case studies, heavy reliance on FDI leads to rapid productivity improvements in the short and medium terms. However, in the long term it may create fragile economies whose narrow specializations in FDI-related activities and weak national systems of innovation may become an obstacle to further upgrading. The trade-off between short-term efficiency and long-term strategic orientation and flexibility are the key emerging issues for the front-runner economies of Central-East Europe like Hungary, the Czech Republic and Poland. Other East European economies (Romania, Bulgaria, Russia, Ukraine) will have to engage with FDI as the way to gain quick access to new technologies. In both groups of countries, however, the key long-term issue is how to achieve complementarity between domestic and foreign sources of knowledge.

References

Evangelista, R., T. Sandven, G. Sirilli and K. Smith, "Measuring the cost of innovation in European industry." Paper presented at the International Conference *Innovation Measurement and Policies*, Luxembourg, EC, Eurostat, DGXIII, 20–21 May (1996).

Evangelista, R., G. Perani, F. Rapiti and D. Archibugi, "Nature and impact of innovation in manufacturing industry: Some evidence from the Italian innovation survey." *Res. Pol.* **26**, 4–5, 521–536 (1997).

Gokhberg, L., "Transformation of the Soviet R&D system." In L. Gokhberg, J.M. Peck and J. Gacs (eds.), *Russian Applied Research and Development: Its Problems and its Promise*, Laxenburg, IIASA, RR-97-7 (1997).

Kubielas, S., "Polish macroeconomic and S&T policies: Interlinkages for growth and decline." *J. Int. Relat. Develop.* **6**, 2, 156–184 (2003).

Nauwelaers, C. and A. Reid "Learning policy in a market-based context: Process, issues and challenges for EU candidate-countries." *J. Int. Relat. Develop.* 2002, **5**, 4, 352–356 (2002).

Radošević, S., "Patterns of innovative activities in countries of Central and Eastern Europe: An analysis based on comparison of innovation surveys." SPRU Electronic Working Papers Series, No. 34, www.sussex.ac.uk/spru (1999).

Radošević, S., "Patterns of preservation, restructuring and survival: Science and technology policy in Russia in the post-Soviet era." *Res. Pol.* **32**, 6, 1105–1124 (2003).

Radošević, S. and L. Auriol, "Patterns of restructuring in research, development and innovation activities in Central and Eastern European countries: Analysis based on S&T indicators." *Res. Pol.* **28**, 351–376 (1999).

Sirilli, G., "Old and new paradigms in the measurement of R&D." *Sci. Public Pol.* **25**, 5, 305–311 (1998).

CHAPTER 7

CAN EU POLICY INTERVENTION HELP PRODUCTIVITY CATCH-UP?

Peter Holmes, Javier Lopez-Gonzales, Johannes Stefan and Cordula Stolberg

Introduction

The EU has endorsed the objective of assisting the whole of the EU economy to improve industrial competitiveness, with a particular focus on knowledge, innovation, and entrepreneurship. The instruments targeted at these objectives include mainly competition policy and enterprise policy. In addition, within the framework of structural and cohesion policy, the EU has set itself the objective of facilitating rapid catch-up in real economic terms in the less advanced regions of the Union. With the integration of the CEE economies into the Union, the main focus for EU cohesion policy will in the future rest with its new member states.

In focusing on the conditions for real economy catch-up in the new member states in CEE, the aim of this chapter is to assess the current design of EU policy intervention. To verify the efficiency and effectiveness of policies to this end, a clear picture of the reasons for lower levels of real economy competitiveness in CEE is needed. Here, we make use of the results generated by the other work packages of the *East–West Productivity Gap* project. This research directs our attention mainly to sectoral specialization patterns, technology (including R&D, technology transfer and absorption), and to mainly management-related firm-specific factors as principal reasons for lower productivity levels and key drivers of productivity growth.

Stylized facts: Setting the agenda

Since the demise of socialism, the economies in CEE have, by and large, experienced higher income and productivity growth rates than the average of the EU-15. However, the new member states still lag behind seriously in terms of overall competitiveness. Measured in terms of average national labor productivity, the CEE/EU-15 gap at the end of 2002 ranged from about 80% of the EU-15 average in the Baltic countries, through around 70% in Poland, the Czech Republic and Hungary, to 55% for Slovenia (value added at current prices per employed person and annual average market exchange rates).

Since the early 1990s, CEE countries have been gradually integrating into the European market, with the implementation of the Europe Agreements, and with the achievement of Union membership in May 2004 have been granted full single market status. Additionally, the new EU members received pre-accession financial support within the framework of PHARE, ISPA, and SAPARD. While those programs were largely governed by the EU Commission and mainly geared to institutional integration, the integration of the CEE economies into EU industrial policy and EU cohesion policy in particular is more devolved to the competence of the member states, and has a more pronounced focus on increasing competitiveness and assisting real economy catch-up.

Structure of the chapter

As a first step, we briefly discuss the theoretical foundations of economic policy intervention in favor of preventing economic divergence and/or supporting swift economic convergence. In its second part, the chapter reviews the emphasis placed by the EU on 'institutional framework conditions' in policy assistance. Here, some reference is made to experience in East Germany, where financial support from the West was mainly invested into institution-building and social transfers. In the next part, the design of EU industrial policy is checked against the particular conditions pertaining in CEE, and the specific sources of productivity gaps and drivers of productivity growth in the new member states. Here, the focus is on competition policy, FDI and trade policy and the horizontal instruments of enterprise policy. The final part of the chapter assesses the sectoral effects of horizontal policies, and whether those policies are well suited to the particularities of CEE. The paper closes with a set of conclusions for a coherent and effective policy-mix design for the EU level conducive to catch-up in real economic terms in the new CEE members-states.

Theoretical Foundations of Economic Policy Interventions

To provide sound economic policy recommendations, it is necessary to determine the political goals of the state or union and to assess — from the point of view of market mechanisms — what policies are efficient to promote the designated political goal. The aim of this section is briefly to assess the theoretical foundations that underlie the EU's concept for policy interventions.

The overriding aim of EU policy intervention can be summed up in terms of the so-called 'Lisbon strategy', which predicates that the Union should become 'the most dynamic and competitive knowledge economy'. More precisely, today's EU policy interventions involve two sub-aims: enterprise growth and innovation in Europe as a whole on the one hand; and reduction of economic disparities between economic regions on the other. From an economic point of view, we are prompted to question whether those two sub-aims are in fact compatible in terms of policy instruments, or whether achieving one aim is likely to compromise the other.

In general, we can distinguish between two schools of thought with respect to the overriding aim of the Lisbon strategy. Conflicting predictions on the effects of economic integration follow from different theoretical concepts:

- One group assumes that technology, being exogenous, is freely available across the integrated economic area. Hence, less advanced regions either catch up with higher growth rates by using freely available and more advanced foreign technology (absolute convergence), or are able to catch up conditionally on the ability to absorb and implement the foreign technology in their own production systems (weak convergence). While the supply of technology is exogenous, differences in development levels are, in this interpretation, endogenous, and depend on the respective endowments of regions with immobile factors. European integration itself (i.e., the deepening and enlargement of the European single market as well as the introduction of a common currency) is sufficient to secure *both* convergence of levels of economic development within the common market via trade and competition *and* a higher level of economic development for the whole region via a more efficient allocation of scarce resources.

The implications for economic policy in this convergence hypothesis involve the promotion of unrestricted trade and mobility of factors of production. With regard to less developed regions, the concept would suggest reducing the barriers to the exploitation of more advanced and foreign technology, but no specific intervention in market mechanisms.

- A second group assumes increasing return to scale in the aggregate (decreasing long-run cost curves) and beneficial externalities at the micro level; technology is endogenous and localized. With deepening integration, the most productive factors will tend to flow toward the more favored regions offering higher returns, and hence improve the allocation of scarce resources; agglomerations will benefit from integration whereas disadvantaged peripheries might well fall further behind. In the strong case of this non-convergence story, the existence of a sufficiently large development gap causes divergence, whereas in the weaker version, convergence can only set in if a minimum regional-specific threshold level of economic development has been achieved (below which private investment cannot yield the rate of return required by the market). Hence, European integration secures a higher level of economic development via reallocation of scarce resources to their most efficient use, but benefits are not necessarily distributed equally across regions.

  In terms of economic policy, regional concentration through liberalization of trade and movement of factors within the integration area is accepted in this interpretation as the optimal policy (efficiency argument). However, the result may be a higher level of regional concentration, which might go against the second objective of the Lisbon agenda, if deepening integration resulted in an uneven distribution of agglomerations between European regions. With reduction of economic disparities between economic regions being an explicit European goal, the non-convergence concept might justify policy intervention on those grounds.

  This line of reasoning raises two further questions: first, a political decision has to be taken on the precise form of the target for the reduction of economic disparities, i.e., whether convergence of per capita GDP via relatively higher growth in lagging regions is the aim, or whether the establishment of equal economic welfare is to be achieved. Whereas the former case would justify policy intervention to reduce the *gap,* or to achieve a minimum required *level* in regions with weak agglomerations, the optimal policy for an equalization of welfare between regions might best be served by allowing the maximum level of efficiency via concentrations, and a surrogate redistribution of generated income to lagging regions in the form of transfers. In the case of the EU, it seems safe to assume that for regional policy, the former type of convergence is preferred. Second, the regions for which the aim of convergence is postulated have to be defined: if the sizes of regions are too divergent, if population densities are very heterogeneous between regions, if endowments in natural resources are too divergent, and/or if the territorial size of a region is too small to assure a meaningful relationship between the activities taking place in the region and what is reported by statistics, then it is unrealistic to expect economic convergence. In the context of EU regional policy, the so-called NUTS2 regions have been defined as the geographical level at which inequalities should be measured, yet some of the NUTS2 regions are indeed too divergent in their underlying potentials to serve as meaningful regions in terms of policies for economic convergence (see e.g., Boldrin and Canova, 2001).

From the design of EU cohesion policy, and from public statements in support of policy interventions, we may posit that the theoretical foundation thereof is deduced from the concept of possible non-convergence, and that regional policy does take the form of compromising overall economic efficiency for the sake of interregional equality. Empirical analysis of effects of regional policy alone on economic convergence (in particular income levels) is rather inconclusive (Boldrin and Canova, 2001). However, some of the evidence suggests that interaction between economic integration (primarily trade liberalization), macro policy, micro policy and institutional reform, and EU policy intervention, may be important (Pischke, 2001).[40] Moreover, cohesion policy has lately received a 'Lisbon agenda makeover' (see the speech of Commissioner Barnier to the enlarged presidency of the Parliament on 18 February 2004): we should note that the proposed renationalization of large parts of cohesion policy to some degree dilutes the potential conflict between the two sub-aims. This allows us to assess EU

[40]EU assistance for the development of infrastructure has undoubtedly been a positive-effect story.

structural and cohesion policy in the broader framework of policy interventions in general.[41]

The Implications of Policies Aimed at 'Institutional Framework Conditions'

During the phase of preparation for membership, the EU placed particular weight on installing the institutional framework of the Union in CEE economies. The pre-accession phase was clearly dominated by the insertion of community law from the *acquis communautaire* into the national laws of the new members. However, the German experience after reunification shows that institution-building, however necessary a condition for catching up, is far from sufficient to improve the conditions for real economy convergence. Rather, in post-socialist economies, we observe specific conditions which suggest the need for similarly specific policies. The analysis below suggests that EU policies as planned have the potential to meet those particular needs. Maybe, however, a different mix of policies aimed at increasing skills and know-how, production networks and inter-firm interaction, R&D and innovation, entrepreneurship, infrastructure, etc. would promise to be more effective.

The (near-)complete introduction of the *acquis communautaire* has, indeed, highlighted the need for economic policy to embrace more specifically the particular deficiencies of the CEE economies, as discussed in previous chapters. That conclusion holds *a fortiori* to the extent that the overall productivity gap is a function of the length of the 'tail' that follows the best-practice activities documented in Chapter 4.

The Design of EU Industrial Policy in Light of the Particular Conditions Pertaining in CEE Economies

Industrial policy is essentially within the competence of the member states. The role of the EU in EU industrial policy is therefore confined to the 'open method of co-ordination', in which the Commission serves as something

[41]Of course, the trade-off resurfaces at the level of member states. In that connection, a recent competitiveness report suggests that European regional policy should embrace a stronger focus on promoting knowledge and innovation in the weaker regions, if the gap between the most and least competitive regions in Europe is not to grow even wider (*European Competitiveness Index*, 2004).

like a conductor of discussions, a sponsor of policy developments and improvements. Within the framework of the Lisbon agenda, the discussion pertaining to EU industrial policy centers around industrial competitiveness: knowledge, innovation and entrepreneurship are held to be the three key factors (see EC COM (2002) 714). The overarching 'philosophy' of EU policies can be summarized thus:

> '...the Lisbon goal calls for policies that establish an environment conducive to enterprise growth and innovation while ensuring that the market players are subject to uniform rules. Enterprise policy focuses on the first objective, while competition policy emphasizes the second. But both policies contribute to high and sustainable productivity growth' (EC COM, 2002, 262, p. 14).

More specifically, the assessment of individual instruments of EU industrial policies suggests the predominance of three important characteristic principles:

- Policy intervention can only compensate (where necessary) for market failure (enterprise policy) or protect/safeguard the market (competition policy).
- Enterprise policy and competition policy are to work in a complementary way (EC COM, 2002, 262). Potential areas of conflict, such as, e.g., cooperation in R&D and innovation, are dealt with specifically in the EU competition policy, in our example below in the form of technology transfer block exemptions.
- Industrial policy is strictly confined to a horizontal approach. Hence the leitmotiv of 'framework conditions'. This concept originates from the definition of the broad principles of EU industrial policy in 1990 (see EC COM, 90, 556) and resurfaces throughout the latest publications outlining future EU policy, including policies for CEE economies (e.g., EC COM, 2002, 714). Specific interventions aimed at supporting particular firms or sectors of the economy are either ruled out explicitly or embraced only if aimed at reducing over-capacity (e.g., the steel sector).[42]

This conceptualization of industrial policy appears to offer all possibilities of devising a coherent and effective policy-mix in the new CEE members

[42]One prominent exception to this rule, however, is the EU Common Agricultural Policy. We will later argue that this policy in particular could in fact be potentially harmful for the goal of real economy catch-up in some of the CEE member economies.

to assist swift real economy convergence. Of particular importance for the new member states is the fact that none of the instruments in EU industrial policy serve to restrict flexibility: none appear to change market scarcities or prices, in such a way as to send distorted signals to market agents, in particular investors.[43]

For the post-socialist economies, flexibility in the reallocation of resources is a particularly important condition of real economy catch-up (Stephan, 2003a): because of the historically rooted distortions both in sectoral structures and within industrial firms in post-socialist economies, profound restructuring is a necessary precondition for a dynamic process of catch-up development. The contemporary patterns of comparative advantages of those economies are hence also subject to change, and it is impossible to determine which comparative advantages will in fact lead the new members into real-economy convergence: today, those economies feature lower unit labor costs in industrial production, yet some CEE industries appear to be developing particular strengths in capital-intensive and knowledge-driven manufacturing industries. Any policy in support of, e.g., more standard labor-intensive production would hence intervene unduly in the market.

Additional EU industrial policy specifically targeted at new members

Some additional policy instruments of EU industrial policy are targeted at the particular needs of new member countries. Those mainly focus upon improving infrastructure, know-how and skills, and local institutions.

Clearly, investment in infrastructure is well targeted at the specific deficiencies of the region. Indeed, accessibility and quality of transport infrastructure proved to be among the key firm-specific sources of lower CEE levels of productivity in a comparison of pairs of similar firms from West and East (Stephan, 2003b) forming part of the *East–West Productivity Gap* project. Policies aimed at improving know-how and skills of

[43]A possible exception are instruments targeted at improving the access to finance by way of 'a wider availability of guarantees' (EC COM, 2000, 771, p. 7). Such policy intervention can easily give rise to adverse motivational effects as moral hazard. At the same time, however, provision of seed- and early-stage financing and micro-loans have the potential to increase flexibility by assisting the emergence of new firms.

entrepreneurs and workers alike also correspond well to the specific needs of the economies of the new member-states. Of course, the level of formal education is comparatively high in the new member states; but management deficiencies and a weakness in entrepreneurship are amongst the most important competitive disadvantages in CEE, as we saw in Chapter 4. The EU plans to focus policy in this field on 'creating an environment conducive to entrepreneurship, skills upgrading and SME development' (EC COM, 2002, 714, p. 28). Further measures include 'supporting the development of business services, promoting the culture of inter-firm cooperation and enhancing the development of innovative clusters' (*Ibid*. p. 28). Once again, the above-cited analysis on firm-specific determinants of productivity gaps reveals that amongst the most important sources of gaps between comparable firms in East and West are a low intensity of use of communications technologies (e-mail, internet, e-business) for inter-firm networking and a general lack of networking between the firms and their customers, suppliers and other stakeholders (Stephan, 2003b).

For CEEs, local institutions servicing business in tasks such as, e.g., applying for assistance from EU structural funds, or channeling of potential investors to profitable locations and potential local partners, are complete novelties. Hence, EU support in the development of local institutions and the training of their employees can have a very important, if indirect, effect on the competitiveness of CEE industry.

EU enterprise policy in light of CEE development conditions

The instruments of EU enterprise policy focus in particular on the three objectives of entrepreneurship, innovation, and access to markets (see ECSEC, 2000, 771). The instruments promoting entrepreneurial activity include predominantly institutional framework reforms (in the field of bankruptcy legislation and simplification of administrative and regulatory procedures for start-ups, and by promoting new legal forms of entrepreneurship), but also more direct measures like improving access to finance for seed- and early-stage financing and micro-loans, knowledge and skills-related activities (education schemes at all levels, vocational training in firms), and also business support activities (presentations laying out the possibilities of inter-firm cooperation and networking, supply-chain management, e-commerce, etc.).

The instruments targeted at supporting innovation and change focus on a removal of obstacles to the dynamic development of research and technology (including issues such as intellectual property rights and patenting, as well as the removal of obstacles to the introduction of new products), on the encouragement of support mechanisms and exchange of good practice (at both the regional level, in the 'Regional Innovation Policy Network' and 'Network of Regions of Excellence', and the firm level, with the emphasis on innovation finance and technology transfer), and on promoting business services in general — in terms of the taxonomy used in Chapter 6, seeking to create at least some of the elements of a national innovation system.

The instruments related to ensuring access for goods and services to markets are mainly concerned with improving the efficiency of the single market project: elimination of remaining barriers, liberalization in the fields of utilities, improvements in public procurement, competition and state-aid rules and other single market legislation. In addition, the policy-mix envisages some strategies to help small and medium enterprises using the whole potential of the Single Market.

Most of those instruments are conducive to dynamic economic development, not only in established European industries, but in particular in the new member states: here, entrepreneurship and innovative activity are particularly underdeveloped, while practicing and potential entrepreneurs are at the lower end of the learning curve in terms of management and market know-how and experience. In this respect, promoting a bankruptcy framework that allows entrepreneurs a fresh start after failure is necessary to accommodate the risky character of entrepreneurship, and helps to disentangle inefficient allocations of scarce resources in the Schumpeterian sense. Given the high intensity of enterprise restructuring in the formerly state-governed economies, such a dynamic approach to that task is particularly important. This dynamic approach can be further promoted by easing the pain of absorbing administrative and regulatory procedures which are all new to business agents in CEE: here, know-how on how best to operate in a highly regulated environment is particularly scarce. The experience with the promotion of new forms of entrepreneurship in Germany seems to suggest, however, that such initiatives have only limited effectiveness if they are not underpinned by the actual training of potential entrepreneurs: the introduction in that country of the so-called 'Ich-AG', aimed at making it easier for individuals to start their own one-person company has not been conspicuously successful. Hence, it remains doubtful whether the introduction of such additional forms of entrepreneurship is actually needed.

Without doubt, access to finance for (in particular small) entrepreneurs (whether for start-up, restructuring, or innovation) is a particular European problem (by comparison with the US); it is especially grave in CEE: here, incumbent banks are often over-burdened with poor-quality loan-portfolios from larger client enterprises, and hence unable to provide more risky seed and micro-loans (Dyker, 2001). Any measures to ease this bottleneck are likely to have a very substantial effect. Additionally, knowledge and skills-related activities in the form of education schemes and vocational training in firms, as well as business support activities through the use of 'road-shows' laying out the possibilities of inter-firm cooperation and networking, supply-chain management, e-commerce, etc., can help entrepreneurs in CEE to bridge the experience gap vis-à-vis their Western competitors.

With firms in CEE only gradually integrating into Western markets and East–West firm networks, Western technology in the East is often new, hence innovative activity is generally lower (see Chapter 6 in this book and Cserháti and Takács, 2002, for an analysis of the factors driving innovation in CEE firms). The production of new knowledge or the combination of existing knowledge in new ways can result in marketable new methods of production (process innovations) and/or in newly developed products. Innovations are typically held to be amongst the most important sources of productivity growth, and are consequently an essential factor in the drive by the new member economies to become internationally competitive. Hence, policies aimed at dynamic development of research and technology are of particular importance in CEE economies. In particular, the region- and network-related instruments for the exchange of 'good practices' can help CEE firms to leapfrog up the learning curve.

In terms of enhanced access to markets, CEE firms will benefit particularly from the instruments aiming to improve use of the potentials of the European Single Market. Having begun gradually to integrate into the Single Market from as early as 1992, after the conclusion of the Europe Agreements, some CEE economies still record deficits in foreign trade with West Europe (see Fig. 7.1). This is partly simply a reflection of the high rate of inflow of investment into the region, but it may also partly reflect the lowly status that most CEE firms still occupy in European networks (see Chapter 4).

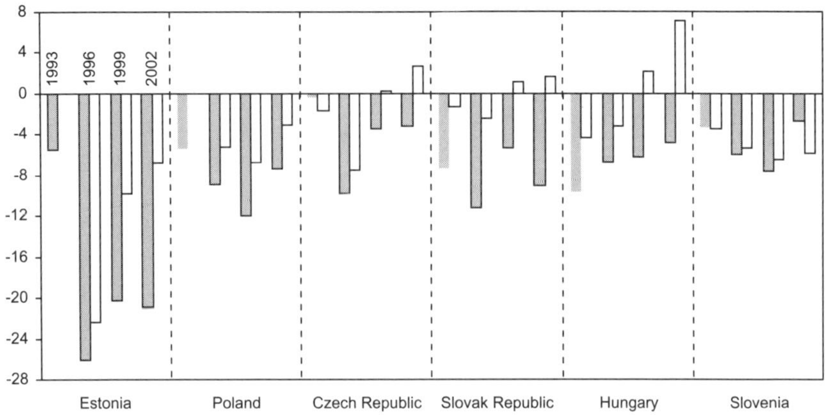

Note: grey...total balance; white...balance with EU-15

Fig. 7.1. Trade balances of the transition countries with the rest of the world, and with the EU. *Source:* WIIW, National Statistical Offices, own calculations.

EU Competition Policy in the Perspective of CEE Development Conditions

We now turn to the EU's principal policy towards industry, namely competition policy. Here, the new member states have been obliged to adopt rules compatible with the Rome Treaty ever since the Europe Agreements were signed. It might therefore be tempting to conclude that the effects of accession have already occurred. In reality, however, the pattern of change has been quite subtle. The Europe Agreements did not in fact impose any requirements on candidate countries with respect to domestic competition laws, but only with respect to matters covered within the EU by Articles 81 (on restrictions of competition) and 82 (on abuses of dominant position) for private actions, which affect cross-border trade, and the corresponding state aids rules. Paradoxically, the functions of the newly created competition agencies carried out under the rubric of the Europe Agreements would have disappeared upon accession, leaving them with only internal tasks, had accession not been the occasion for a major re-think of the way the EU deals with competition issues, namely the creation of a network of national competition agencies to complement DG Competition. (We explain this and the questions it raises below).

With accession, trade policy now becomes an EU matter for the new member states. Interestingly, the pre-accession phase was not a customs union (CU), but a form of free trade area (FTA) (like the European Economic Area). Only with accession did the new member-countries actually join the EU CU. For most countries, the tariff structures had anticipated membership, so that there should be no serious obstacles to a smooth transition. The major impact is likely to be on anti-dumping (AD), where all EU measures applied against candidate countries (barring use of the new transition mechanism) were dropped upon accession. But the new member countries are now obliged to take on the EU's AD measures instead of their own, thus losing their residual pre-accession trade policy autonomy. This raises two questions:

- Had the CEECs been able to use their residual trade instruments as a policy to affect location of investment?
- More problematically, if so, is the loss of this instrument likely to be bad for catch-up?

Table 7.1 highlights the main changes in competition, trade, and industrial policy following on accession.

Competition law reform

Eastwards enlargement of the EU has coincided with a major reform of competition law enforcement across the EU. The overall objectives of the Competition Law Reform focus on a more transparent and more directly applicable competition law enforcement mechanism, with simpler procedures, a decrease in bureaucracy, and closer co-operation between national competition authorities (NCAs) and the Commission, as well as amongst NCAs.

Eastern enlargement made a reform of competition law highly opportune. The CEEC competition authorities were set up with the Europe Agreement rules very much in mind. They required that the CEECs, then as associates, should put in place some form of competition regime which would replicate the impact on trade between member states of articles 81 and 82 (formerly 85, 86) of the Rome Treaty. These articles are directly effective within the EU (being enforceable by DG Competition and if necessary by action in the courts). But the corresponding clauses of the EAs could not be directly effective in the same way unless implemented by legislation in

Table 7.1. Shifting policy responsibilities after accession.

	Pre-accession		Post-accession		
	National	EU	National	EU	
				Network	DG Comp
Competition	Must ensure 81/82 and state aids equivalence where effect on trade.	No formal powers	National markets only.	Regional markets.	EU-25 cases.
	Can treat local cases as it wishes. Monitors and approves aids.		EA-related tasks.		Preamble and SME policies of EU apply in full.
					Control of state aids.
Trade	National rules apply	FTA rules only.	Must apply CET including AD.	CEECs lose voice at WTO 2003; gain vote in EU 2004.	
		Rules on NTBs as they affect product norms.	National transition measures?		
Industry	Gives state aids; must accept.	Sets technical norms.	Norms?	EU technology etc. policies apply in full to CEECs.	
			Scope for national derogations?		

AD = anti-dumping; CET = common external tariffs; EA = Europe agreements; FTA = free trade area; NTBs = non-tariff barriers.

the partner countries. The partners chose to set up competition laws and competition agencies. The new competition policies went beyond the literal requirement of the EAs, which only necessitated controls on restrictive business practices which might affect cross border trade between the EU and partners.

It is interesting to note in this connection that many existing member states (e.g., Italy) had until recently no competition authority. While the Commission was empowered to tackle cross-border cases, the Rome Treaty is silent on purely domestic matters. And member states *with* competition policies were free to use principles different from Treaty rules for purely domestic matters. (The UK, for example, has only just removed a blanket public interest provision from its *domestic* competition rules.) By the same token, the new competition agencies in CEE would have found that, upon accession, their sole tasks were to resolve purely domestic cases; indeed, it would have been possible for accession countries to abolish their agencies, had they wished to do so, on the grounds that they could rely on the pro-competitive effect of regional free trade on a small open economy — an option that could certainly have appealed to the Baltic states.

In the event, a decision was taken at the overall EU level that will radically transform the potential role of the fledgling agencies. The Modernization Regulation of 2003,[44] which came into force on the day of enlargement, follows the logic of the jurisprudence of the European Court of Justice, holding that EU competition law is directly effective within member states and can therefore be invoked by parties other than the Commission (though the scope for actors other than the Commission to apply article 81(3) (governing the rules for exemptions from Article 81) is more complex). But we should note once again that the new arrangements only apply to the application of Community law: matters with no possible effect on trade remain in domestic hands.

Vissi (1998) argues further that, whereas under the pre-accession regime, cross-border competition cases in the CEECs had to be judged according to the wording of articles 81 and 82 alone, the application of the full Rome Treaty to these cases implies that the early general articles of the Treaty, regarding cohesion etc., will now become relevant to the interpretation of the competition provisions. Frazer (1996) argues that this has been

---

[44]See *Modernization of EC Antitrust Enforcement Rules.* Council Regulation (EC) No 1/2003; and the Modernisation Package http://europa.eu.int/comm/competition/publications/publications/modernisation_en.pdf

problematic even within the EU, and it is a particularly delicate burden to impose on the new competition authorities.

The modernization of Regulation 17 (1962), which governs the restriction of competition (Article 81) and abuses of a dominant position (Article 82), forms the core of the Competition Law Reform. A new European Competition Network (ECN) serves as key player within the new enforcement system. At the same time, more responsibility is shifted to companies, as they will have to ensure that their actions either do not restrict competition or qualify under the provisions of Article 81(3) without being able to rely on 'comfort letters' from the Commission.

The ECN will operate on the principle of best-placed authority. The provisions of Article 81(3) will become directly applicable in the new member states as in the EU-15, and, based on this, there will be joint enforcement of the rules governing restrictive practices by the Commission, the NCAs, and national courts. This represents a major change to the present enforcement system. Whereas prior to the reform, only the Commission was able to apply Article 81(3), NCAs and national courts are now able to and expected to apply the provisions of Article 81(3) when the Competition Law Reform comes into force. National courts thus play an important role in the enforcement of competition law and complement the role of NCAs. Equally important is the change to the handling of block exemptions granted by the Commission. If the Commission has granted such a block exemption, by which Article 81(1) (governing restriction of competition) is declared inapplicable to certain agreements, decisions, or practices, and if these agreements, decisions or practices cause effects that are incompatible with Article 81(3), not only the Commission, but also the NCAs, have the power to withdraw the block exemption from a particular case. Thus NCAs are, under the circumstances described above, empowered to quash the block exemption granted by the Commission.

With regard to the relations among the members of the network and their competences, the Commission maintains a leading function. National competition law has to act within the boundaries of EU competition law. NCAs cannot apply national competition law to agreements or practices covered by the provisions of Article 81(1) such as would prohibit such agreements or practices, if the same is not also prohibited under EU competition law. Member states are, however, free to apply *stricter* national competition laws that prohibit unilateral conduct by companies, e.g., abusive behavior toward economically dependent undertakings. NCAs are, moreover, obliged to inform the Commission before or immediately after, commencing a formal investigation under the provisions of Articles 81/82. This information about proceedings has also to be made available to the other member states. The Commission can also directly intervene in the proceedings of NCAs or national courts: if the Commission initiates proceedings under the provisions of Articles 81/82, NCAs and/or national courts are relieved of their competencies over those cases. Furthermore, if the Commission has reached a decision in particular cases under the provisions of Articles 81/82, NCAs and/or national courts must not adopt decisions relating to those cases that go against the ruling of the Commission.

In proceedings under Articles 81/82 that might affect trade between member states, the application of national competition law must not lead to the prohibition of agreements/practices that affect trade between member states, but are allowed under Article 81(1) or fulfill the conditions of/are covered by Article 81(3).

According to the principle of best-placed authority, each case should only be dealt with by one (namely the most appropriate) authority. Hence, competition authorities are able to suspend or close a case on the ground that another competition authority has dealt or is dealing with the case. In practice, this requires the exchange of information — even confidential information — between the different authorities. The Competition Law Reform provides for an exchange of information conditional on the sole use of such information for the application of Articles 81 or 82, or for the application of national competition law if it refers to same case.

The Competition Law Reform and the concept of the ECN in principle provide a basis for a more direct approach to the enforcement of competition policy. At the same time, it places more responsibilities on the shoulders of the NCAs and national courts, in terms of applying and enforcing competition law. This could potentially prove difficult for some NCAs in CEE, as competition authorities are relatively new in those countries and are not as experienced in the enforcement of competition law as NCAs in other member states.

The ECN aims at a more direct approach to the enforcement of competition policy. However, the new system leaves some open questions with regard to responsibilities and competencies within the network, as well as with regard to the relationships between the members of the network. These issues become particularly interesting in cases with cross-border implications.

The principle of best-placed authority, and the handling of each case by a single authority, should make competition law enforcement more transparent (both for competition authorities and firms) and offer a more direct application. Nevertheless, it is not always clear which authority should initiate proceedings in cases with cross-border implications, or should have the competency to deal with such cases. It is ambiguous as to whether NCAs can take decisions that affect other member states too, in cases with cross-border implications, or whether such decisions are legally binding only within national boundaries.[45] If decisions by NCAs *are* only legally binding within national boundaries, it might well come to multiple and contradictory enforcement (which is precisely what the competition law reform aims to avoid). It is worth noting here that the jurisdictional overlap issue arises in the EU in a very different one from the US, where both the Federal Trade Commission and the Anti-Trust Division of the Department of Justice enforce federal law. In this case, they normally act as prosecutors only, and coherence is assured by the fact the initial decisions, not only appeal decisions, are made by the courts. In fact, anyone with standing — usually aggrieved competitors, consumer groups and individual states — can bring a competition case to a US court. The principle of direct effect of EC competition law actually opens up the prospect of additional private enforcement of EC competition law, as has indeed occurred occasionally in the UK. We discuss below the issues raised by the private enforcement of the *state aid* element of competition law.

The issue of market definition is an important one, too. The outline of the Competition Law Reform does not state which authority should define the relevant market in cases with cross-border implications. The market definition is, however, highly relevant in such cases, as the decision on whether a firm conducts anticompetitive behavior can change with the definition of the relevant market. In their paper on the ECN, Mavroidis and Neven (2000) point out some further potential problems that the implementation of the Competition Law Reform might bring about, viz.,

- A possible 'disintegrating effect' of the reform, as the NCAs face different incentives in exercising their power, and probably have no incentive to consider effects outside their national boundaries, except in their own interest.

[45]See also Mavroidis and Neven (2000) on this issue. They interpret the White Paper to mean that decisions by NCAs are only binding within national boundaries.

- The issue of accountability is not specifically addressed; the authors suggest accountability standards and standards of independence.
- Balancing between positive and negative net benefits might become difficult under multiple enforcement. If one country experiences a negative effect from a decision (although the net effect over all countries affected might be positive), it may block the implementation of the decision.

Some hypothetical scenarios and their likely outcomes[46] can help to highlight the potential problems and questions the new system of competition law enforcement raises:

- In case two firms from two different countries have an agreement which would impose vertical restraints, which NCA would have the competency to deal with the case/initiate proceedings? Or is this otherwise a case that the Commission would deal with?

No set rules exist for such a scenario. Two or more NCAs might deal with one case. NCAs might continue to deal with cases that are already dealt with by other authorities or might indeed initiate proceedings even though another NCA/the Commission is already dealing with the case. Generally, the member state/NCA that is better placed to deal with the case should take the case on.

- Considering the same case as above, one of the two countries has now granted an exemption for that agreement. Would such an exemption only be binding within national boundaries, or would it also be applicable across borders, i.e., in the second country? What would happen if the second country disagreed with the granting of the exemption? Would the Commission intervene and, more importantly, would the Commission undertake a cost-benefit analysis of the case in light of its effect on both countries/all member states? Alternatively, would one of the two countries have to undertake such an analysis?

If the Commission has issued a decision concerning an agreement, NCAs and national courts cannot — in cases with cross-border implications — issue a divergent decision (as mentioned above, this does not — under the

[46]These scenarios were presented to Adam Zolnowski of the Polish Competition Office, who kindly outlined the operations of the ECN with regard to the cases and highlighted where such operational procedures have yet to be put in place. The text above represent a summary of the answers.

provisions outlined above — apply to purely domestic agreements under block exemptions). If, however, an NCA or national court grants such an exemption, another member state is free to assess the matter without considering previous rulings. The outcome of such a process is nevertheless entirely unforeseeable at the moment, as the issue of the scope of jurisdiction of a state in itself remains unclarified. Complicated by the exemption issue, there are neither formal nor informal guidelines on how to deal with such a case.

- How is the question of defining the relevant market in any potential case handled? Which authority defines the relevant market and which criteria are used to do so? What happens if there is disagreement about the definition of the relevant market among NCAs, or between NCAs and the Commission?

Apart from the general criteria of the homogenous conditions of competition and the substitutability of the concerned products, which NCAs will use in a similar fashion when applying EC law, there are no further guidelines as how the relevant market should be determined. Therefore, different and mutually contradictory market definitions might emerge, which could considerably hamper the identification of cases. *N.B.*: the issue of market definition may be subject to discussion on the forum of the ECN (discussions of this issue between the US and the EC have, for example, proven to be successful).

- How big is the potential for 'forum shopping', i.e., NCAs only taking up cases that are of national interest? Will there be a mechanism in place to prevent such behavior?

It should not be possible to bring complaints before an authority with little interest in the matter. On the principle that cases should be dealt with by the best-suited authority, that authority should have an interest in the case, and the outcome of the case (especially if unresolved) should have a potential impact on the economy. There exists, however, the risk that in some circumstances no authority would want to, or could afford to, deal with a given case.

- How will the principle of best-placed authority operate in practice? Assuming there is a horizontal agreement between two firms in two countries, which authority will deal with the case? What happens if the NCA of a third country has an interest in intervening because some of its industries/consumers would be affected by the agreement, too?

The future functioning of the ECN is still very much in the melting-pot. Generally, cases should be dealt with by the authority that has the biggest interest/is most affected by the case and has the best resources to deal with it. There has been some controversy recently over merger cases in Poland (banks) and Slovenia (beer) where the suggestion was made that the national interest might be better served if the local NCA alone could make the decision.

State aid

The state aid regimes of the CEECs changed completely with EU accession, although the economic impact of this may turn out to be modest. During the transition period, the CEECs had already established *national* authorities managing the state aid system in accordance with EU rules. With accession, those national authorities still have a monitoring function. Final decisions, however, are taken in Brussels. All new state aid and all plans to alter existing aid (including aid under Article 87(2), formerly Article 92) have to be notified to the Commission. Proposed measures cannot be put into effect until the Commission has approved of them. Moreover, under Article 88(3) (formerly Article 93(3)), the Commission has the power to prevent the distribution of aid or stop an ongoing payment. The only exception is new aid that is classified as being too small to affect trade between member states.

Under the EAs, all CEECs were allowed to apply the regional exception rule in the distribution of state aid provided under Article 87(3). That article lists three additional conditions under which state aid can be granted:

1. For regions where the standard of living is low.
2. To promote the execution of an important project of common European interest.
3. To facilitate the development of certain economic areas.

Similar measures are, for example, applied to East Germany, for which Article 87(2) explicitly provides grounds for granting state aid in order to promote regional development. The measures under Article 87(3) are, however, only applicable for a certain time period laid down in the EAs. The regional exception rule can be considered to be of particular relevance to CEECs: here, industries are often infant, agglomerations often insufficiently large to provide cluster advantages and scale economies (in the sense described in the introductory section of this chapter). Here, additional support for investment, and tax incentives not least for FDI, can help to improve conditions for catch-up development in CEECs. Looking at the Treaty of Accession of 2003 for the new member countries, we find that only Hungary, Poland, and Slovakia (plus Cyprus) appear to have further transitional periods for competition policy and, more specifically, state aid. Those transitional rules lay down particular measures that can be applied as well as the time frame in which these measures can be applied. Poland, for example, will, under the special economic zones provision, be able to continue disbursing aid authorized before 2000 and not exceeding 75% of the eligible investment costs for firms not classified as SMEs, but only aid up to 30% of the eligible investment costs to the motor vehicle sector. Specific corporate tax exemptions were allowed for SMEs until 2010. For the other CEECs listed under the transitional measures in competition policy, equally specific measures apply.[47]

As mentioned above, the CEECs had already been adapting to the post-accession state aid system prior to accession by establishing the necessary institutional framework. Within that framework, the establishment of state aid monitoring authorities was thus a central task. Table 7.2 below shows which authorities in the CEECs are in control of state aid, and which are responsible for monitoring it.

In the following, we take a closer look at the state aid system in practice, and we discuss whether and where problems in the state aid regimes of the CEECs are likely to arise in light of EU accession. In particular, we consider the following issues:

- The new state aid regimes in practice.
- The amount of aid granted and the instruments used.
- State aid to the manufacturing sector versus horizontal objectives.
- State aid used by firms as a strategic instrument.
- State aid and productivity.

[47]See Accession Treaty, http://www.europarl.eu.int/enlargement_new/treaty/doc_en/aa00039en03.doc

Table 7.2. Institutional arrangements for state aid in CEECs.

Country	Control of state aid	Monitoring of state aid
Bulgaria	Commission for the Protection of Competition	Ministry of Finance
Czech Republic	Office for the Protection of Economic Competition	
Estonia	Ministry of Finance	
Hungary	State Aid Monitoring Office	
Latvia	State Aid Surveillance Commission	
Lithuania	Competition Council	
Poland	Office of Competition and Consumer Protection	
Romania	Competition Council	Competition Office
Slovakia	State Aid Office	
Slovenia	Ministry of Finance	

Source: Anti-trust and State Aid Authorities and Legislation in the Candidate Countries, http://www.europa.eu.int/comm/competition/enlargement/candidate_countries/.

The new state aid regimes in practice

As mentioned above, the main impact of EU accession on the state aid systems in the CEECs is that the CEECs have acquired a monitoring function in relation to state aid. Moreover, although general provisions as to the functioning of the state aid system after accession are outlined for the CEECs (see above), further provisions such as potential cooperation between the state aid monitoring authorities (analogous to the cooperation within the ECN) are not specified. Given the short time that the new system has been in operation, it is not possible at the present time to say much more about the state aid regimes in practice.

The amount of aid granted and the instruments used

One sign of potential problems facing the CEECs after accession could be the overall amount of state aid granted by the CEECs compared to the overall amount granted by the EU. If there existed a striking discrepancy between those two amounts, and in particular, if the amount of aid granted by the CEECs was considerably higher than that of the old EU, this might indicate that the CEECs would face pressure to reduce the amount of granted aid after accession. A comparison between the amount of state aid granted by the old EU and the CEECs in 2000 reveals that the old EU

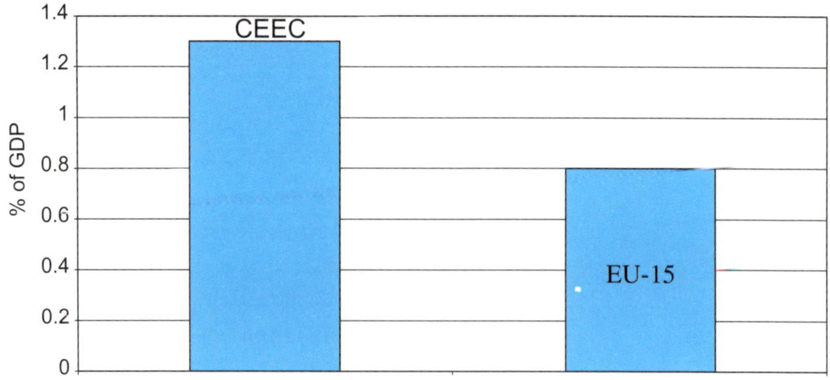

Fig. 7.2. State aid in the EU-15 and CEECs as percentage of GDP, 2000.
Note: Total state aid less agriculture, fisheries, and EU funding.
Source: State Aid Scoreboard, autumn 2002 update, special edition on the candidate countries (http://europa.eu.int/comm/competition/state_aid/scoreboard/).

granted an average of 0.8% of their GDP whereas the CEECs granted an average of 1.3% of their GDP (see Fig. 7.2); measured in Purchasing Power Standards (PPS), the old EU on average granted 185 PPS per person and the CEECs 105 PPS per person.

There exist, certainly, considerable variations across the CEECs, ranging from 0.4% of GDP in Slovakia and 0.5% of in Estonia to 1.7% of GDP in Hungary and 1.9% in Romania. Nevertheless, considering the limited financial means of the CEECs compared to EU-15 countries, it is unlikely that the amount of state aid granted will now, after accession, prove problematic in general. Individual CEEs might have to reconsider some of their state aid disbursements (see Fig. 7.3). But while countries at the higher end of the scale, such as Romania, Hungary, and the Czech Republic, might have to aim at decreasing the amount of state aid granted, the other countries do not lie to any considerable extent above the old EU average or the separate amounts granted by each of the old EU member states.

It is evident that these aggregate indicators are not well suited to making predictions about potential problems for the state aid regimes in the CEECs after accession. An analysis at the sector level would be much better suited to that task, as it would reveal whether certain sectors seem to be unreasonably 'favored' by state aid, and how the CEECs perform with

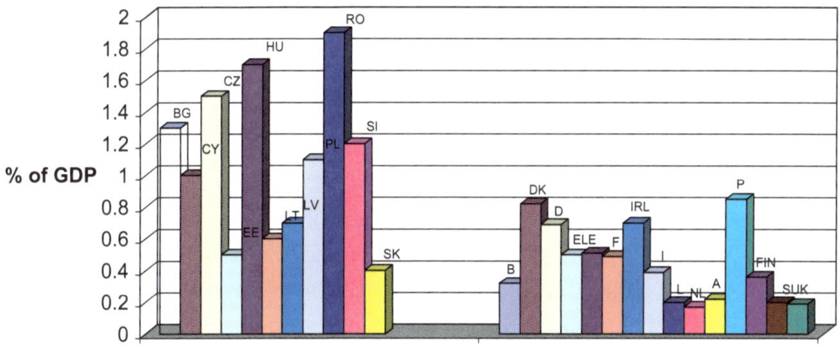

Fig. 7.3. State aid as percentage of GDP for EU-15 and CEECs, 2000.
Note: Total state aid less agriculture, fisheries, and EU funding.
Source: State Aid Scoreboard, autumn 2002 update, special edition on the candidate countries http://europa.eu.int/comm/competition/state_aid/scoreboard/

regard to the EU objective of tackling horizontal objectives. We return to this in the following section.

The *instruments for the distribution of state aid* can be divided into 4 categories:

- direct grants and tax reductions
- capital and investment subsidies
- 'soft credits'
- credit guarantees.

In 2000, the CEECs generally made more use of tax exemptions (51% of all state aid was granted through use of this instrument compared to 29% in the old EU) than the EU. The intensive use of this instrument may partly be explained by government budget restrictions (note that, again, the use of instruments varied across the CEECs); however, there does not appear to exist a significant discrepancy in the pattern of usage of state aid instruments between the CEECs and the old EU such as could become problematic after accession.

State aid to the manufacturing sector versus horizontal objectives

The main objective of the distribution of state aid is to increase competitiveness. This is highly relevant for the CEECs, as they lag behind most of the old member states in terms of competitiveness, as defined in technology and productivity terms. At the same time, as the CEECs are gradually adapting to the EU state aid system, they also have to adopt the state objectives imposed by the EU. The EU has highlighted the need to target horizontal objectives across its member states (and subsequently across the CEECs), and has developed the strategy of 'less and better aid' to '... reduce the general level of state aids, shifting the emphasis from supporting individual companies or sectors towards tackling horizontal objectives of Community interest, such as employment, regional development, environment and training or research.'[48] At this point, it is important to stress that the targeting of horizontal objectives does not preclude aid being granted to the manufacturing sector per se, as this might actually facilitate the fulfillment of horizontal objectives (e.g., aid to enhance R&D/training facilities or reducing unemployment).

A look at the general structure of state aid granted by the CEECs should help us to analyze how the CEECs perform with regard to pursuing horizontal objectives. Moreover, it could reveal potential problems in terms of the amount of state aid granted in total in relation to the old EU, and the amount of aid granted to the manufacturing sector in relation to the old EU. Figures 7.4 and 7.5 show the amounts of aid granted to the manufacturing sector and to horizontal objectives.

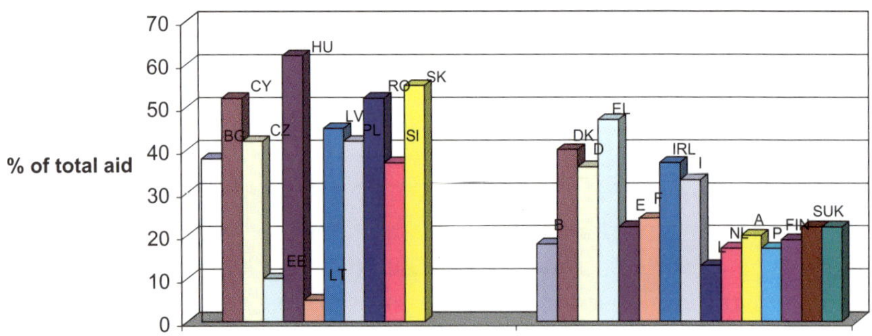

Fig. 7.4. State aid to the manufacturing sector as percentage of total aid for EU-15 and CEECs, 2000.
Source: State Aid Scoreboard, autumn 2002 update, special edition on the candidate countries http://europa.eu.int/comm/competition/state_aid/scoreboard/

[48]Lisbon European Council Conclusions, March 2000.

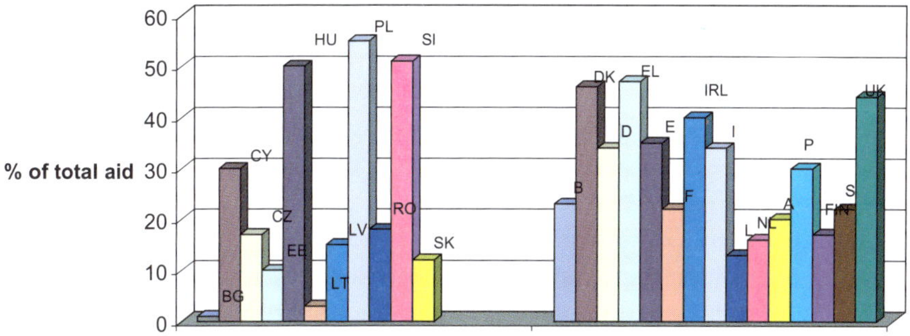

Fig. 7.5. State aid for horizontal objectives as percentage of total aid for EU-15 and CEECs, 2000.
Source: State Aid Scoreboard, autumn 2002 update, special edition on the candidate countries http://europa.eu.int/comm/competition/state_aid/scoreboard/

The average percentage share of state aid to manufacturing in total state aid in 2000 was 46% for the CEECs and 35% for the EU. Again, it is important to consider the variations across the CEECs. Moreover, and as mentioned above, aid to the manufacturing sector per se is not negative as such; aid might well facilitate the creation of a level playing field (which is another state aid objective of the EU).

Alternatively, one has to consider that, even in 2000, at least some of the CEECs were still undertaking some restructuring. The aid might have gone into the sectors concerned. Unfortunately, no industry-specific data is available to make a more detailed analysis. Furthermore, the data only shows the aid distribution for a single year. A time series approach would clearly be desirable as a basis for more profound statements, but cannot be done within the scope of the present enquiry.

The data does, however, give some indications. Hungary, Romania, Slovakia and the Czech Republic granted the highest percentages of aid to the manufacturing sector. A detailed analysis of the receiving industries would reveal whether some sector seem to be especially 'favored' by aid. This would certainly have to be changed, if it were the case. Quite apart from that, however, those countries might have to reconsider their state aid distribution with regard to the manufacturing sector, as they grant considerably more than any old EU member state.

The picture changes slightly when we take horizontal objectives into account, too. Here, Hungary scores very high, with 50% of its total aid being granted for the fulfillment of horizontal objectives, which is, indeed, above the level of any EU-15 country. Thus, Hungary's state aid system seems to be well in line with EU requirements. The Czech Republic, Romania, and Slovakia (and especially Bulgaria, Latvia, and Estonia), on the other hand, score much lower in terms of horizontal objectives, and might therefore have to reconsider their state aid systems for that reason. Bulgaria and Latvia in particular will have to increase their share of state aid going to horizontal objectives. It should, however, be stressed that, on average, the CEECs spent in 2000 a higher percentage of their total aid on horizontal objectives (39%) than the old EU (24%). Poland, Hungary, and Slovenia stand out here, with considerably higher percentages spent on horizontal objectives than any of the old EU member states. Thus, although some CEECs might have to aim for higher rates of aid directed to horizontal objectives, on average, the CEECs seem to perform very well with regard to horizontal objectives, and indeed better than the EU.

The general picture emerging from this discussion seems to be that, in general terms, the CEECs have adapted well to the state aid system required by the EU, and should not face any major challenges in light of EU accession. Some CEECs however, seem still to be underperforming in some areas, and will have to initiate corresponding changes.

State aid rules used as a strategic instrument

Another issue, which is also highly relevant for the CEECs, is that of firms using the state aid system as a strategic tool for pursuing their interests. This might take the form of challenges to aid granted to competitors, or of claims for aid to the firms themselves. With regard to the situation in the CEECs, foreign investors might also 'bind' their investment decisions to the granting of certain forms of state aid (e.g., tax exemptions). This would hit the CEECs particularly hard, as they still place a high priority on attracting foreign investment. Such cases are, however, very hard to prove, and all we can do here is to make suggestions as to the possible use of the state aid system by private firms. The Commission itself has taken up that subject in its 'Report on the Application of EC State Aid Law by the Member State Courts' (EU/DG Competition, 1999), and notes there that surprisingly few companies seem to make use of the opportunity to challenge the granting of aid legally. They suggest that a lack of knowledge about the system might be the reason. Unfortunately, no such analysis for the CEECs is available. It might be worth considering this topic for further research and analysis.

State aid and productivity

The EU has established the principle of the level playing field. This objective implies that state aid should not be used to increase a region's productivity, but that aid might be granted for redistributive or social purposes, under which the region's economic performance would probably not be enhanced. On the other hand, it can be assumed that the CEECs will want to use the regional exception provisions of Article 87(3) within their state aid system. Under this rubric, the CEECs could actively promote an industry's or region's productivity and competitiveness without directly contravening the principle of the level playing field.

Other Union Policies with Impact on Industrial Competitiveness

Industrial policy instruments are not the only ones orchestrated in support of the aim of competitiveness: under the provisions of the EU Treaty, all other policies and activities the EU pursues form part of today's EU industrial policy approach. Those include mainly trade policy, R&D policy, regional policy with EU Structural and Cohesion Fund policies, and vocational training policy (see EC COM, 2002, 714, pp. 26–28).

FDI, trade and trade policy

The relationship between FDI, trade, and trade policy is one that is also vitally important for the CEECs in light of EU accession. As mentioned earlier, the CEECs are trying to attract FDI, at least partly, in order to increase productivity and national competitiveness. Moreover, FDI should contribute to a country's economic growth prospects and should possibly also trigger spillover effects to domestic industries. (See Chapter 4 on this point.) It is therefore interesting to analyze the impact that trade policy measures may have on FDI. The CEECs had to adopt EU trade policies before acceding, so that these are now the current trade policies of the CEECs. Do these current trade policies of the CEECs, with their potential effects on FDI, support the EU's emphasis on horizontal trade policy?

In an initial investigation of the relationship between trade and FDI, we looked at a few simple relationships from the Polish case (Figs. 7.6 and 7.7).

The one feature that stands out is that the trade pattern of 'foreign' firms by sector seems to match that of the rest of firms. Where foreign firms have a high share of total exports, there would, of course, inevitably be a high correlation between total exports of a sector and exports by foreign firms, so we plotted the relationship between exports by foreign firms and exports by 'domestic firms' across sectors. We found a positive correlation. The same is also true for imports. These correlations could be spurious if all that is happening is that we are measuring the size of large and small sectors. However, we do also observe a strong positive correlation between the trade balances of foreign firms and those of other firms.

It is not easy to draw policy implications from such a simple analysis, but it does seem to offer some reassurance about the nature of the growth and FDI process. It implies (weakly) that foreign investors are in fact investing in firms where Poland has a comparative advantage, and while we would be hard pressed to use this simple result to argue that foreign net exports have a positive spillover effect on other firms, we can at least suggest that there is in the Polish case no sign of a crowding-out

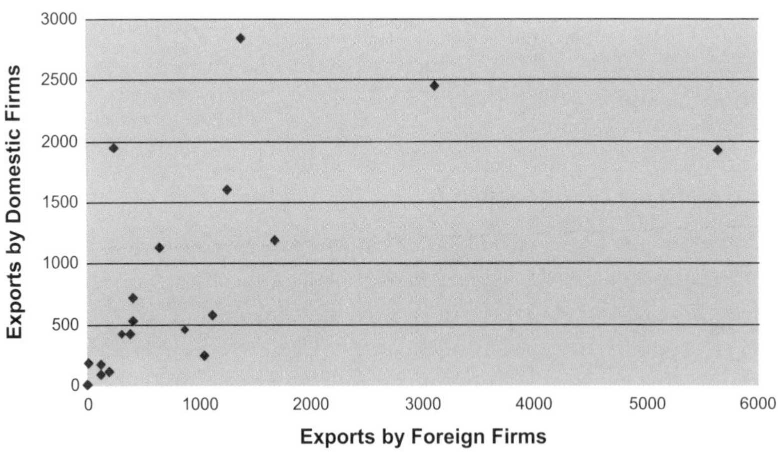

Fig. 7.6. Exports by foreign firms against exports by domestic firms: Poland, 2001 ($ m).
Source: Foreign Investment in Poland, Annual Report by the Foreign Trade Research Institute, 2002; *Trade Policy Review for Poland 1999*, WTO.

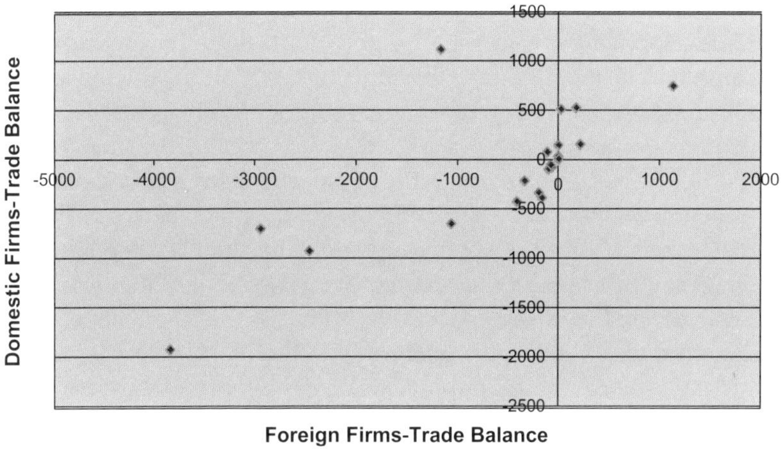

Fig. 7.7. Trade balances of domestic firms against trade balances of foreign firms; Poland, 2001 ($ m).
Source: Foreign Investment in Poland, Annual Report by the Foreign Trade Research Institute, 2002; *Trade Policy Review for Poland 1999*, WTO.

effect. On the face of it, the similarity of foreign and other firms supports rather than undermines the case for accepting the EU philosophy of horizontal rather than discriminatory industrial policy, at least in the Polish case.

Institutional changes

From April 2004, the CEECs cease to have a voice at the WTO; they must now let the EU speak and negotiate for them. This means that, as they gain a voice and vote in the EU, they lose their voice and vote at the WTO.

The new member states must now apply EU common external tariffs (CET), and also EU anti-dumping (AD) measures, rather than their own. In the past, CEECs have used AD very little. (Their main targets were the former Soviet Union (FSU), China and each other.) Now, they will be obliged to adopt all the EU measures. (There will also be the possibility of transitional anti-dumping measures after accession). The effect on the CEECs will be many more measures on more countries. Inside the EU, the accession countries will not be able to invoke AD unilaterally; but for many products they will find ready allies. This is, however, unlikely to be a plus for the economies concerned in terms of productivity enhancement and economic development in general. The freedom to introduce anti-dumping measures has in most cases had similar effects on productivity as the freedom to subsidize declining sectors. A burden is imposed on both consumer and user industries.

The new member states have, of course, now been relieved of AD and safeguard duties imposed by the EU on *them*. In fact, between 1998 and end 2002, out of 202 new AD investigations by the EU, 31 were against candidate countries (Bulgaria, Croatia, Czech Republic, Estonia, Hungary, Lithuania, Poland (the leader with six), Romania, Slovakia, Slovenia). It is worth noting that Sweden, having been a victim of AD before it joined the EU, became a fierce internal opponent of AD after it joined. It is not yet clear whether this will also be true of the new member states. In the next but one section, we investigate the trade effects of accession to the EU of the CEECs with regard to AD policies, and in particular the removal of EU anti-dumping measures towards the CEECs. But first, we must pause to review the state of AD legislation in the EU.

Anti-dumping law in the EU

The current legal regime under which an AD duty can be imposed by the EU follows the agreement on the code of practice of anti-dumping set out during the Uruguay Round. The antidumping agreement is formally known as the *Agreement on Implementation of Article VI of the General Agreement on Tariffs and Trade 1994*. It has dominance over all other agreements in the international trade arena on AD.

Article VI allows members of the WTO/GATT to apply AD measures on other contracting parties. This can be done when sufficient evidence has been brought forward demonstrating the presence of *dumping* and the presence of injury to the domestic industries. Dumping, as defined under the agreement, is considered as introducing a good into an export market at a lower price than its normal comparable value for like[49] products in the exporting country in the ordinary course of trade.

[49]A like good as defined by WTO/GATT rules is 'a product which is identical, i.e., alike in all respects to the product under consideration, or in the absence of such a product, another product which, although not alike in all respects, has characteristics closely resembling those of the product under consideration'.

An AD investigation has the following possible outcomes.

- *Provisional measures*: These can take the form of a price undertaking or the imposition of a duty once preliminary examination has provided sufficient evidence of the existence of some form of injury caused. However, they are only valid for four months. Under special circumstances, they can be extended for a further two-month period.[50]
- *Definite measures*: These can be used once the investigation has finished, and evidence shows that dumping has occurred and that injury has been caused to the domestic industry. Duties are imposed by the Council following recommendations of the Commission after consultation with the member states.[51] A definite measure can be a price undertaking or a duty, depending on what is judged to be more suitable to undo the harm that dumping has caused.
- *Termination*: An AD investigation is terminated when there is insufficient evidence to prove the act of dumping, or when dumping does not pose a threat to the domestic industry.

A price undertaking is described under the GATT as a binding commitment by the foreign firm to raise export prices so that either the dumping or the injury suffered by the domestic industry is eliminated' (WTO). The size of the duty tends generally to be equal to that of the dumping margin. However, for the EU, this is not the case. Here, the *lesser duty rule* takes precedence. That rule posits that the size of the penalty must be set at just enough to remove the injury caused to the domestic firm and not at the full dumping margin.

In 1968, the first community-wide legislation on anti-dumping was enacted. Since then, as with the AD law of most countries (notably the US), it has been modified several times. The current legislation governing AD practices in the EU is, certainly, based on the agreements reached in the international trade arena set up by the WTO, as discussed above.[52] The AD laws governing practice in the EU do, however, feature a couple of amendments to the laws agreed upon during the Uruguay Round. These are the *Community interest test* and the *lesser duty rule*. The latter we have

[50] *Thirteenth Annual Report from the Commission to the EU Parliament on the Community's AD and Anti-Subsidy Activities*, 1995, p. 15.
[51] *Ibidem*.
[52] *Seventeenth Annual Report from the Commission to the EU Parliament on the Community's Anti-Dumping and Anti-Subsidy Activities*, Brussels 08/09/99 COM (1999) 411 final.

already discussed. The former aims to satisfy all interested parties within the community. It thus incorporates into the implementation of *Article VI* of the GATT the principle that measures against dumped imports will only be undertaken when the appropriate interests of domestic consumers and producers have been considered.

Upon accession, new member states have to adapt their trade policy to that of the EU, thus incorporating the community interest test and the lesser duty clause into their current AD policy.

The trade diversion effects of EU anti-dumping policy towards new member states

The accession agreements concluded by the EU and the CEECs conceded duty-free access to 95%[53] of CEEC imports towards the EU-15 (the remaining 5% including mainly agricultural products). Thus, the trade balance between the NMS and the EU-15 is not likely to change enormously following accession. The main change that will affect trade between the two parties is the removal of all contingent protection from the side of the EU. Anti-dumping and anti-subsidy activities will cease. We here analyze the possible effects of the removal of anti-dumping actions from the EU targeted at the new member states.

The European Union was a prolific user of anti-dumping measures; during the 1990s, the EU initiated 349 proceedings, of which 38 were against future accession countries. Of those 38, 17 (44.7%) of these investigations ended in the imposition of definitive duties, 8 (21.05%) were resolved by price undertakings and 13 (34.2%) investigations were terminated with no imposed penalties.

The apparent trend in AD filings from the EU to the then accession countries is significantly biased towards Chapter 73 of the Combined Nomenclature (CN), namely *articles of iron or steel*, with 36.8% of all investigations. Table 7.3 demonstrates the distribution of AD initiations by sector.

The share of targeted chapter exports in total exports by prospective member states to the EU shows the possible range of trade distortion that AD could have upon trade between the two parties during the period under

[53]According to the *Revue de l'Elargissement*, No. 59, English edition, 9 February 2004.

Table 7.3. Incidence of AD initiations vis-à-vis prospective member states, by sector, 1991–2000.

Chapter	Product Specification	Number of Times Targeted	Share of total Exports of Prospective Member States to the EU
73	Articles of iron and steel	14	3.9464%
31	Fertilizers	7	0.8068%
44	Wood and articles of wood; wood charcoal	5	4.6556%
72	Iron and steel	5	3.6990%
56	Wadding, felt and nonwovens: special yarns; twine, cordage, rope and cables	3	0.1290%
25	Salt; sulfur; earths and stone; plastering material, lime and cement	3	0.9464%
79	Zinc and articles thereof	1	0.1590%
Total		38	14.3422%

Note: 'Prospective member states' refers to Cyprus, the Czech Republic, Estonia, Hungary, Latvia, Lithuania, Malta, Poland, Slovakia and Slovenia.
Source: Authors' calculations, based on data from the EU annual report on antidumping and antisubsidy activities.

investigation. The results obtained show that the seven specified chapters represent 14.34% of exports from prospective member states to the EU for the given period. In the following sub-sections, we try to analyze the possible distortions to that 14.34% of trade that *may* be affected by AD. Note that this figure by no means sets a maximum on the effects of AD on the prospective member states. But it indicates what proportions of trade we are talking about in the following sub-section.

Revealed comparative advantage in targeted chapters

In order to deepen our understanding of the nature of AD targeting vis-à-vis the prospective member states, we look at the Revealed Comparative Advantage[54] (RCA) of the above mentioned chapters, so as to ascertain the level of competitiveness of the targeted industries.

[54]The RCA is calculated using the Balassa (1965) index. This measures the degree of specialization of countries in given sectors by comparison to the rest of the economy. We compare the trade of the prospective member states with the EU as a benchmark, and thus calculate the RCA relative to the EU.

The revelations of analysis using the method explained in Box 7.1 for the chapters under investigation are presented in Table 7.4.

As can clearly be seen, all the targeted chapters show a very significant positive RCA. This shows that AD targeting was mainly towards those sectors which show a revealed comparative advantage. The removal of AD measures will allow the targeted sectors to reap the benefits of their comparative advantage. Hence, accession to the EU can be expected to yield an additional benefit to CEECs in the form of discontinuation of AD measures levied against them.

The negative impact of AD can be measured by analyzing the diversion of trade from countries that are named by the petition to those that are not; this is known as the *trade diversion* effect, and it is to this that we turn in the next sub-section.

Trade diversion

The trade diversion effect as analyzed by the literature[55] discriminates between named and non-named countries. It reports the apparent trend of non-named countries *taking over* trade from named countries, thus reducing the effectiveness of AD as a tool for keeping imports out. Our concern lies on the direction of this trade diversion within CEE, the EU and the rest of the world.

By separating the non-named category into three sections, we can investigate whether trade is diverted to non-named countries within the EU, in CEE or towards other world producers. We shall also discriminate as to the outcomes of the investigations. The results are reported below. Using the method described in Box 7.2 allows us to create a comparable framework within which to analyze the effects of AD on prospective member states. The results are as follows.

When an AD investigation ended in the *imposition of definite duties*, the results reveal the following reaction in trading patterns.

As can be seen from Fig. 7.8, there is a negative effect of AD duties on named CEECs in the form of a reduction in trade with the EU for the goods under investigation by over 20% in the first year. After that, we see a recovery of trading patterns. We use the evolution of trade through time as a counterfactual showing how trade should have evolved during the period under investigation, and thus deduce that the negative effect of AD

[55]See Prusa (1996), Konings *et al.* (2001), Brenton (2001) and Lasagni (2000).

Box 7.1: Calculation of Revealed Comparative Advantages (RCA)

RCA commonly bears the name of its inventor, viz., Balassa index. It is calculated on the basis of the following equation:

$$RCA = \left(\frac{X_{i,j}}{\sum_i X_{i,j}}\right) \div \left(\frac{\sum_j X_{i,j}}{\sum_i \sum_j X_{i,j}}\right) \tag{1}$$

with $X_{i,j}$ = exports (imports to the EU) of sector i from country j. The numerator represents targeted chapter exports to the EU divided by overall chapter (all chapters) exports of prospective member states to the EU. The denominator is chapter imports of the EU from all countries divided by overall chapter (all chapters) imports of the EU. When RCA $>$ 1, the sector under investigation is said to have a revealed comparative advantage. Conversely, when RCA $<$ 1, the sector does not benefit from a revealed comparative advantage.

Box 7.2: Calculation of effects of anti-dumping actions on trade between prospective member states and the EU

In order to calculate the trade effects of AD, the framework introduced by Prusa (1996) and expanded by Lasagni (2000) for the EU is used.[56] This is based on creating a dataset containing trade values of imports towards the EU of both named and non-named countries. However, cross-case comparison is not always appropriate when large differences in trading volumes exist, which is the case for most of the data under consideration. This called for the use of modified techniques so as to allow comparison. Time was normalized using t_0 as the year of initiation and subsequent years with the corresponding suffix depending on how many years had passed since initiation, so that t_1, t_2 t_3 and t_4 represent respectively trade values 1, 2, 3 and 4 years after the initiation of the investigation. These points in time lie between 1992 and 2001. Furthermore, to allow for cross-case comparison, percentage changes of trading volumes were computed using the year of initiation of the AD investigation (t_0) as the benchmark, following this equation:

$$\Delta\ \text{imports}^j_{i,t} = \frac{(\text{imports}^j_{i,t} - \text{imports}^j_{i,t0})}{\text{imports}^j_{i,t0}} \tag{2}$$

with $i = (1, \ldots, 38)$, $t = (t_0, \ldots, t_4)$, and j = (named, non-named EU, world and CEE). Thus, the proportionate change in imports of good i at time t is equal to the imports of the product at time t minus the import of the products at time t_0 (initiation of AD investigation) divided by the value of imports at time of initiation. The j differentiates between named countries and non-named countries (in the EU, in CEE and in the world).

Table 7.4. Revealed comparative advantage for targeted chapters.

Chapter	Product Specification	Average RCA*
73	Articles of iron and steel	3.4
31	Fertilizers	2.986
44	Wood and articles of wood; wood charcoal	2.785
72	Iron and steel	2.535
56	Wadding, felt and nonwovens; special yarns; twine, cordage, rope and cables	1.263
25	Salt; sulfur; earths and stone; plastering material, lime and cement	2.163
79	Zinc and articles thereof	2.328

Note: *The value reported is the average RCA for the period 1992–2001.
Source: COMEXT.

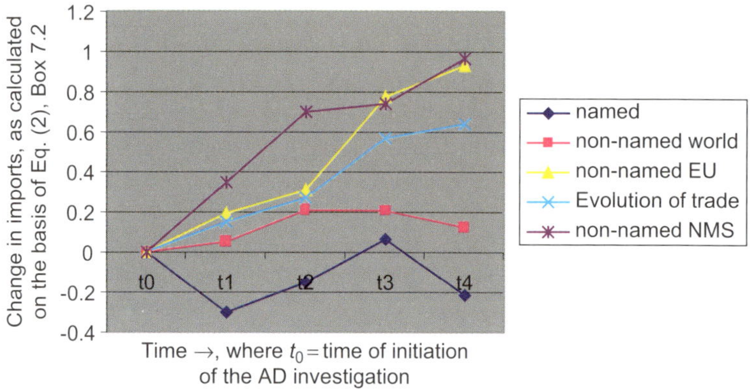

Fig. 7.8. The trade effects of AD duties on named and non-named countries.
Source: Authors' calculations using EUROSTAT.

on named CEECs is actually greater than 20%. We also note that the share of trade of non-named CEECs goes up quite significantly. We can thus deduce that there is a significant diversion of trade to non-named CEECs when AD is imposed on a named CEEC. This allows us to draw inferences on the similarity of composition of industry across CEE. The imposition of duties on named CEECs also seems to benefit EU producers, but only very slightly.

[56]See also Brenton (2001) and Konings *et al.* (2001).

When an AD investigation ended in a *price undertaking*, the deviation of trade from its value before investigation reveals little change in trading patterns over the period studied. The data show a fall in named country exports for the goods under investigation in t_1, followed by a quick rise in the following year tending towards the evolution of trade line. Prusa (1997) suggests that there may have been a negative effect on trade during the period of investigation, largely caused by the uncertainty of the outcome of the investigation. This he terms the *investigation effect*.

When an investigation is *terminated*, there appear to be no negative effects on named country exports for the goods under investigation. However, non-named CEEC exports show a significant increase.

These results must be put into perspective. We must look at the actual trade values in order to assess the magnitude of the effects of AD on trade. Named country trade with the EU represents but a fraction of total trade both within and outside the EU for the goods under investigation. Total trade for the period under investigation between the prospective member states and the EU amounted to an average of €53 billion. The average amount of trade directly affected by AD was but €795 million. This amounts to a mere 1.5% of total trade with the EU. We thus conclude that, although the effects of AD on the prospective member states in the period 1991–2000 were individually quite significant, the amount of trade that directly affected by them represented only a minor proportion of total trade between the two parties.

We have, of course, been investigating only the *direct* effects of AD on named products. There may be other effects of AD which our methodology does not pick up. In particular, the possibility of *trade deflection* must be considered. Trade deflection occurs because countries tend to adjust their trading patterns as a result of AD. Due to the highly specific nature of AD, countries can switch production at low costs from a highly disaggregated good which has suffered the imposition of AD duties to a *like* good that does not face AD duties. The countervailing effect is the so-called *deterrence effect*, which reflects the probability of new AD filings on the import-deflected goods, and thus deters the targeted industry from following this path. No quantitative estimates of the significance for trade of the trade deflection

---

Here and *passim* strictly ECU.

A like good in this instance can be described as a good of a parallel 8- or higher digit category, normally within the same 4-digit category.

and deterrence effects are available. But they can, of course, only represent a fraction of the 14.34% of trade affected by AD in the first place.

We can thus conclude that:

- The impact of AD on NMS produces significant distortions in targeted industries, and whether these are from named or non-named producers.
- The overall direct effect is very small, with just 1.5% of trade being distorted.
- The trade deflection and deterrence effects may affect a greater share of trade and certainly need more investigation. But they probably do not alter the basic picture.
- We have identified that the trade diversion effect is present between named and non-named CEECs. Thus, when a named CEEC suffers the imposition of duties, there is a counteracting benefit to non-named CEE industries, which 'take over' named country exports.
- Our analysis of the trade diversion effect of AD shows that the trade effects of the elimination of this factor upon accession are going to be of small magnitude. However, the analysis of the RCA of the targeted industries reveals that the removal of AD measures will allow those industries to reap the benefits of their comparative advantage and grow without artificial constraint. This will be a significant factor of productivity enhancement, and ultimately of East–West catch-up.

Finally in this section, we should note that a comprehensive analysis of the trade policy effects of enlargement on the CEECs would have to consider also the effects on the CEECs of adopting the EU AD policy. Such an investigation would, however, take us beyond the limits of the present study.

Regulation

The creation of the new network of competition authorities coincides with a new phase in EU regulatory structures, namely an attempt to introduce a degree of subsidiarity into the rule-making system. In a variety of areas such as telecoms, competition and food safety, the EU is introducing a system whereby the Community authorities will act as a supervisor of national authorities rather than the final legislator in every case. The area where there is most pressure here is food safety. This is of particular interest to CEECs, as their food and food-processing industries may be subject to very strict regulations in the rest of the EU. It seems, however, that the new flexibility will not necessarily be to the advantage of the CEECs, in that it will mostly allow a margin of flexibility *upwards*. In the long run, this may be in the interest of CEEC consumers and producers, but in the medium term, it will mean higher costs for producers, and for consumers with less risk-averse tastes. So the impact on productivity will likely be negative in the short-to-medium run, if possibly positive in the long run.

Conclusions

Competition

The new European Competition Network opens up possibilities for using the full flexibility of existing EU policies within CEECs (e.g., priority for SMEs, referred to in the treaty, but not in Articles 81/82 directly.) What is less clear is whether the decentralization of enforcement will actually allow this discretion to be used effectively in practice. Much will depend on national courts, as well as national agencies. The impact on productivity should ultimately be positive across the board, but in the short run could be rather mixed.

Industrial policy

The CEECs are now generally subject to EU rules in this regard, and it seems likely that it is this rule-based system that has the most to contribute to convergence. There is little evidence from CEE or from the EU-15 to suggest that policy tools lost on accession have been major factors of catch-up. Nor, it must be added, have EU funds. In the outstanding Irish case, for instance, it is clear that that catch-up was due primarily to national horizontal policies. Certainly a high level of state aids does not seem to be correlated within the EU-15 with the ability to pick winners, but rather with the political strength of particular lobbies or the depth of social problems in certain sectors. The implication is that state aids control should still be an aim. But we must be wary of private actions in this area which could tilt the playing field towards those with ability to pay lawyers.

The somewhat technological bias of horizontal EU industrial policy means that lock-in of CEE economies into low-wage comparative advantage is hardly an issue in policy terms. The danger, as highlighted in Chapter 6, is rather that that technology-oriented bias might — in the worst case — not correspond to existing or (short-term emerging) abilities/capabilities in CEE economies, and hence 'go over the heads of' the

CEE economies. To that extent, more sector- and existing-comparative-advantage specific policies with all their well documented vulnerability to capture by vested interest, might be better attuned to CEE specificities.

One specific area where accession and a new policy framework could possibly have an impact relates to technical norms. Eastward enlargement occurred at a time when the EU was trying to adopt a slightly more devolved approach to, for example, food safety standards. There is a real risk that CEEC firms and consumers will have to pay extra to reduce risk levels below those deemed acceptable. On the other hand, accession will mean that, for the first time, CEECs get a vote in relation to the relevant regulations, and will be able to defend national measures before the ECJ. But in practice, it seems likely that most tolerated derogations will be upwards rather than downwards.

Trade policy

The CEECs are now inside the EU net. Steel safeguard measures, for example, can no longer be applied against them. Certainly, it is not entirely sure that this is in the long run interest of productivity catch-up. EU rules risk leading to (slightly) more protectionism at EU level, *but*, on the other hand, because measures can only be introduced at EU level, the pay-off to investing in rent-seeking is likely to be limited. The most reasonable assumption is that firms will feel that they cannot relax on productivity improvement merely by hoping for protection.

Does any of this suggest that enlargement will bring about major changes in EU policy towards industry, whether in terms of what can be done nationally or what should be done at a community level? In terms of the constraints on national policies, we would still argue that the great virtue of the EU system is that it provides a rule-based framework for economic actors: predictability for investors may well be worth more than discretionary policy powers when political actors are weak, financially constrained or inexperienced. Holmes and Seabright (2000), following Krugman (1987), argue that the tying of hands may be the greatest benefit of EU rules. At the EU level, the introduction of any new policies towards industry was made subject to unanimity by the Maastricht Treaty. This is probably just as well, since the Community's record in micro economic intervention is not really so good as to suggest that its specific programs as such are the best instruments for promoting catch-up. At this stage, our working hypothesis must be:

- The biggest contribution enlargement itself will make to catch-up will be through the consolidation of policy credibility on the basis of the direct effect of EU law and the binding nature of EU law on its members.

References

Balassa, B., "Trade liberalisation and 'revealed' competitive advantage," Manchester School of Economics and Social Studies, **33**, 99–123 (1965).

Boldrin, M. and F. Canova, "Inequality and convergence in Europe's regions: Reconsidering European regional policies." *Econ. Pol.* **32**, April, 207–253 (2001).

Brenton, P., "Antidumping policies in the EU and trade diversion." *Europ. J. Polit. Economy* **17**, September, 593–608 (2001).

Commission of the European Communities, State Aid Scoreboard, autumn 2002 update, special edition on the candidate countries (2002).

Council Regulation (EC) No 1/2003, *Official J. Europ. Comm.* (2003).

Council Regulation (EC) No 659/1999, *Official J. Europ. Comm.* (1999).

Cserháti, I. and T. Takács, "Innovation at the firm level: A central european comparative study." ECOSTAT, mimeo (2002).

Dyker, D.A., "The dynamic impact on the Central-Eastern European economies of accession to the European Union: Social capability and technology absorption." *Europe-Asia Stud.* **53**, 7, 1001–1021 (2001).

European Commission, Directorate-General for Competition, Competition Law in the European Communities, Vol. IIA, Rules Applicable to State Aid, Situation at 30 June 1998 (1998).

European Commission COM (90) 556.

European Commission staff paper SEC (2000) 771.

European Commission COM (2002) 714.

European Commission COM (2002) 262.

European Competitiveness Index 2004, Robert Huggins Associates, Wales, United Kingdom, mimeo (2004).

European Union, Consolidated Versions of the Treaty on European Union and of the Treaty Establishing the European Community, Brussels (2002).

European Union/DG Competition, Report on the Application of EC State Aid Law by the Member State Courts, 4 June (1999).

Frazer, T., "Competition policy, the regions and the Central and Eastern European countries." Paper presented to the conference *Rules of competition for the Economic Integration of Countries in Transition into the EU*, Technical University, Bergaka demie Freiburg, Germany, 5–7 July (1996).

Holmes, P. and P. Seabright, "Industrial policy after Maastricht: What is possible?" In D.J. Neven and L.-H. Roller (eds.), *The Political Economy of Industrial Policy in Europe and the Member States*, Berlin, Edition Sigma (2000).

Konings, J., H. Vandenbussche and L. Springael, "Import diversion under European antidumping policy." *J. Industry Competition and Trade* **1**, 3, 283–299 (2001).

Lasagni, A., "Does country targeted antidumping policy by the EU create trade diversion." *J. World Trade* **34**, 4, 137–159 (2000).

Mavroidis, P.C. and D.J. Neven, "The modernisation of EU competition policy: making the network operate," Université de Lausanne, *Cahier de Recherches Economiques* 00/17 (2000).

Prusa, T., "The trade effects of US antidumping actions." NBER Working Paper 5440 (1996).

Pischke, J.-S., Discussion of Boldrin, M. and F. Canova, "Inequality and convergence in Europe's regions: Reconsidering European regional policies." *Econ. Pol.* **32**, April, 245–248 (2001).

Stephan, J., "Evolving structural patterns in the enlarging European division of labor: Sectoral and branch specialisation and the Potentials for closing the productivity gap." IWH Sonderheft 5/2003, Halle/Saale: IWH (2003a).

Stephan, J., "Firm-Specific Determinants of productivity gaps: A report of results of field study involving manufacturing firms in West and East Germany, the Czech Republic, Hungary, and Poland." Discussion Paper 183, Halle/Saale: IWH (2003b).

Vissi, F., "Central issues of Hungarian competition policy in the light of association with the European Union." In S. Estrin and P. Holmes (eds.), *Competition and Economic Integration in Europe*, Cheltanham: Edward Elgar (1998).

CHAPTER 8

SUMMING-UP: PRODUCTIVITY CATCH-UP AND INTERNATIONAL COMPETITIVENESS

David A. Dyker

Main Conclusions

- Subsidiaries of MNCs in CEE generally enjoy a high degree of operational autonomy, while strategic functions are centered at head office. So productivity-oriented measures nearly always come in the form of top-down investment and technology transfer strategies based on state-of-the arts global business and technological practice.
- The experience of FDI in Eastern Europe, as documented by our case studies, provides strong evidence that the East–West productivity gap on main production lines is relatively small, and can be closed quite quickly on the basis of these top-down investment and technology transfer strategies. That means that, as long as wages in the host countries remain well below West European levels, there should be ample scope for further, profitable investments. The triangulation process has thrown up nothing to contradict this conclusion.
- The implication is that social capability and technological congruence have not been critical problems on these main production lines.
- It should be stressed that these strong conclusions emerge in the first place from a set of interviews involving exclusively West-Central European investor-firms and largely East-Central European host countries. It would be dangerous to extend them to the whole transition region. Our global triangulation exercise reinforces this caveat.
- Investor companies have invested massive resources in training programs, ranging from full-time secondments to on-the-job training,

sometimes on site in the host country, sometimes back at headquarters. These programs have covered blue-collar as well as white-collar workers. This suggests that one of the reasons why social capability has not been a critical problem is simply that *it has been seriously addressed by the companies involved*. This conclusion is generally confirmed by intra-project triangulation, though other work programs within the *East–West Productivity Gap* project do raise doubts as to whether training is a factor which significantly differentiates one firm from another.

- The positive experience with main-production-line productivity is not matched by performance in relation to ancillary sectors, with subsidiaries stuck within essentially dyadic relationships. Investor-firms have generally struggled to build adequate supply networks in the host countries. Where they have persevered, they have done so in the face of a stubborn productivity deficit. Given that lead-company programs for building social capability have been largely restricted to the in-house dimension, this is, perhaps, hardly surprising. There is also a hint that technological congruence problems may be much more stubborn once we move beyond the sphere of Fordist and post-Fordist production lines. Whether that is primarily an effect of fear of technological incongruity on the part of investing firms, or of more objective technological factors, remains unclear. The global literature suggests that the latter factor may be the most important, with the impact of FDI on growth in developing countries strongly and inversely correlated with the size of the 'objective' technology gap between home and host country. Our global case studies suggest a more specific form of that hypothesis — that there is a threshold in terms of initial human capital endowment under which economies and companies will not be able to absorb the upgrading that FDI offers. They also suggest the possibility of an extreme scenario where FDI fails to generate strong linkages at host-country level, while progressively strengthening linkages within the MNC network itself. In the case of East Asian electronics, indeed, the pattern seems to be that backward linkages are stronger where there is less FDI. Comparison with other work packages within the project confirms our overall conclusion here, but urges caution in relation to its generalizability. Individual country studies reveal wide differences in precise patterns of linkage, possibly related to differences in underlying resource endowments and related differences in corporate strategy.
- Investor companies have been eager to exploit local training and R&D facilities, but have done so on an essentially casual basis. Teaching of

foreign languages and software development are the only two areas where local educational/research expertise is brought in systematically. The implication is that local human capital formation organizations are not playing the role they ought to be playing in the solution of social capability problems in CEE. Detailed investigation of the operation of these organizations suggests that internal weaknesses have been a major cause of this failure. And behind those internal weaknesses have lain serious failures of innovation policy. This is confirmed by intra-project triangulation.

- Consideration of the likely institutional effects of CEEC accession to the EU highlights the importance of the previous point. Past experience suggests that, pure Single Market effects apart, it is horizontal measures, whether in terms of industrial policy, trade policy or whatever, that have been most effective in terms of catch-up, at both Union and national level. The Irish case is cited as an outstanding example of this pattern. The East Asian electronics case demonstrates the same point. It is clear that horizontal measures cannot be effective, if there is no adequate network of horizontal institutions in the given catch-up countries. This 'horizontal hiatus' could be a key factor hindering the process of productivity catch-up. It is equally clear that untargeted horizontal policies are likely to be ineffective.
- Our material generally confirms the hypothesis that vertical industrial policies (trying to 'grow' national champions etc.) do not work. But while global triangulation generally reinforces this conclusion, the Indian and Chinese experience in the car and IT sectors interposes an important footnote here. Vertical industrial policies may not produce national champions, but they can have a significant impact in terms of strengthening local learning capacities, and possibly bringing the given economy, company or sector above the critical human-capital threshold.
- While investor companies have shown great willingness to help local suppliers to raise their game, they have been short of ideas as to how to actually do it. In practice, help often reduces to simply helping the local supplier to be taken over by another foreign company. This pattern is strongly confirmed by the global literature.
- With strong FDI impacts on productivity trends in FIEs and weak impacts elsewhere, the overall effect of FDI on productivity convergence is likely to be mixed. In FDI target sectors, the tendency to convergence, East–West and inter-country, will be strong. Elsewhere, convergence to West European levels will be slow and difficult, and significant differences

between individual East European countries will survive into the long term. This mirrors the global experience.

- The pattern of supply hierarchy in CEE whereby local companies are largely relegated to the status of second- and third-tier suppliers, with first-tier suppliers usually wholly or partly foreign-owned, is not universally reflected in global experience. Indeed, in China, the problem is exactly the opposite — domestically owned first-tier suppliers (in the case reviewed to the auto industry) are strong, but second- and third-tier suppliers are weak. This in no way invalidates our conclusion on CEE, which is strongly supported by other research on CEE. But it does suggest that patterns of strength and weakness in supply hierarchies may be as much a function of specificities in development paths as of any universal developmental tendency. It is noteworthy that the pattern in Portugal has been more like the East European than the Chinese experience.
- The global experience strongly confirms the case-study results on the importance of two-way technology transfer, or rather on the reverse technology transfer element within that. It does, however, raise serious questions as to whether reverse technology transfer is a positive factor of host country development. Too often, this seems to reflect an imbalance between intra-MNC linkages (strong) and intra-host-country linkages (weak).

These conclusions are, in a sense, not surprising. It is not surprising that Czech and Hungarian production-line workers can quite easily be brought up to the standards of German workers, and it is not surprising that companies with shareholders to keep happy are not prepared to take on the job of retraining whole nations. There are, nevertheless, critical problems and gaps in the FDI-driven process of catch-up in Eastern Europe. These problems are as much a function of weaknesses in local infrastructure (especially R&D) as of any shortcomings in the management of major foreign investments. The fact remains that, in the outcome, the countries of Eastern Europe may experience uneven, dualistic development, rather than the smooth convergence to West European levels of development which catch-up theory (in principle) predicts. It is now common within individual East European countries for levels of productivity and real wages in related sectors to vary by a factor of 2:1 and above, depending on whether the companies in question are foreign- or domestically-owned. This is clearly sub-optimal for the host countries themselves. To the extent that it generates social tensions and ultimately impacts on political stability, it could also significantly change the outlook for further foreign direct investment in this critically important area of the 'new' Europe in ways wholly beyond the control of the firms concerned.

Finally, in this section, let us return to the main 'unexpected' result of our interviews. The strategies of the companies we interviewed are predominantly global strategies. This does not prove that global strategies are generally dominant among firms investing in CEE, but it does suggest that the global outlook is significantly represented among them. Intra-project triangulation strongly confirms that conclusion. The global literature suggests that the global-strategic orientation is, indeed, the dominant one among MNCs the world over.

How is this likely to affect the impact of EU accession on the CEECs? To the extent that multinational investments in the region are cost-driven, and to the extent that enlargement tends to increase real wages in CEE, it will tend to mean a higher degree of onward mobility of investment, which means less FDI in the region. To the extent that the investments are network-building (if, in principle, on a global scale), the removal of frontier barriers and the (putative) improvement of infrastructure, particularly transport, in the new member-states may swing the balance of effectiveness towards pan-European strategies. To the extent that eastwards enlargement unleashes rapid growth in GDP and a boom in consumption in CEE, and to the extent that the new member states retain significant peculiarities of taste, specifically CEE strategies may emerge — for the first time — in the case of some consumer-oriented companies. In a word, the net impact on levels of FDI could go either way. In that context, we should be that much more cautious about our assessments of the likely overall impact of FDI on productivity in the accession countries.

Closing the Productivity Gap and Competitiveness

Competitiveness is a slippery concept, and no less an economist than Paul Krugman has suggested that we should not use it (Krugman, 1996). But the EU uses it, and indeed the Lisbon Agenda, which lays out the framework for the whole EU approach to catch-up within an enlarged Union, focuses precisely on the goal of making the EU 'the most dynamic and competitive knowledge economy'. Here, competitiveness is evoked as a dimension of a process of human capital accumulation which is itself a key condition of real convergence. We can identify this understanding of the word 'competitiveness' as 'real economy' or 'dynamic' competitiveness. We can also identify 'static' or 'Heckscher–Ohlin' competitiveness. At the level of the business firm, this simply means the capacity to stay in business by making profits. At the level of the national economy, it means parametric congruence, i.e., that prices of factors of production, and the exchange rates which translate those prices into other currencies, should reflect underlying factor availability.

The most striking thing about the region under investigation is that it presents virtually diametrically opposite pictures of competitiveness, depending on whether we are looking at dynamic or static competitiveness. In terms of real economy competitiveness, the CEECs remain weak. Their human capital endowment flatters to deceive, their level of technological capability is at best uneven, and they are heavily dependent on exogenous sources of technological and managerial upgrading. In terms of Heckscher–Ohlin competitiveness, they are strong. Wages remain very low by West European standards, and, as the material presented forcefully illustrates, productivity levels can, under West European, US or Japanese tutelage, quickly converge to West European levels. So in globalized, middle-tech, relatively labor-intensive industries like the automotive industry and the mass-electronics industry, the CEECs have a Heckscher–Ohlin competitive advantage which they are likely to retain into the medium-to-long term, as long as exchange rate developments are not allowed to distort effective factor prices in those countries.[59] That, in turn, means that those sectors are likely to 'bed down' in CEE, with obvious implications for employment in the same sectors in the EU-15.

What about the 'sensitive' sectors pin-pointed in Chapter 7, which have suffered from systematic backdoor protectionism through anti-dumping actions on the part of the EU in the past, and will do so no more? The most striking thing about those sectors is that, wood products and textiles apart, they are not especially labor-intensive. Rather they are raw-material-intensive (non-ferrous metals, earths and stone) or capital-intensive (iron

---

[59]Once the CEECs have joined the Single Currency, the possibility will arise of real exchange rate appreciation, with local inflation rates continuing to be higher than the EU average under the influence of the Balassa–Samuelson effect, whereby prices of non-tradables rise disproportionately in catch-up countries. That could significantly damage CEE static competitiveness in labor-intensive industries. In practice, CEEC accession to the Single Currency is likely to be a long-term matter. On the most optimistic scenario, most of the real economy catching up will have been accomplished by that time.

and steel, base chemicals, cement — the classic communist heavy industries). Thus, much of the revealed comparative advantage of the CEE economies comes from natural endowment and the capital endowment inherited from the communist period, rather than from cheap labor. Integration into the Single Market will hardly change patterns in relation to raw-material-intensive industries. In relation to capital-intensive sectors, the pattern which has already emerged, whereby Western companies invest in traditional, capital-intensive sectors in CEE in order to upgrade inherited capacities, is likely to be reinforced, as the remaining barriers to FDI disappear. So these revealed comparative advantages can be expected to strengthen as the process of integration of the CEE economies into those of the EU-15 proceeds. That, in turn, will tend to accelerate the process of productivity catch-up in those sectors, subject to the caveat introduced in Chapter 7 in relation to EU-wide protectionism.

As we have seen, the process of productivity enhancement in CEE has been very uneven, and is likely to remain so. And this fundamental fact heightens the divergence between the two competitiveness indicators, almost to the point of paradox. The more uneven the process of productivity enhancement in CEE, the bigger the gap between the foreign-owned and domestically-owned sectors, the longer the 'tail' in these economies, whether in terms of companies or R&D institutes, the weaker will be the trajectory of convergence of dynamic competitiveness. The more uneven the process of productivity enhancement in CEE, the more will low productivity in the weaker sectors tend to hold down wages. And as long as there are not too many imperfections in local labor markets, that means that wages will stay low in the high-productivity, foreign-owned sectors as well. On this basis, Heckscher–Ohlin competitiveness can be maintained indefinitely. To repeat and reinforce the analysis of Chapter 4, therefore, the danger is that the CEECs will 'clamp on' (Verspagen, 1999) rather than catching up — reaching a certain level of development significantly higher than their current level, but still significantly lower than that of the EU-15, and then becoming stuck at that point. That, in turn, will tend to institutionalize a division of labor between Eastern and Western Europe which will threaten the jobs of unskilled workers in the West and the living standards of everyone in the East. This is in no sense an inevitable outcome, but it will take good policies and good companies to ensure that it is avoided.

References

Krugman, P., *Pop Internationalism*. Cambridge, Massachusetts, MIT Press (1996).

Verspagen, B., "A global perspective on technology and economic performance, and the implications for the post-socialist countries." In D.A. Dyker and S. Radošević (eds.), *Innovation and Structural Change in Post-Socialist Countries: A Quantitative Approach*. Dordrecht, Kluwer (1999).

About the Authors

David A. Dyker is Professor of Economics at the University of Sussex, UK.

Katie Higginbottom is Senior Section Assistant in the Seafarers' Section of the International Transport Workers' Federation London, UK.

Peter Holmes is Jean Monnet Reader in European Integration at the University of Sussex, UK.

Leonardo Iacovone is research officer in the Department of Economics, University of Sussex, UK.

Neils Kofoed was a research officer in the Economics Department, University of Sussex when he wrote his contributions to the book. He is currently Assistant Economist at the UK Department for Education and Skills (DfES).

Javier Lopez-Gonzales is project coordinator for Africa and Latin America at Altair Asesores, Spain.

Boris Majcen is director of the Institute for Economic Research, Ljubljana.

Slavo Radošević is Reader in Industrial and Corporate Change at the School of Slavonic and East European Studies, University College, London, UK.

Matija Rojec is Senior Research Fellow, Faculty of Social Sciences, University of Ljubljana.

Johannes Stefan is Head of Department for Industrial and Regulatory Economics at the Halle Institute for Economic Research, Germany.

Cordula Stolberg is an analyst with JP Morgan Chase, London, UK.

INDEX